LF

MANUAL OF
PEDIATRIC NUTRITION

W. ALLAN WALKER, M.D.

KRISTY M. HENDRICKS, R.D., M.S.

Both of
Combined Program in Pediatric Gastroenterology
and Nutrition
Massachusetts General Hospital
Boston, Massachusetts

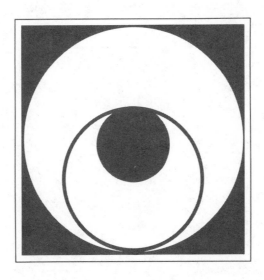

W. B. SAUNDERS COMPANY

1985

Philadelphia   London   Toronto   Mexico City   Rio de Janeiro   Sydney   Tokyo   Hong Kong

W. B. Saunders Company: West Washington Square
                          Philadelphia, PA 19105

Library of Congress Cataloging in Publication Data

Walker, W. Allan

Manual of pediatric nutrition

1. Children—Nutrition.   2. Diet therapy for children.
   3. Parenteral feeding of children.   4. Enteral feeding
   of children.   I. Hendricks, Kristy M.   II. Title.
   III. Title: Pediatric nutrition. [DNLM: 1. Child Nutrition.
   2. Diet Therapy—in infancy & childhood.
   3. Enteral Feeding—in infancy & childhood.
   4. Parenteral Feeding—in infancy & childhood. WS 115
   W186m]

RJ206.W26 1985   615.8'54'088054   84–23674
ISBN 0–7216–9101–3

Manual of Pediatric Nutrition   ISBN   0–7216–9101–3

Last digit is the print number: 9   8   7   6   5   4   3   2   1

PREFACE

The importance of nutrition in pediatrics has become more apparent in recent years as a result of significant observations that have helped both to define the specific needs of young infants to attain optimal growth and development and to prevent the expression of nutritionally related diseases at a later age. Of particular importance to industrialized societies is the awareness of subtle malnutrition present in pediatric patients in general as well as in underprivileged children of large cities and the hospitalized pediatric patient population. We now know that specific nutrient deficiency (e.g., zinc, essential fatty acids) can occur in virtually any pediatric patient as well as in unique patient populations such as premature infants, food faddists, or families obsessed with weight reduction. Thus, the increased awareness of nutrition as an important component of the practice of pediatrics has prompted the creation of this handbook.

The purpose of this handbook is to provide a comprehensive and practical guide to dietitians, house officers, nutritional fellows, and pediatricians in managing clinical nutritional problems in pediatric patients. The handbook is divided into six sections, each of which has an abundance of tables and practical guides to evaluation and management of specific clinical nutritional issues. Chapter 1 involves nutritional assessment and includes current parameters of anthropometric evaluation along with control values. In addition, laboratory and dietary evaluations and an assessment of feeding skills are provided. In Chapter 2, an approach to the evaluation of energy needs is provided along with appropriate illustrations of actual cases. Chapters 3 and 4 provide, in tabular form, a pragmatic and easily followed guide to enteral and parenteral nutrition management using the most updated guidelines available. Finally, the last two sections (Chapters 5 and 6) provide practical approaches to the nutritional support of patients with altered intestinal function and those with normal gastrointestinal function. These conditions have been selected not to be comprehensive but to be representative of the most common nutritional problems encountered in gastroenterology and other disciplines and, we hope, to provide an adequate basis for the nutritional approach to other medical problems.

Although this handbook reflects the approach used principally by the Combined Division of Gastroenterology and Nutrition at Harvard Medical School (Children's Hospital and Massachusetts General Hospital), we are grateful for the comprehensive review by several established nutritionists from various institutions and disciplines to assure its general use in pediatrics. Dr. Lewis Barness, Professor and Chairman of Pediatrics at the University of South Florida Medical School; Dr. John Reynolds, Professor of Pediatrics and Chief of Neonatology at the University of Oregon School of Medicine; Dr. Paul Pencharz, Associate Professor of Pediatrics and Nutrition at the University of Toronto School of Medicine, and Head, Division of Clinical Nutrition, Hospital for Sick Children, Toronto, Canada; Dr. Susan Baker,

27.95

Assistant Professor of Pediatrics at Harvard Medical School and member of the Nutritional Support Team at Children's Hospital, Boston, Massachusetts; and Ms. Alice Smith, Nutritionist at Children's Memorial Hospital, Northwestern University School of Medicine, Chicago, Illinois, have diligently reviewed these chapters and provided meaningful suggestions to make them more appropriate to the projected audience. We are grateful for their effort on this handbook.

W. ALLAN WALKER, M.D.
KRISTY HENDRICKS, R.D., M.S.

CONTENTS

1

NUTRITIONAL ASSESSMENT

Nutritional assessment is the evaluation of an individual's nutrient deficiencies and requirements. Assessment permits early intervention in the treatment of deficiencies and prevention of them in individuals identified as being at risk. It allows comparison of the growth of an individual against some norm and provides a basis for objective recommendations and evaluation of nutritional support. Although much information has been published on the use of increasingly sophisticated techniques,[1-3] objective clinical judgment remains an important component of nutritional assessment.[4] Selection of standards that are relevant to a specific population, appropriate techniques and equipment for measurement, and perceptive history taking are important.[5]

A combination of anthropometric, clinical, laboratory, and dietary information can aid in the evaluation. In each category, various tests monitor different aspects of nutrition. A few pragmatic guidelines are provided to help determine where to begin in the assessment of an individual (Table 1–1), what type of assessment is likely to yield valuable information, and how to proceed with a more extensive and costly evaluation.[6] An example of a work sheet for data collection and assessment in general pediatrics is included (Fig. 1–1),[7] and the various indices of anthropometry, reference standards, techniques, and interpretation as well as classification of malnutrition are detailed. This chapter also describes clinical evaluation of nutrient deficiency and excess and includes laboratory values and immunologic parameters useful in nutritional assessment. Finally, dietary evaluation and recommendations for normal infant feeding are detailed.

TABLE 1–1. Approach to Identification of Nutritional Problems

	Clinical	Anthropometric	Laboratory	Dietary
Screening	Physical and dental history and examination, sexual maturation, use of medication	Weight, length, head circumference, weight for height	Hemoglobin, hematocrit	Typical pattern, vitamin & mineral supplements
Midlevel, add:	More extensive examination (e.g., skin, hair, nails)	Tricep skinfold, arm circumference, prediction of mature height	MCV, albumin, total protein, total lymphocyte count	24-hour recall and 3- to 7-day food records, developmental evaluation of feeding skills
In-depth, add:	Bone mineralization (e.g., epiphyseal enlargement, cranial bossing)	Bone age, height velocity	Specific vitamin, mineral, and lead levels, delayed cutaneous hypersensitivity	Same, observation in hospital

Pediatric Nutritional Assessment Data

Name _____

Date _____

Birth Date _____

Anthropometric Data

Height _____ cm _____ percentile

Weight _____ kg _____ percentile

Weight for Height _____ percentile

Head circumference _____ cm _____ percentile

Triceps Skinfold Thickness _____ cm _____ percentile

Arm Muscle Circumference _____ cm _____ percentile

Laboratory Data

Hematocrit/Hemoglobin _____   WBC/Total Lymphocyte Count _____

Albumin/Total Protein _____   _____

Transferrin Sat./MCV _____   _____

_____   _____

History

Diagnosis/Presenting Problems: _____

_____

Recent Weight Change: _____ loss/gain: over _____ weeks, months _____

Feeding Skills and Behavior: _____

_____

Estimated Caloric Intake (CI): _____

_____ kcal _____ kcal/kg

_____ g protein _____ g/kg _____ % cal

_____ g fat _____ % cal

_____ g carbohydrate _____ % cal

Specific nutrient deficiencies/problems _____

_____

Potential problems _____

Vitamin/mineral supplements _____

Recommendations

Ideal Body Weight (IBW) _____ kg   Recommended kcal/day _____

for present height   Protein g/day _____

Recommendations: _____

_____

_____

_____

_____ R.D.

Figure 1–1. Chart for recording pediatric nutritional assessment data.

ANTHROPOMETRIC EVALUATION

Physical growth is, from conception to maturity, a complex process influenced by environmental, genetic, and nutritional factors. Anthropometry is the measurement of physical dimensions of the human body at different ages. Comparison with standard references determines abnormalities in growth and development that may have resulted from nutritional deficiencies or excesses. Reference standards (included here) represent optimal growth of a normal population. Repeated measurements of an individual over time provide objective data on nutrition, health, and well-being. Errors in comparison of measurements taken at different times can be caused by poor technique and equipment; examples of standardized techniques and equipment can be found in other sources.[2, 3, 5, 8, 9]

Weight

Body weight is a simple, reproducible growth parameter and a good index of acute nutritional status. An accurate age, sex, and reference standard is necessary for evaluation. Weight is plotted on two graphs: weight for age and weight for height.

Standards. Figures 1–2 through 1–5 are National Center for Health and Statistics (NCHS) Growth Charts.[10] All measurements were done between 1962 and 1974 by the United States Public Health Service on large samples of children throughout the United States. These data represent the most comprehensive measurements available for comparison.

Interpretation. Weight below the 10th percentile or above the 90th percentile may indicate weight deficit or excess, respectively. Weight for height can be calculated as a percentage of standard weight (the 50th percentile for height and sex, or age and sex) as follows:

$$\% \text{ standard} = \frac{\text{actual weight}}{\text{standard weight}} \times 100$$

$$>120\% \text{ standard} = \text{excess}$$
$$80–90\% \text{ standard} = \text{marginal deficiency}$$
$$60–80\% \text{ standard} = \text{moderate deficiency}$$
$$<60\% \text{ standard} = \text{severe deficiency}$$

Recent change in weight (loss or gain) is also important to note and is often an indicator of acute nutritional problems. Weight loss is calculated to be[1]:

$$\% \text{ usual body weight} = \frac{\text{current weight}}{\text{usual weight}} \times 100$$

$$85–95\% = \text{mild weight loss}$$
$$75–84\% = \text{moderate weight loss}$$
$$<75\% = \text{severe weight loss}$$

Percent weight change can also be calculated:

$$\text{percent weight change} = \frac{\text{usual weight} - \text{current weight}}{\text{usual weight}}$$

The severity of weight loss over time can be assessed with Table 1–2.

Technique. Subject stands, lies, or sits in center of balance scale platform. Minimal clothing and no shoes should be worn. Weight is taken to the nearest 0.1 kg or 1.0 oz.[2, 3]

Text continued on page 8

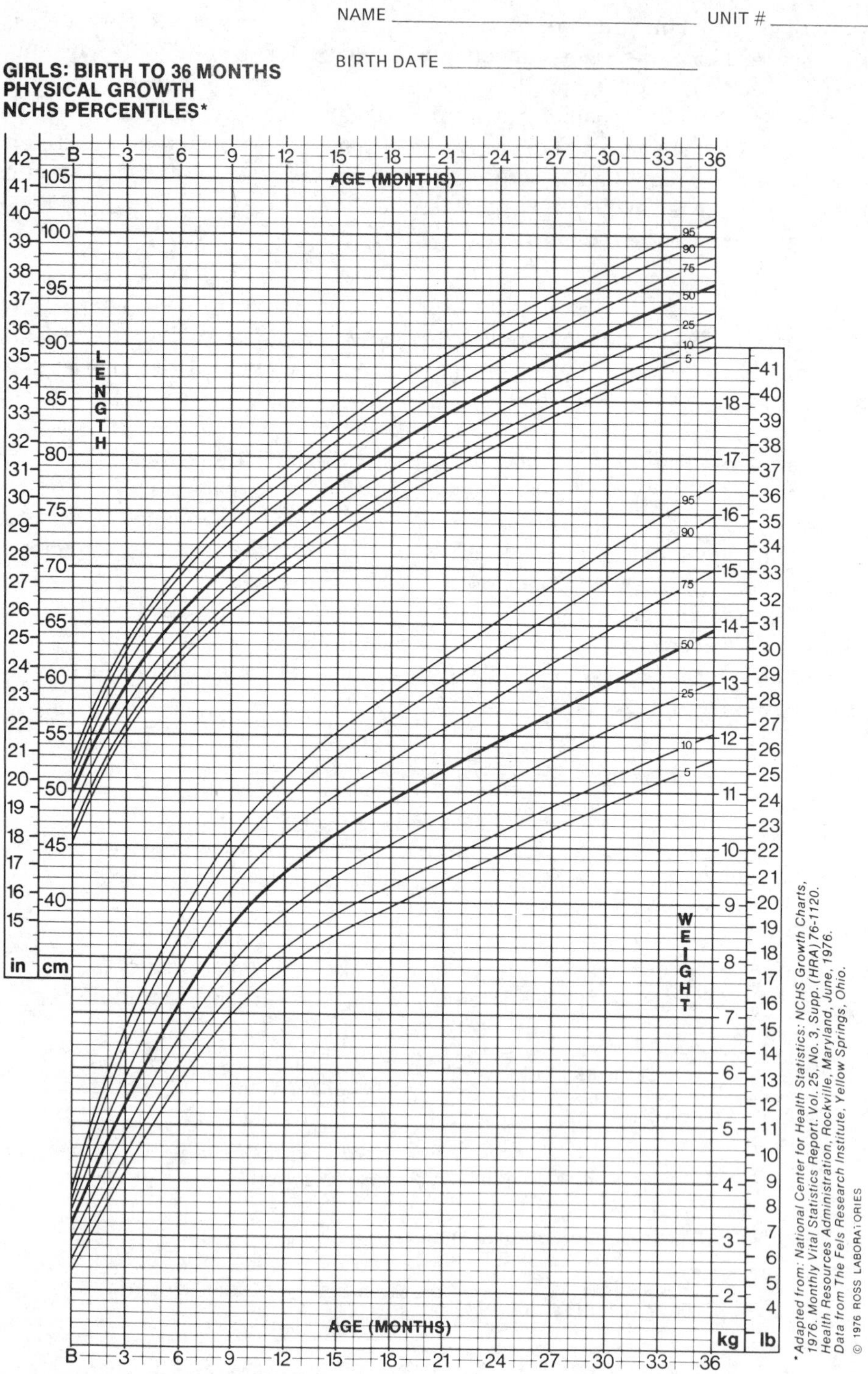
NAME
UNIT #
BIRTH DATE
GIRLS: BIRTH TO 36 MONTHS
PHYSICAL GROWTH
NCHS PERCENTILES*
AGE (MONTHS)
B 3 6 9 12 15 18 21 24 27 30 33 36
LENGTH
in
cm
95
90
75
50
25
10
5
WEIGHT
kg
lb
AGE (MONTHS)
*Adapted from: National Center for Health Statistics: NCHS Growth Charts, 1976. Monthly Vital Statistics Report. Vol. 25, No. 3, Supp. (HRA) 76-1120. Health Resources Administration, Rockville, Maryland, June, 1976. Data from The Fels Research Institute, Yellow Springs, Ohio.
© 1976 ROSS LABORATORIES

Figure 1–2. Physical growth chart for girls, birth to 36 months. Reprinted with permission of Ross Laboratories, Columbus, Ohio 43216.

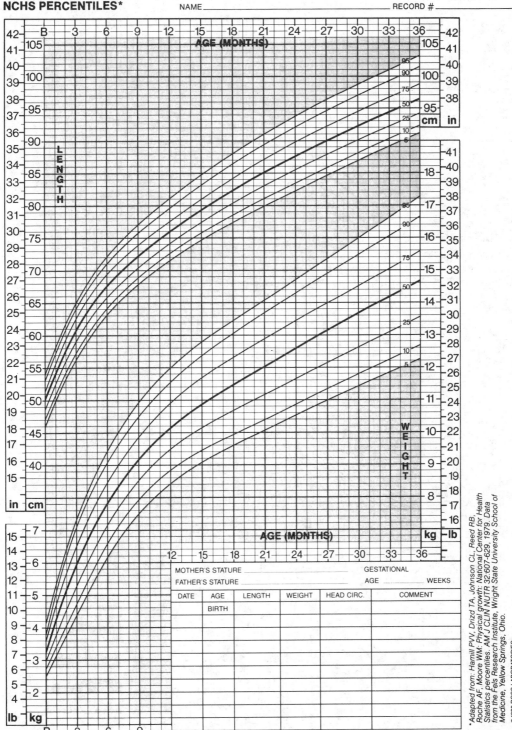

Figure 1–3. Physical growth chart for boys, birth to 36 months. Reprinted with permission of Ross Laboratories, Columbus, Ohio 43216.

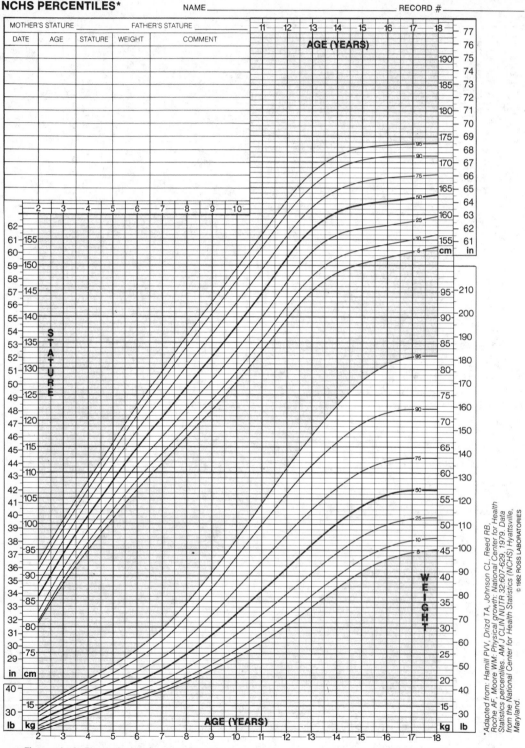

GIRLS: 2 TO 18 YEARS
PHYSICAL GROWTH
NCHS PERCENTILES*

NAME _____ RECORD # _____

Figure 1—4. Physical growth chart for girls, 2 to 18 years. Reprinted with permission of Ross Laboratories, Columbus, Ohio 43216.

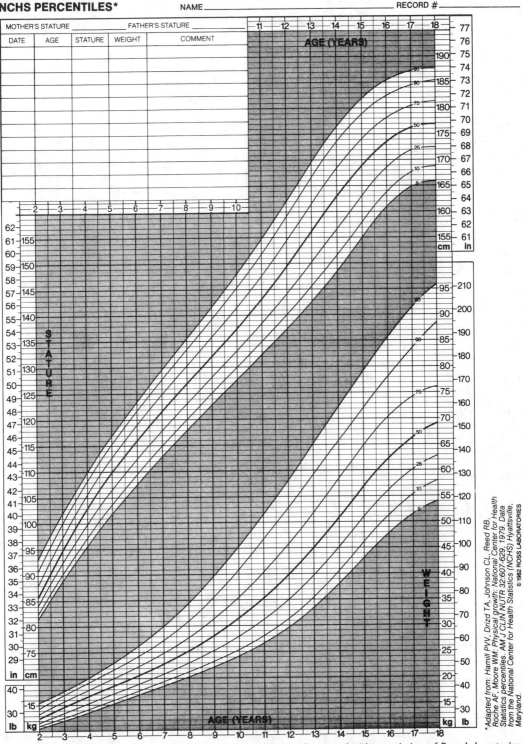

Figure 1–5. Physical growth chart for boys, 2 to 18 years. Reprinted with permission of Ross Laboratories, Columbus, Ohio 43216.

TABLE 1–2. Assessment of Weight Loss Over Time

Time	Significant (%)	Severe (%)
1 week	1–2	>2
1 month	5	>5
6 months	10	>10

Adapted from Roberts SLW: Nutrition Assessment Manual. Iowa City: University of Iowa Hospitals, 1977; Grant A: Nutritional Assessment: Guidelines for Dieticians. Seattle, WA: Northwest Kidney Center, 1977.

Length

Measured with appropriate equipment and proper methodology, length is a simple and reproducible growth parameter that provides, in conjunction with weight, significant information for the clinician.

Standards. Figures 1–2 through 1–5, the 1979 NCHS Growth Charts, are used for standards of length as well as weight.[10]

Interpretation. Length for age below the 5th percentile indicates a severe deficit, and measurements that range between the 5th and 10th percentiles should be evaluated further. Evaluation of growth velocity can be helpful in determination of chronicity or constitutional short stature in such cases. Length assesses growth failure and chronic undernutrition, especially in early childhood.

Technique. Despite its simplicity, there is a high percentage of error in measurement of length because of improper technique or equipment. The patient should be standing erect, without shoes, on the scale platform or floor. Shoulders should be straight and the subject should look straight ahead. Children younger than 2 years of age should be measured recumbent on a wooden length board.[11] Measurements should be to the nearest 0.5 cm or 0.125 in.

Head Circumference

Head circumference is influenced by nutritional status until age 36 months, but the effects on brain growth lag behind those on weight and height. The examination is routinely done to screen for other possible influences on brain growth as well.

Standards. Figures 1–6 and 1–7 are NCHS Growth Charts.[18] All measurements were done between 1962 and 1974 by the United States Public Health Service on large samples of children throughout the United States.

Interpretation. Measurements below the 5th percentile may indicate chronic undernutrition during fetal life and early childhood.

Technique. A flexible, narrow tape measure is placed firmly around the head above the supraorbital ridges and over the frontal bulge, where the circumference is greatest. Measurements should be taken to the nearest 0.25 cm or 0.125 in.[11]

Weight for Height

This ratio is important, as it more accurately assesses body build and distinguishes wasting from dwarfism.

Standards. Figures 1–6 through 1–9 chart weight for height from measurements taken by the National Center for Health Statistics.[10] All measurements were done between 1962 an 1974 by the United States Public Health Service on large samples of children throughout the United States.

Interpretation. Measurements that fall within the 50th percentile indicate appropriate weight for height; the farther the deviation from this, the more over- or undernourished the individual. The percentiles are not extended far enough to

NAME _____ UNIT # _____

BIRTH DATE _____

**GIRLS: BIRTH TO 36 MONTHS
PHYSICAL GROWTH
NCHS PERCENTILES***

* Adapted from: National Center for Health Statistics: NCHS Growth Charts, 1976. Monthly Vital Statistics Report. Vol 25, No. 3, Supp. (HRA) 76-1120. Health Resources Administration. Rockville, Maryland, June, 1976. Data from The Fels Research Institute, Yellow Springs, Ohio.

DATE	AGE	LENGTH	WEIGHT	HEAD C.
	BIRTH			

DATE	AGE	LENGTH	WEIGHT	HEAD C.

Figure 1–6. Physical growth and head circumference chart for girls, birth to 36 months. Reprinted with permission of Ross Laboratories, Columbus, Ohio 43216.

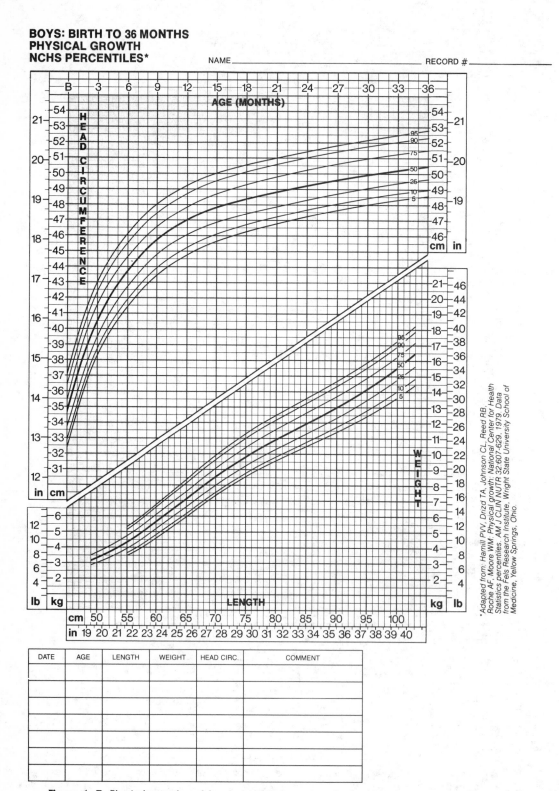

Figure 1–7. Physical growth and head circumference chart for boys, birth to 36 months. Reprinted with permission of Ross Laboratories, Columbus, Ohio 43216.

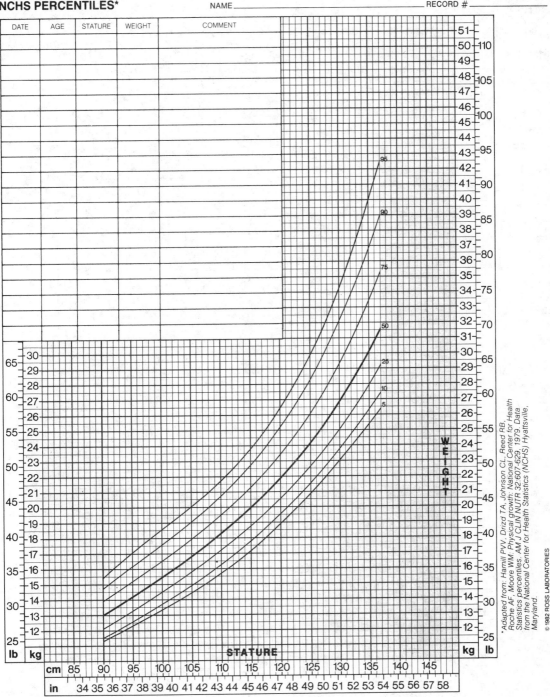

Figure 1–8. Physical growth chart for prepubescent girls. Reprinted with permission of Ross Laboratories, Columbus, Ohio 43216.

**BOYS: PREPUBESCENT
PHYSICAL GROWTH
NCHS PERCENTILES***

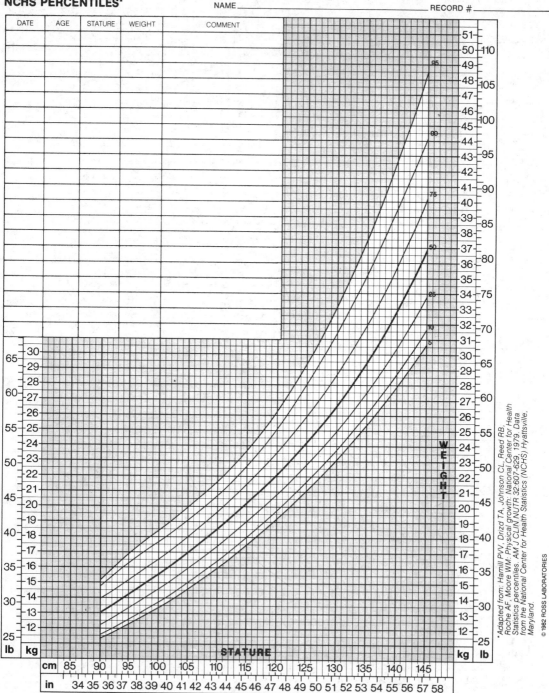

Figure 1–9. Physical growth chart for prepubescent boys. Reprinted with permission of Ross Laboratories, Columbus. Ohio 43216.

evaluate weight for height of adolescents (males taller than 145 cm, females taller than 138 cm). Weight for height is not very useful in this range because of the preadolescent "fat growth spurt." For suggested guidelines on desirable weight for height above these ranges, see Table 2–10.

Growth Velocity

Growth velocity is a simple and reproducible measure that evaluates change in rate of growth over a specified time period; it generally is expressed in centimeters per year. It is a more sensitive way of assessing growth failure or slowed growth and is particularly helpful in the early identification of children with undernutrition.

Standards. Figures 1–10 and 1–11 are Tanner growth velocity charts, based on growth data of British children from birth to maturity.[12]

Interpretation. Increments in growth may occur at different times but follow a similar sequence in most instances. Growth velocity charts are constructed from and used for longitudinally obtained incremental data. They are more sensitive to slight changes in growth status.

Prediction of Mature Height

There are several methods available for prediction of mature height; each one considers different variables and is an estimate only.

Standards. Tables 1–3 and 1–4 are Fel's parent-specific standards for height. They are sex- and age-specific and are based on mean parental height.[13] Tanner found that height at age 3 years, more so than at any other age, showed a good correlation with mature height,[14] and constructed the following formulas:

Height (cm) at maturity (male) = 1.27 × height at age 3 years + 54.9 cm

Height (cm) at maturity (female) = 1.29 × height at age 3 years + 42.3 cm

Interpretation. For genetic reasons, some children may be taller or shorter than average. These estimations may be helpful in evaluating constitutional short stature. The growth patterns of other family members may also be helpful in determination of the correct diagnosis in such instances.

Skinfold Thickness

Nearly half of the body fat in humans is in the subcutaneous layer, and measurements of this deposit can lead to accurate estimations of total body fat. Skinfold thickness measurements are accurate, simple, and reproducible and can be used to monitor changes in total body fat.

Standards. The measurements in Table 1–5 were compiled by Karlberg and coworkers[15] and are based on longitudinal data of 200 Swedish children in the first three years of life. Measurements for childhood through adult life (Table 1–6) were compiled by Frisancho[16] and are based on the National Center for Health Statistics measurements of large samples of American children thoughout the United States.[10]

Interpretation. Skinfold thickness measurements assess current nutritional status and body composition; they provide an index of body energy stores and can be used in conjunction with weight for height to determine chronic undernutrition. Measurement sites vary, and edema or intravenous fluids may affect accuracy. Measurements are most useful on children who can be followed for a period of time.[17]

Technique. Measurement of skinfold thickness is taken at the midpoint between the acromion and olecranon on the nondominant arm while it is relaxed. The layer

Text continued on page 19

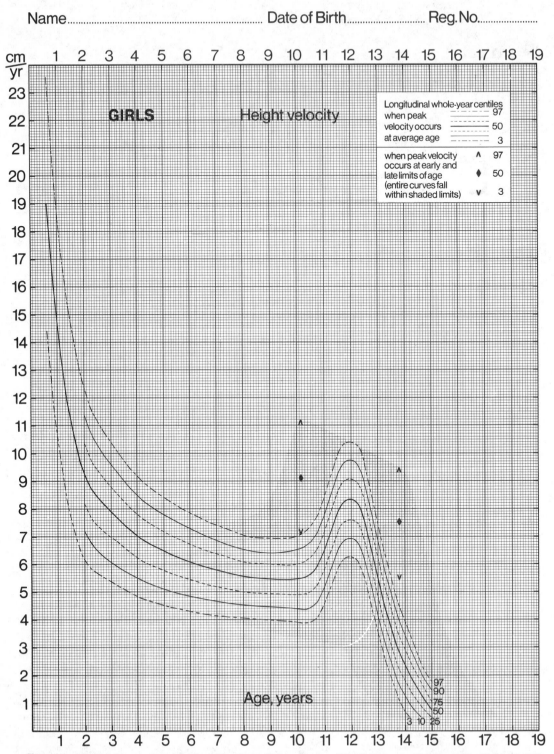

Figure 1–10. Height velocity chart for girls. Compiled by Tanner JM, Whitehouse RH: Arch Dis Child 51:170, 1976. Chart Ref. 4A, copyright Castlemead Publications.

Name... Date of Birth......................... Reg. No. ....

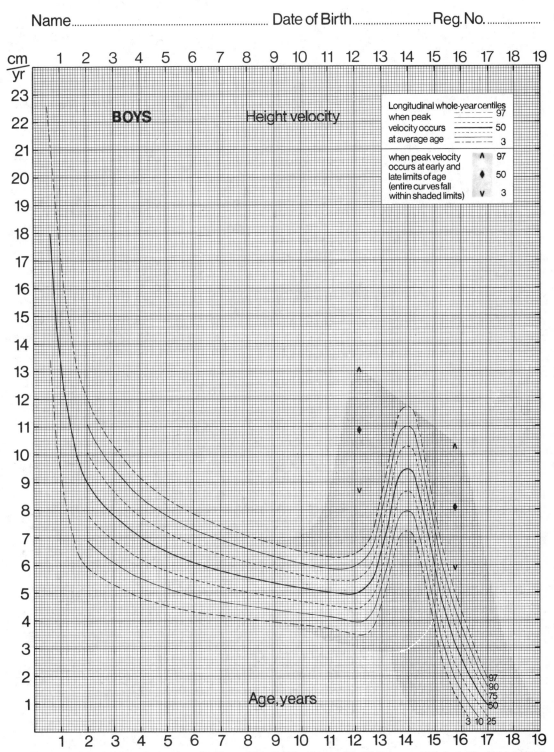

Figure 1-11. Height velocity chart for boys. Compiled by Tanner JM, Whitehouse RH: Arch Dis Child 51:170, 1976. Chart Ref. 2A, copyright Castlemead Publications.

TABLE 1–3. Fels Parent-Specific Standards for Height: Girls' Stature by Age and Parental Midpoint States*

Age (yr–mo)	Parental Midpoint (cm)									
	161	163	165	167	169	171	173	175	177	178
Birth...	47.3	48.9	49.0	49.2	49.2	48.8	49.7	49.1	49.0	47.5
0–1 ...	53.0	53.4	54.2	52.0	53.3	53.1	53.5	53.2	55.8	52.8
0–3 ...	57.4	58.4	59.6	57.4	59.4	59.6	59.4	58.0	61.5	57.6
0–6 ...	64.4	64.7	65.6	65.7	64.6	66.5	66.6	67.4	67.3	65.8
0–9 ...	68.2	69.0	70.2	70.1	69.8	71.5	71.5	71.0	72.2	69.8
1–0 ...	72.3	73.0	73.8	74.0	74.0	75.2	75.5	74.6	77.3	73.2
1–6 ...	78.8	79.5	80.6	81.4	80.2	81.7	82.6	81.6	84.0	81.0
2–0 ...	84.6	84.0	86.5	87.4	85.5	88.8	88.7	88.2	89.5	87.6
2–6 ...	89.1	87.2	91.0	91.6	89.9	93.2	92.9	92.6	93.9	92.0
3–0 ...	93.2	90.4	94.5	95.8	93.8	97.1	96.5	96.5	98.5	96.2
3–6 ...	96.7	93.5	98.3	99.6	97.8	101.4	100.3	102.0	102.4	103.0
4–0 ...	100.1	96.8	102.4	103.5	103.9	104.9	104.0	103.8	105.8	104.3
4–6 ...	103.5	100.2	106.0	106.7	105.8	108.6	107.5	107.4	109.4	108.0
5–0 ...	106.8	103.5	108.9	109.9	109.1	111.6	110.9	111.0	112.6	111.7
5–6 ...	110.0	107.0	112.2	113.2	112.0	114.8	114.4	114.2	115.8	115.4
6–0 ...	113.2	110.2	115.0	116.2	115.0	118.2	117.8	117.3	119.1	118.8
6–6 ...	116.1	113.4	117.8	119.4	117.6	121.6	121.2	120.8	122.6	122.3
7–0 ...	118.8	116.5	120.6	122.4	120.2	124.4	124.4	124.0	125.0	125.5
7–6 ...	121.7	119.4	123.5	125.7	122.9	127.6	127.6	127.3	127.8	128.7
8–0 ...	124.6	122.4	126.3	128.8	125.8	130.7	130.8	130.2	130.8	132.0
8–6 ...	127.3	125.5	129.4	131.8	128.5	133.8	133.8	133.4	133.9	135.0
9–0 ...	130.1	128.6	132.2	134.7	131.4	137.1	136.7	136.6	137.0	138.2
9–6 ...	132.7	131.6	135.6	137.5	134.2	140.2	139.8	139.8	139.9	140.9
10–0 ...	136.0	135.1	139.0	140.3	136.9	143.8	142.9	143.1	143.8	143.6
10–6 ...	139.1	138.5	142.3	143.2	140.0	147.4	146.0	146.6	147.4	146.4
11–0 ...	141.9	141.6	145.9	146.0	143.4	150.3	149.0	149.6	151.3	149.4
11–6 ...	145.0	144.8	149.4	148.9	146.6	153.2	152.1	152.8	155.3	152.2
12–0 ...	148.0	147.8	152.8	151.8	150.3	156.4	155.2	155.8	159.0	154.9
12–6 ...	150.8	151.1	155.8	154.4	154.0	159.0	158.2	158.8	161.1	158.0
13–0 ...	152.9	154.2	158.8	157.0	157.0	161.0	161.1	161.7	162.3	160.5
13–6 ...	154.5	157.2	161.0	159.1	159.0	163.0	163.3	164.0	163.0	162.5
14–0 ...	155.4	158.8	161.7	160.9	160.4	163.7	165.0	165.9	163.9	164.1
14–6 ...	155.7	159.4	162.2	162.5	161.5	164.0	166.2	167.4	164.5	165.5
15–0 ...	155.9	159.8	162.6	163.7	162.2	164.0	167.1	168.4	165.0	166.5
15–6 ...	156.1	160.1	162.7	164.7	162.9	164.0	167.5	169.2	165.3	167.8
16–0 ...	156.0	160.5	162.8	165.5	163.4	164.1	167.8	169.7	165.5	168.7
16–6 ...	156.1	160.7	162.9	166.1	163.8	164.2	167.8	170.3	165.6	169.4
17–0 ...	156.2	160.8	163.0	166.5	164.0	164.3	167.9	170.9	165.7	170.0
17–6 ...	156.2	160.9	163.0	166.9	164.2	164.4	167.9	171.4	165.7	170.4
18–0 ...	156.2	161.0	165.0	167.2	164.3	164.4	167.9	171.8	165.7	170.8

*No attempt to eliminate sampling fluctuations

From Garn SM, Rohman CG: Interaction of nutrition and genetics in timing of growth. Pediatr Clin North Am 13:353, 1966.

TABLE 1–4. Fels Parent-Specific Standards for Height: Boys' Stature by Age and Parental Midpoint States*

Age (yr–mo)	161	163	165	167	169	171	173	175	177	178
Birth		47.1	49.7	50.3	50.0	48.3	50.7	50.0	51.5	51.4
0–1		52.7	54.6	54.7	57.6	53.2	53.6	52.2	55.6	55.9
0–3		58.9	60.8	60.0	62.2	57.4	60.8	61.2	61.4	62.6
0–6		65.1	66.2	66.8	67.4	65.8	70.2	69.0	70.2	70.3
0–9		70.7	72.9	73.8	73.2	71.0	74.8	75.2	77.1	75.7
1–0		73.1	75.6	75.7	75.1	73.4	76.6	77.1	79.6	77.8
1–6		79.9	82.4	81.7	82.0	81.2	82.6	83.4	86.8	85.2
2–0		85.4	87.2	87.0	87.4	87.8	88.0	88.9	92.0	91.3
2–6		88.8	91.3	92.0	92.1	93.2	93.5	94.0	96.7	96.0
3–0		93.2	94.9	96.1	96.0	97.2	98.1	98.3	100.7	99.9
3–6		96.3	98.4	100.0	99.5	101.0	102.3	102.6	104.5	103.5
4–0		99.5	102.2	103.5	103.1	104.6	106.0	106.3	108.0	107.0
4–6		102.7	105.4	107.1	106.6	108.0	109.6	109.6	111.4	110.4
5–0		105.6	108.5	110.6	110.0	111.5	113.2	112.7	114.6	113.8
5–6		108.3	111.3	113.4	112.7	114.5	116.3	115.8	117.4	116.8
6–0		110.9	114.1	116.4	115.4	117.4	119.4	118.7	120.4	119.8
6–6		113.6	116.9	119.3	118.4	120.3	122.4	121.7	123.4	122.8
7–0		116.2	119.7	122.3	121.3	123.2	125.6	124.6	126.6	125.6
7–6		118.9	122.5	125.1	124.3	126.1	128.8	127.6	129.5	128.4
8–0		121.6	125.0	127.8	126.8	128.8	131.6	130.4	132.8	131.6
8–6		124.2	127.6	130.7	129.3	131.5	134.9	133.2	135.9	134.6
9–0		126.9	130.4	133.3	131.9	134.1	138.0	136.0	138.8	137.5
9–6		129.9	132.9	136.1	134.6	136.9	141.0	138.8	142.0	140.5
10–0		132.5	135.8	138.8	137.4	139.8	143.8	141.5	145.3	143.2
10–6		135.6	138.8	141.5	140.3	142.6	146.8	144.3	148.6	146.0
11–0		138.5	141.8	144.1	143.0	145.4	149.9	146.8	151.9	148.9
11–6		141.6	144.9	146.9	145.6	148.3	152.8	149.6	155.4	151.6
12–0		144.7	148.0	149.7	148.4	151.4	155.7	152.4	158.8	154.5
12–6		147.7	151.1	152.6	151.6	154.6	158.3	155.8	162.6	157.5
13–0		151.0	154.2	155.7	154.9	158.0	161.7	159.6	166.3	160.5
13–6		154.5	157.7	158.9	158.1	161.6	164.6	163.6	170.1	163.8
14–0		158.8	161.7	162.3	161.6	165.7	167.6	167.8	173.4	166.9
14–6		162.6	164.9	165.9	164.8	169.6	170.3	172.0	175.2	171.3
15–0		165.8	168.1	169.1	167.9	172.9	173.0	174.7	176.4	175.2
15–6		168.0	171.3	172.0	170.6	174.5	175.6	175.8	177.0	178.6
16–0		169.4	173.3	174.3	172.8	177.3	177.5	176.6	177.4	181.2
16–6		170.3	174.2	175.8	174.4	178.4	178.7	177.3	177.4	182.8
17–0		170.9	174.7	176.8	175.4	179.2	179.4	177.8	177.5	184.3
17–6		171.2	174.9	174.4	176.0	180.0	179.9	178.2	177.6	185.4
18–0		171.5	175.0	177.9	176.2	180.5	180.2	178.6	177.6	186.3

*No attempt to eliminate sampling fluctuations.
From Garn SM, Rohman CG: Interaction of nutrition and genetics in timing of growth. Pediatr Clin North Am 13:353, 1966.

TABLE 1–5. Thickness of Triceps and Subscapular Skinfolds at 1 to 36 Months of Age

Age (months)	Percentiles	SD	Triceps (mm)		Subscapular (mm)	
			Males	*Females*	*Males*	*Females*
1		−2	2.9	3.5	3.1	3.8
	10		4.0	4.5	4.2	4.9
	25		4.7	5.2	4.8	5.4
	50		5.3	5.8	5.6	6.2
	75		6.2	6.7	6.5	7.0
	90		7.0	7.6	7.5	7.9
		+2	8.1	8.3	8.3	9.0
3		−2	4.5	5.0	3.5	4.7
	10		6.0	6.2	4.9	5.9
	25		6.8	7.2	5.8	6.9
	50		8.1	8.2	6.9	8.0
	75		9.2	9.2	8.1	8.6
	90		10.3	10.5	9.0	9.4
		+2	11.7	11.8	10.7	11.1
6		−2	6.3	6.7	3.8	4.0
	10		7.8	8.2	5.5	5.9
	25		8.6	9.0	6.2	6.9
	50		9.7	10.4	7.1	8.1
	75		11.1	11.3	8.4	8.9
	90		11.8	12.7	10.1	10.3
		+2	13.5	13.9	11.0	12.4
9		−2	6.0	6.7	3.4	4.7
	10		7.5	7.9	5.3	6.0
	25		8.7	8.8	6.0	6.7
	50		9.9	10.1	7.1	7.6
	75		11.2	11.3	8.5	8.8
	90		12.5	12.5	9.7	10.1
		+2	14.0	13.5	11.4	11.1
12		−2	6.2	6.4	3.8	4.5
	10		7.8	7.6	5.3	6.0
	25		8.6	8.7	6.0	6.5
	50		9.8	9.8	7.2	7.5
	75		11.1	11.2	8.6	8.7
	90		12.2	12.2	9.6	9.8
		+2	13.8	13.6	11.0	10.9
18		−2	6.4	6.8	3.9	4.2
	10		7.7	7.9	5.3	5.7
	25		8.6	8.9	6.0	6.2
	50		9.9	10.3	6.8	7.1
	75		11.4	11.3	7.9	8.0
	90		12.2	12.3	9.3	9.0
		+2	13.6	13.6	10.3	10.2
24		−2	5.8	6.5	3.0	3.9
	10		7.4	8.3	4.6	5.3
	25		8.5	8.9	5.4	5.6
	50		9.8	10.1	6.5	6.5
	75		11.6	11.6	7.4	7.3
	90		13.1	12.8	8.3	8.4
		+2	14.2	14.1	10.2	9.5
36		−2	6.6	6.4	2.9	2.6
	10		7.8	8.2	4.5	4.7
	25		9.0	9.4	5.0	5.2
	50		9.8	10.3	5.5	6.1
	75		11.0	11.5	6.4	7.2
	90		12.2	12.5	7.1	8.6
		+2	13.4	14.4	8.9	10.6

Adapted from Karlberg P, et al.: The development of children in a Swedish urban community. A prospective longitudinal study. III. Physical growth during the first three years of life. Acta Pediatr Scand (Suppl) 187:48, 1968; courtesy of Acta Pediatr Scand in Palmer S and Ervall S, eds.: Pediatric Nutrition in Developmental Disorders, 1978. Courtesy of Charles C Thomas, Publisher, Springfield, IL.

TABLE 1–6. Percentiles for Triceps Skinfold (mm²)*

Age Group	n	5	10	25	50	75	90	95	n	5	10	25	50	75	90	95
					Males								*Females*			
1–1.9	228	6	7	8	10	12	14	16	204	6	7	8	10	12	14	16
2–2.9	223	6	7	8	10	12	14	15	208	6	8	9	10	12	15	16
3–3.9	220	6	7	8	10	11	14	15	208	7	8	9	11	12	14	15
4–4.9	230	6	6	8	9	11	12	14	208	7	8	8	10	12	14	16
5–5.9	214	6	6	8	9	11	14	15	219	6	7	8	10	12	15	18
6–6.9	117	5	6	7	8	10	13	16	118	6	6	8	10	12	14	16
7–7.9	122	5	6	7	9	12	15	17	126	6	7	9	11	13	16	18
8–8.9	117	5	6	7	8	10	13	16	118	6	8	9	12	15	18	24
9–9.9	121	6	6	7	10	13	17	18	125	8	8	10	13	16	20	22
10–10.9	146	6	6	8	10	14	18	21	152	7	8	10	12	17	23	27
11–11.9	122	6	6	8	11	16	20	24	117	7	8	10	13	18	24	28
12–12.9	153	6	6	8	11	14	22	28	129	8	9	11	14	18	23	27
13–13.9	134	5	5	7	10	14	22	26	151	8	8	12	15	21	26	30
14–14.9	131	4	5	7	9	14	21	24	141	9	10	13	16	21	26	28
15–15.9	128	4	5	6	8	11	18	24	117	8	10	12	17	21	25	32
16–16.9	131	4	5	6	8	12	16	22	142	10	12	15	18	22	26	31
17–17.9	133	5	5	6	8	12	16	19	114	10	12	13	19	24	30	37
18–18.9	91	4	5	6	9	13	20	24	109	10	12	15	18	22	26	30
19–24.9	531	4	5	7	10	15	20	22	1060	10	11	14	18	24	30	34
25–34.9	971	5	6	8	12	16	20	24	1987	10	12	16	21	27	34	37
35–44.9	806	5	6	8	12	16	20	23	1614	12	14	18	23	29	35	38
45–54.9	898	6	6	8	12	15	20	25	1047	12	16	20	25	30	36	40
55–64.9	734	5	6	8	11	14	19	22	809	12	16	20	25	31	36	38
65–74.9	1503	4	6	8	11	15	19	22	1670	12	14	18	24	29	34	36

*Data collected from whites in the United States Health and Nutrition Examination Survey I (1971–1974)

From Frisancho AR: New norms of upper limb fat and muscle areas for assessment of nutritional status. Am J Clin Nutr 34:2540, 1981. © Am J Clin Nutr, American Society for Clinical Nutrition.

of skin and subcutaneous tissue is pulled away from the underlying muscle and held until measurement with the calipers at the midpoint is complete. Readings should be taken to 0.5 mm, made 3 seconds after application of the calipers. Lange or Harpenden skinfold calipers are recommended for accurate measurements.[2, 11]

Arm Circumference and Muscle Mass

In conjunction with triceps skinfold thickness, arm circumference can be used to determine muscle area and fat area. As with skinfold thickness, it correlates well with other more sophisticated and difficult measures of body composition.

Standards. Tables 1–7 and 1–8 were compiled by Frisancho[16] and are based on the National Center for Health Statistics measurements of large samples of American children throughout the United States.[10]

Interpretation. Simple nomogram calculation[18] requires arm circumference and triceps skinfold measures to determine muscle circumference and cross-sectional muscle and fat areas (Figs. 1–12 and 1–13). Arm circumference and muscle mass correlate highly with weight for height and weight for age.[19]

Bone Age

Epiphyseal closure is a measure of how far the bones have progressed toward maturity. Roentgenograms of the hand and wrist are generally used for convenient determination of this measure. The percentage of maturity attained indicates potential for "catch-up" growth.

Standards. Measurements for epiphyseal closure can be found in *Radiographic Atlas of Skeletal Development of the Hand and Wrist,* by Gruelich and Pyle.[20]

Text continued on page 24

TABLE 1–7. Percentiles of Upper Arm Circumference and Estimated Upper Arm Muscle Circumference*

Age Group	Arm Circumference (mm)							Arm Muscle Circumference (mm)						
	5	10	25	50	75	90	95	5	10	25	50	75	90	95
Males														
1–1.9	142	146	150	159	170	176	183	110	113	119	127	135	144	147
2–2.9	141	145	153	162	170	178	185	111	114	122	130	140	146	150
3–3.9	150	153	160	167	175	184	190	117	123	131	137	143	148	153
4–4.9	149	154	162	171	180	186	192	123	126	133	141	148	156	159
5–5.9	153	160	167	175	185	195	204	128	133	140	147	154	162	169
6–6.9	155	159	167	179	188	209	228	131	135	142	151	161	170	177
7–7.9	162	167	177	187	201	223	230	137	139	151	160	168	177	190
8–8.9	162	170	177	190	202	220	245	140	145	154	162	170	182	187
9–9.9	175	178	187	200	217	249	257	151	154	161	170	183	196	202
10–10.9	181	184	196	210	231	262	274	156	160	166	180	191	209	221
11–11.9	186	190	202	223	244	261	280	159	165	173	183	195	205	230
12–12.9	193	200	214	232	254	282	303	167	171	182	195	210	223	241
13–13.9	194	211	228	247	263	286	301	172	179	196	211	226	238	245
14–14.9	220	226	237	253	283	303	322	189	199	212	223	240	260	264
15–15.9	222	229	244	264	284	311	320	199	204	218	237	254	266	272
16–16.9	244	248	262	278	303	324	343	213	225	234	249	269	287	296
17–17.9	246	253	267	285	308	336	347	224	231	245	258	273	294	312
18–18.9	245	260	276	297	321	353	379	226	237	252	264	283	298	324
19–24.9	262	272	288	308	331	355	372	238	245	257	273	289	309	321
25–34.9	271	282	300	319	342	362	375	243	250	264	279	298	314	326
35–44.9	278	287	305	326	345	363	374	247	255	269	286	302	318	327
45–54.9	267	281	301	322	342	362	376	239	249	265	281	300	315	326
55–64.9	258	273	296	317	336	355	369	236	245	260	278	295	310	320
65–74.9	248	263	285	307	325	344	355	223	235	251	268	284	298	306
Females														
1–1.9	138	142	148	156	164	172	177	105	111	117	124	132	139	143
2–2.9	142	145	152	160	167	176	184	111	114	119	126	133	142	147
3–3.9	143	150	158	167	175	183	189	113	119	124	132	140	146	152
4–4.9	149	154	160	169	177	184	191	115	121	128	136	144	152	157
5–5.9	153	157	165	175	185	203	211	125	128	134	142	151	159	165
6–6.9	156	162	170	176	187	204	211	130	133	138	145	154	166	171
7–7.9	164	167	174	183	199	216	231	129	135	142	151	160	171	176
8–8.9	168	172	183	195	214	247	261	138	140	151	160	171	183	194
9–9.9	178	182	194	211	224	251	260	147	150	158	167	180	194	198
10–10.9	174	182	193	210	228	251	265	148	150	159	170	180	190	197
11–11.9	185	194	208	224	248	276	303	150	158	171	181	196	217	223
12–12.9	194	203	216	237	256	282	294	162	166	180	191	201	214	220
13–13.9	202	211	223	243	271	301	338	169	175	183	198	211	226	240
14–14.9	214	223	237	252	272	304	322	174	179	190	201	216	232	247
15–15.9	208	221	239	254	279	300	322	175	178	189	202	215	228	244
16–16.9	218	224	241	258	283	318	334	170	180	190	202	216	234	249
17–17.9	220	227	241	264	295	324	350	175	183	194	205	221	239	257
18–18.9	222	227	241	258	281	312	325	174	179	191	202	215	237	245
19–24.9	221	230	247	265	290	319	345	179	185	195	207	221	236	249
25–34.9	233	240	256	277	304	342	368	183	188	199	212	228	246	264
35–44.9	241	251	267	290	317	356	378	186	192	205	218	236	257	272
45–54.9	242	256	274	299	328	362	384	187	193	206	220	238	260	274
55–64.9	243	257	280	303	335	367	385	187	196	209	225	244	266	280
65–74.9	240	252	274	299	326	356	373	185	195	208	225	244	264	279

*Data collected from whites in the United States Health and Nutrition Examination Survey I (1971–1974)

From Frisancho AR: New norms of upper limb fat and muscle areas for assessment of nutritional status. Am J Clin Nutr 34:2540, 1981. © Am J Clin Nutr, American Society for Clinical Nutrition.

TABLE 1–8. Percentiles for Estimates of Upper Arm Fat Area and Upper Arm Muscle Area*

Age Group	Arm Muscle Area Percentiles (mm²)							Arm Fat Area Percentiles (mm²)						
	5	10	25	50	75	90	95	5	10	25	50	75	90	95
Males														
1–1.9	956	1014	1133	1278	1447	1644	1720	452	486	590	741	895	1036	1176
2–2.9	973	1040	1190	1345	1557	1690	1787	434	504	578	737	871	1044	1148
3–3.9	1095	1201	1357	1484	1618	1750	1853	464	519	590	736	868	1071	1151
4–4.9	1207	1264	1408	1579	1747	1926	2008	428	494	598	722	859	989	1085
5–5.9	1298	1411	1550	1720	1884	2089	2285	446	488	582	713	914	1176	1299
6–6.9	1360	1447	1605	1815	2056	2297	2493	371	446	539	678	896	1115	1519
7–7.9	1497	1548	1808	2027	2246	2494	2886	423	473	574	758	1011	1393	1511
8–8.9	1550	1664	1895	2089	2296	2628	2788	410	460	588	725	1003	1248	1558
9–9.9	1811	1884	2067	2288	2657	3053	3257	485	527	635	859	1252	1864	2081
10–10.9	1930	2027	2182	2575	2903	3486	3882	523	543	738	982	1376	1906	2609
11–11.9	2016	2156	2382	2670	3022	3359	4226	536	595	754	1148	1710	2348	2574
12–12.9	2216	2339	2649	3022	3496	3968	4640	554	650	874	1172	1558	2536	3580
13–13.9	2363	2546	3044	3553	4081	4502	4794	475	570	812	1096	1702	2744	3322
14–14.9	2830	3147	3586	3963	4575	5368	5530	453	563	786	1082	1608	2746	3508
15–15.9	3138	3317	3788	4481	5134	5631	5900	521	595	690	931	1423	2434	3100
16–16.9	3625	4044	4352	4951	5753	6576	6980	542	593	844	1078	1746	2280	3041
17–17.9	3998	4252	4777	5286	5950	6886	7726	598	698	827	1096	1636	2407	2888
18–18.9	4070	4481	5066	5552	6374	7067	8355	560	665	860	1264	1947	3302	3928
19–24.9	4508	4777	5274	5913	6660	7606	8200	594	743	963	1406	2231	3098	3652
25–34.9	4694	4963	5541	6214	7067	7847	8436	675	831	1174	1752	2459	3246	3786
35–44.9	4844	5181	5740	6490	7265	8034	8488	703	851	1310	1792	2463	3098	3624
45–54.9	4546	4946	5589	6297	7142	7918	8458	749	922	1254	1741	2359	3245	3928
55–64.9	4422	4783	5381	6144	6919	7670	8149	658	839	1166	1645	2236	2976	3466
65–74.9	3973	4411	5031	5716	6432	7074	7453	573	753	1122	1621	2199	2876	3327
Females														
1–1.9	885	973	1084	1221	1378	1535	1621	401	466	578	706	847	1022	1140
2–2.9	973	1029	1119	1269	1405	1595	1727	469	526	642	747	894	1061	1173
3–3.9	1014	1133	1227	1396	1563	1690	1846	473	529	656	822	967	1106	1158
4–4.9	1058	1171	1313	1475	1644	1832	1958	490	541	654	766	907	1109	1236
5–5.9	1238	1301	1423	1598	1825	2012	2159	470	529	647	812	991	1330	1536
6–6.9	1354	1414	1513	1683	1877	2182	2323	464	508	638	827	1009	1263	1436
7–7.9	1330	1441	1602	1815	2045	2332	2469	491	560	706	920	1135	1407	1644
8–8.9	1513	1566	1808	2034	2327	2657	2996	527	634	769	1042	1383	1872	2482
9–9.9	1723	1788	1976	2227	2571	2987	3112	642	690	933	1219	1584	2171	2524
10–10.9	1740	1784	2019	2296	2583	2873	3093	616	702	842	1141	1608	2500	3005
11–11.9	1784	1987	2316	2612	3071	3739	3953	707	802	1015	1301	1942	2730	3690
12–12.9	2092	2182	2579	2904	3225	3655	3847	782	854	1090	1511	2056	2666	3369
13–13.9	2269	2426	2657	3130	3529	4081	4568	726	838	1219	1625	2374	3272	4150
14–14.9	2418	2562	2874	3220	3704	4294	4850	981	1043	1423	1818	2403	3250	3765
15–15.9	2426	2518	2847	3248	3689	4123	4756	839	1126	1396	1886	2544	3093	4195
16–16.9	2308	2567	2865	3248	3718	4353	4946	1126	1351	1663	2006	2598	3374	4236
17–17.9	2442	2674	2996	3336	3883	4552	5251	1042	1267	1463	2104	2977	3864	5159
18–18.9	2398	2538	2917	3243	3694	4461	4767	1003	1230	1616	2104	2617	3508	3733
19–24.9	2538	2728	3026	3406	3877	4439	4940	1046	1198	1596	2166	2959	4050	4896
25–34.9	2661	2826	3148	3573	4138	4806	5541	1173	1399	1841	2548	3512	4690	5560
35–44.9	2750	2948	3359	3783	4428	5240	5877	1336	1619	2158	2898	3932	5093	5847
45–54.9	2784	2956	3378	3858	4520	5375	5974	1459	1803	2447	3244	4229	5416	6140
55–64.9	2784	3063	3477	4045	4750	5632	6247	1345	1879	2520	3369	4360	5276	6152
65–74.9	2737	3018	3444	4019	4739	5566	6214	1363	1681	2266	3063	3943	4914	5530

*Data collected from whites in the United States Health and Nutrition Examination Survey I (1971–1974)

From Frisancho AR: New norms of upper limb fat and muscle areas for assessment of nutritional status. Am J Clin Nutr 34:2540, 1981. © Am J Clin Nutr, American Society for Clinical Nutrition.

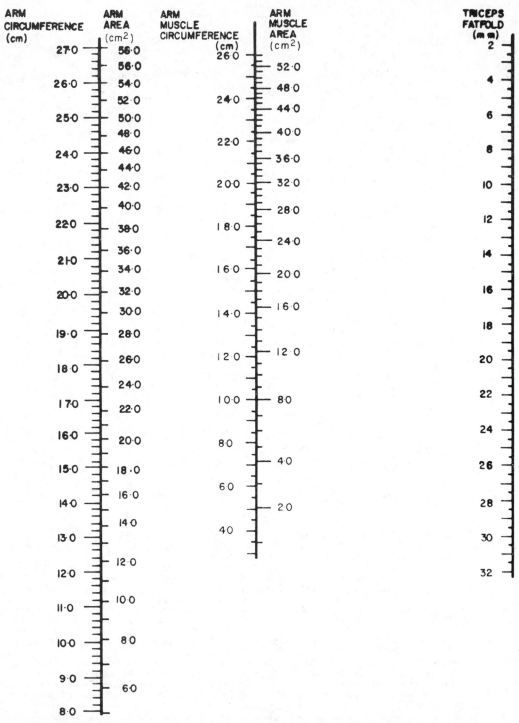

Figure 1–12. Arm anthropometry in nutritional assessment, nomogram for children. To obtain muscle circumference (1) lay ruler between values of arm circumference and fatfold, (2) read off muscle circumference on middle line. To obtain tissue areas (1) read arm and muscle areas, listed to the right of their respective circumferences; (2) fat area = arm area − muscle area. (From Gurney JM, Jelliffe DB: Arm anthropometry in nutritional assessment: nomograms for rapid calculation of muscle circumference and cross sectional muscle and fat areas. Am J Clin Nutr 26:912, 1973. © Am J Clin Nutr, American Society for Clinical Nutrition.)

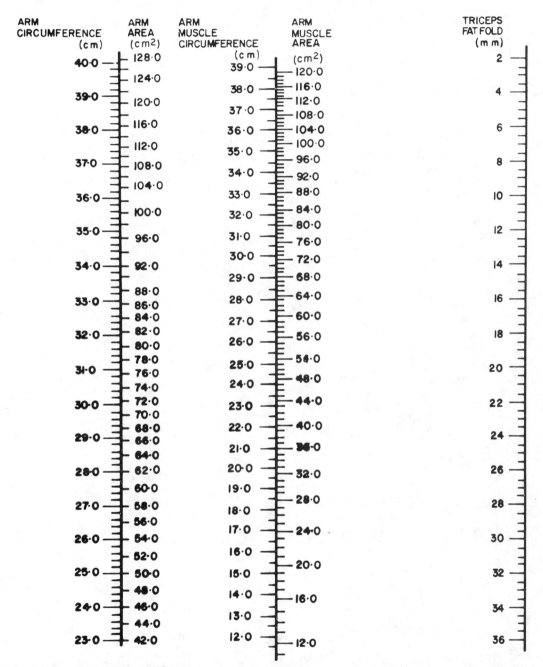

Figure 1–13. Arm anthropometry in nutritional assessment, nomogram for adults. To obtain muscle circumference (1) lay ruler between values of arm circumference and fatfold, (2) read off muscle circumference on middle line. To obtain tissue areas (1) read arm and muscle areas, listed to the right of their respective circumferences; (2) fat area = arm area − muscle area. (From Gurney JM, Jelliffe DB: Arm anthropometry in nutritional assessment: nomograms for rapid calculation of muscle circumference and cross sectional muscle and fat areas. Am J Clin Nutr 26:912, 1973. © Am J Clin Nutr, American Society for Clinical Nutrition.)

Interpretation. Skeletal age is generally retarded in any condition in which growth (measured by height) is slowed secondary to malnutrition, but the percent of retardation may be less for epiphyseal closure than for height. The success of "catch-up" growth depends on the length and age of slowed growth, the adequacy of nutritional repletion, and the control of disease. During this time, height velocity may be twice the average and weight velocity four times the average; the rate of skeletal maturation increases as well.[20]

Sexual Maturation

During adolescence, accelerated growth in height and weight occurs. The appearance of sexual characteristics and the ability to reproduce are followed by a rapid deceleration of growth. Clinical evaluation of sexual maturation is helpful in determining the level of progression through adolescence.[8, 21]

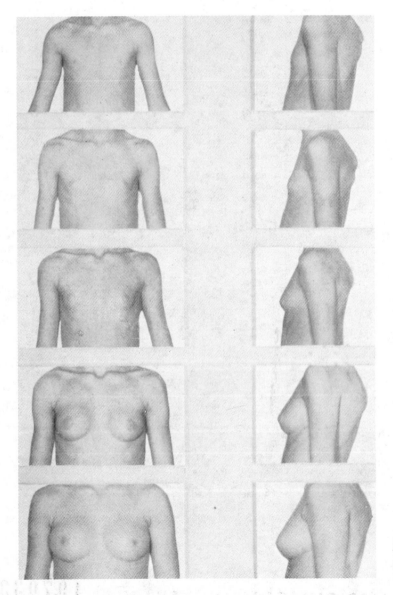

Figure 1–14. Standards for breast development ratings. (From Tanner JM: Growth at Adolescence, 2nd ed. Oxford: Blackwell Scientific, 1962.)

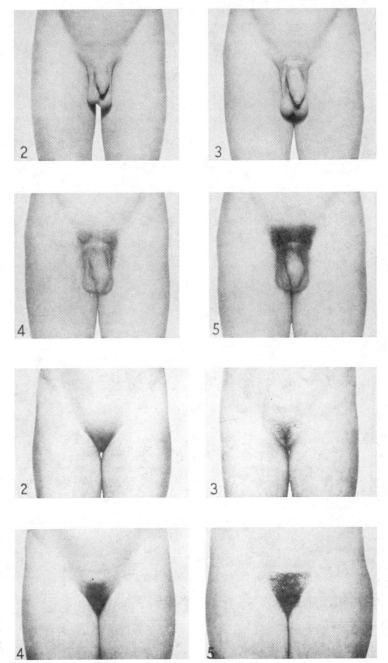

Figure 1–15. Standards for pubic hair ratings in boys and girls. (From Tanner JM: Growth at Adolescence, 2nd ed. Oxford: Blackwell Scientific, 1962.)

Standards. Tanner's stages of sexual development (Figs. 1–14 and 1–15) provide a clinical rating scale (1 = preadolescent; 5 = maturity) for comparison of development. Tables 1–9 and 1–10 also describe various aspects of developmental stages.

Interpretation. Considerable variability exists as to the age at which these events occur. The sequence, however, is fairly uniform.

Additional Growth Charts. Growth information is available for many different populations, and in some instances these may be more appropriate than standard references. The data base in most cases is limited, but scales are available for children who have diabetes[22] or Down's syndrome,[23] who suffer from malnutrition

TABLE 1–9. Stages of Sexual Development: Female

Age	Stages
0–12	I. Preadolescent. Female pelvic contour evident, breast flat, labia majora smooth and minora poorly developed, hymenal opening small or absent, mucous membranes dry and red, vaginal cells lack glycogen.
8–13	II. *Breasts:* Nipple is elevated small mound beneath areola is enlarging and begins pigmentation. *Labia majora:* Become thickened, more prominent and wrinkled; *labia minora* easily identified because of increased size; clitoris, urethral opening more prominent, mucous membranes moist and pink, some glycogen present in vaginal cells. *Hair:* First appears on mons and then on labia majora about time of menarche; still scanty, soft, and straight. *Skin:* Increased activity of sebaceous and merocrine sweat glands; function of apocrine glands in axilla and vulva begins.
9–14	III. Rapid growth peak is passed; menarche most often occurs at this stage and invariably follows the peak of growth acceleration. *Breasts:* Areola and nipple further enlarge and pigmentation becomes more evident; continued increase in glandular size. *Labia minora:* Well developed and vaginal cells have increased glycogen content; mucous membranes increasingly more pale. *Hair:* In pubic region thicker, coarser, often curly (considerable normal variation, including a few girls with early stage II at menarche). *Skin:* Further increased activity of sebaceous and sweat glands; beginning of acne in some girls, adult body odor.
12–15	IV. *Breasts:* Projection of areola above breast plane, and areolar (Montgomery's) glands apparent (this development is absent in about 20% of normal girls); glands easily palpable. *Labia:* Both majora and minora assume adult structure, glycogen content of vaginal cells begins cyclic characteristics. *Hair:* In pubic area more abundant; axillary hair present (rarely present at stage II, not uncommonly present at stage III).
12–17	V. *Breasts:* Mature histologic morphology; nipple enlarged and erect, areolar (Montgomery's) glands well developed, globular shape. *Hair:* In pubic area more abundant and may spread to thighs (in about 10% of women it assumes "male" distribution with extension toward umbilicus); facial hair increased often in form of slight mustache. *Skin:* Increased sebaceous gland activity and increased severity of acne if present before.

Reproduced by permission from Lowrey GH: Growth and Development of Children, 7th ed. Copyright © 1978 by Year Book Medical Publishers, Inc., Chicago.

as a result of overpopulation,[24] who have received a renal transplant,[25] who live in a vegetarian household,[26] or who were born prematurely.[27, 28] Figures 1–16 and 1–17 are growth charts constructed for use with premature infants.

CLASSIFICATION OF MALNUTRITION

Malnutrition is a pathologic state of varying severity; its clinical features are caused by a deficiency, excess, or imbalance of essential nutrients. The cause may be primary (insufficient quantity or quality of food) or secondary (increased requirements or inadequate utilization).

Development of *marasmus* occurs after severe deprivation of both protein and calories, and it is characterized by growth retardation and wasting of muscle and subcutaneous fat. In *kwashiorkor,* the protein deficit exceeds the caloric deficit; edema accompanies muscle wasting that results from acute protein deprivation or loss of protein caused by stress or inadequate calories. Indifference, apathy, and fatigue are present in victims of both conditions, and psychological alterations may be profound. Severe anorexia, apathy, and irritability make these children difficult to feed and manage. Many of the clinical signs (hair and skin changes) lack specificity and are identical to symptoms of other nutrient deficiencies (Table 1–11).[29–32] Hormonal changes are outlined in Table 1–12.[31, 32]

TABLE 1–10. Stages of Sexual Development: Male

Age	Stages
0–14	I. Preadolescent
10–14	II. *Testes* and *penis:* Increasing size is evident (testicle length reaches 2.0 cm or more); scrotum integument is thinner and assumes an increased pendulous appearance. *Hair:* First appearance of pubic hair in area at base of penis. *Skin:* Increased activity of sebaceous and apocrine sweat glands, and function of apocrine glands on axilla and scrotal area begins.
11–15	III. Rapid growth peak is passed; nocturnal emissions begin. *Testes* and *penis:* Further increase in size and pigmentation; Leydig's cells (interstitial) first appear at stage II, are now prominent in testes. *Hair:* More abundant in pubic area and present on scrotum; still scanty and finely textured; axillary hair begins. *Breasts:* Button-type hypertrophy in 70% of boys at stages II and III. *Larynx:* Changes in voice caused by laryngeal growth begin. *Skin:* Increasing activity of sebaceous and sweat glands; beginning of acne, adult body odor.
12–16	IV. *Testes:* Further increase in size (length 4.0 cm of greater); increase in size of penis greatest at stages III and IV. *Hair:* Pubic hair thicker and coarser; in most it ascends toward umbilicus in typical male pattern; axillary hair increases, facial hair increases over lip and upper cheeks. *Larynx:* Voice deepens. *Skin:* Increasing pigmentation of scrotum and penis; acne often more severe. *Breasts:* Previous hypertrophy decreased or absent.
13–17	V. *Testes:* Length greater than 4.5 cm. *Hair:* Pubic hair thick, curly, heavily pigmented, extends to thighs and toward umbilicus; adult distribution and increase in body hair (chest, shoulders, and thighs) continues for more than another 10 years; baldness, if present, may begin. *Larynx:* Adult character of voice. *Skin:* Acne may persist and increase.

Reproduced by permission from Lowrey GH: Growth and Development of Children, 7th ed. Copyright © 1978 by Year Book Medical Publishers, Inc., Chicago.

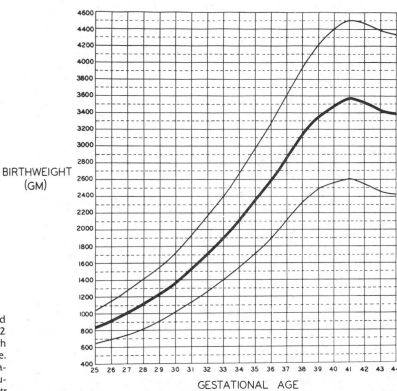

BIRTHWEIGHT (GM)

GESTATIONAL AGE (WEEKS)

Figure 1–16. Smoothed curve values for the mean ± 2 standard deviations of birth weight against gestational age. (From Usher R, McLean F: Intra-uterine growth of live-born Caucasian infants at sea level. J Pediatr 74:901, 1969.)

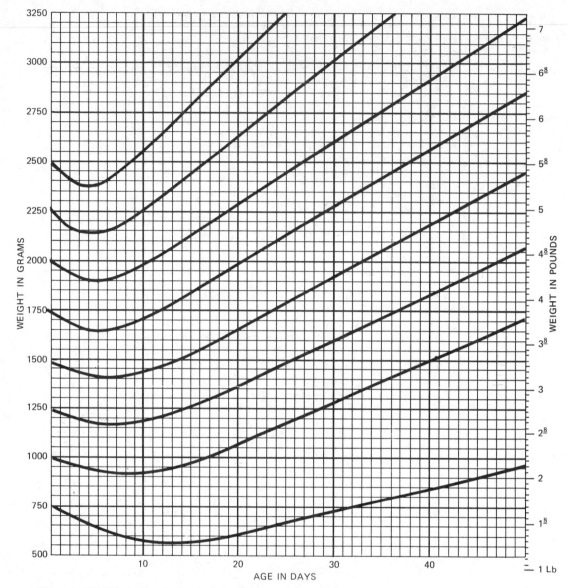

Figure 1–17. Growth chart for low birth-weight infants. (From Lubchenco LO, et al.: Intrauterine growth in length and head circumference as estimated from live births at gestational ages from 26 to 42 weeks. Pediatrics 37:403, 1966. Copyright American Academy of Pediatrics 1981.)

TABLE 1–11. Clinical Signs in Malnutrition

	Marasmus	Kwashiorkor
Growth retardation (linear)	+ +	+
Muscle wasting	+ +	+
Edema	−	+
Apathy, fatigue	+	+ +
Irritability	+	+
Infection	+	+ +
Electrolyte imbalance (hypokalemia)	−	+
Hypoalbuminemia	−	+
Anemia	+	+ +
Fatty liver	−	+
Low body temperature	+	+ +
Gastrointestinal disturbances	+	+ +
Pellagroid dermatoses	−	+

−: not seen; +: seen; + +: seen more frequently or is more marked

TABLE 1–12. Hormonal Changes in Malnutrition

	Marasmus	Kwashiorkor
Insulin	D	D or delayed
Growth Hormone	I, D, or N	I
TSH	N	I
LH and FSH	D	D
ADH	N	I
T_4	N	D or N
Free T_4	D or N	I or N
T_3	D	D
I^{131} thyroid uptake	D	N
Cortisol	I	I
Aldosterone	N	I

D: decreased; I: increased; N: no change

Malnutrition was first defined in terms of a deficit in weight for a child's age. However, height for age and weight for height are often more useful tools for evaluation of acute and chronic malnutrition; for example, a low weight for height is seen in acute malnutrition. In chronic undernutrition, there are frequently no clinical signs other than a low height and weight for age. Children who are over 90 percent of their expected weight for height and less than 90 percent of their expected height for age are termed nutritional dwarfs (Table 1–13), since their height has been stunted but their current weight is appropriate for their height.

The morbidity and mortality associated with malnutrition are more closely correlated with degree of malnutrition than with sex, age, or specific clinical factors,[33] although some studies show a higher mortality rate in infancy than in older age groups.[30] Third-degree (severe) malnutrition has a range of mortality rates from 30 to 60 percent,[33, 34] and second-degree (moderate) malnutrition has a mortality rate of 25 percent.[35] Kwashiorkor has a higher mortality rate than does marasmus,[36] and electrolyte and fluid imbalances increase the death rate significantly.[33, 34]

CLINICAL EVALUATION

Severe nutritional deprivation is easily detectable in most instances. More subtle physical signs, suggesting less severe chronic or subacute deficiencies, are often nonspecific for individual nutrients. Thorough medical and dental history and results of physical examination for signs suggestive of malnutrition (Tables 1–14 and 1–15)[2, 3, 5, 37–40] should be recorded and described as precisely as possible and confirmed by biochemical, anthropometric, or dietary evaluation.

Text continued on page 39

TABLE 1–13. Most Common Classifications of Protein-Calorie Malnutrition

	Normal	Mild	Moderate	Severe
Weight for height*	110–90	90–85	85–75	< 75
Weight for age†	110–90	90–81	80–61	< 60
Weight for age‡	> 90	90–75	75–61	< 60

Presence of edema indicates marasmus; no edema, kwashiorkor
*From McLaren DS, Read WWC: Weight/length classification of nutritional status. Lancet 2:219, 1975.
†From Jelliffe D: The assessment of the nutritional status of the community. World Health Organization Monograph 53, Geneva, Switzerland, 1966.
‡From Gomez F, et al.: Malnutrition in infancy and childhood with special reference to kwashiorkor. Adv Pediatr 7:131, 1955.

TABLE 1–14. Clinical Examination in Nutritional Deficiencies and Excesses

	Major Physiologic Functions	Deficiency Signs	Excess Signs	Important Food Souces
Nutrient				
Protein	Constitutes part of the structure of every cell; regulates body processes as part of enzymes, some hormones, body fluids, and antibodies that increase resistance to infection; provides nitrogen and has a caloric density of 4 cal/g	Dry, depigmented, easily pluckable hair; bilateral, dependent edema; cirrhosis, fatty liver, decreased visceral proteins; skin is dry with pellagroid dermatoses in severe cases	Azotemia, acidosis, hyperammonemia	Meat, poultry, fish, legumes, eggs, cheese, milk and other dairy products, nuts, breast milk, infant formula
Carbohydrate	Supplies energy at an average of 4 cal/g of glucose (sparing protein) and is the major energy source for CNS function; unrefined, complex carbohydrates supply fiber that aids in normal bowel function	Seizures	May cause diarrhea	Breads, cereals, crackers, potatoes, corn, simple sugars (sugar, honey), fruits and vegetables, milk, breast milk, infant formula
Fat	Concentrated calorie source at an average 9 cal/g; constitutes part of the structure of every cell; supplies essential fatty acids and provides and carries fat-soluble vitamins (A, D, E, K)	Essential fatty acid deficiency: dry, scaly skin, poor weight gain, hair loss	Atherosclerosis may be affected by excessive intakes of certain dietary fats; altered blood lipid levels	Shortening, oil, butter, margarine, protein-rich foods (meat, dairy, nuts), breast milk, infant formula
Fat-Soluble Vitamins				
Vitamin A (serum carotene)	Formation and maintenance of skin and mucous membranes; necessary for the formation of rhodopsin (the photosensitive pigment of the rods governing vision in dim light), and regulation of membrane structure and function	Night blindness, degeneration of the retina, xerophthalmia, follicular hyperkeratosis, poor growth, keratomalacia, Bitot's spots	Fatigue, malaise, lethargy, abdominal pain, hepatomegaly, alopecia, headache with increased intracranial pressure, vomiting	Carrots, liver, green vegetables, sweet potatoes, butter, margarine, apricots, melons, peaches, broccoli, cod liver oil, breast milk, infant formula
Vitamin D	Promotes intestinal absorption of calcium and phosphate, renal conservation of calcium and phosphorus	Rickets, osteomalacia, costochondral beading, epiphyseal enlargement, cranial bossing, bowed legs, persistently open anterior fontanelle	Hypercalcemia, vomiting, anorexia, irritability, azotemia, diarrhea, convulsions	Cod liver oil, fish, eggs, liver, butter, fortified milk, sunlight (activation of 7-dehydrocholesterol in the skin), infant formula

	Function	Deficiency	Excess	Food Sources
Vitamin E	Acts as an antioxidant and free radical scavenger to prevent peroxidation of polyunsaturated fatty acids in the body; enhances absorption and utilization of vitamin A	Hemolytic anemia in the premature and newborn, enhanced fragility of red blood cells, increased peroxidative hemolysis	None known	Oils high in polyunsaturated fatty acids, milk, eggs, breast milk, infant formula
Vitamin K	Necessary for prothrombin and the three blood-clotting factors VII, IX, and X; half of the vitamin K in man is of intestinal origin, synthesized by gut flora; necessary for bone mineralization	Hemorrhagic manifestations (especially in newborns), cirrhosis	Hemolytic anemia, nerve palsy	Green leafy vegetables, fruits, cereals, dairy products, soybeans, breast milk, infant formula
Water-Soluble Vitamins				
Vitamin C	Forms collagen cross-linkages of proline hydroxylase, thus strengthening tissue and improving wound healing and resistance to infection; aids utilization of iron; is a water-soluble antioxidant and thus protects other lipid-soluble vitamins	Joint tenderness, scurvy (capillary hemorrhaging), impaired wound healing, acute periodontal gingivitis, petechiae, purpura	Increased incidence of renal oxalate stones	Heat-labile; broccoli, papaya, orange, mango, grapefruit, strawberries, tomatoes, potatoes, leafy vegetables, breast milk, infant formula
Thiamine (B$_1$)	Aids in energy utilization as part of a coenzyme component to promote the utilization of carbohydrate; promotes normal functioning of the nervous system; coenzyme for oxidative carboxylation of 2-keto acids	Beriberi, neuritis, edema, cardiac failure, anorexia, restlessness, confusion, loss of vibration sense and deep tendon reflexes, calf tenderness	None known	Pork (lean), and nuts, whole grain and fortified cereal products, breast milk, infant formula
Riboflavin (B$_2$)	Functions primarily as the reactive portion of flavoproteins concerned with biologic oxidations (cellular metabolism)	Cheilosis, glossitis, photophobia, angular stomatitis, corneal vascularization, scrotal skin changes, seborrhea, magenta tongue	None known	Dairy products, liver, almonds, lamb, pork, breast milk, infant formula
Niacin	Aids in energy utilization as part of a coenzyme (NAD+ and NAFP+) in fat synthesis, tissue respiration, and carbohydrate utilization; aids digestion and fosters normal appetite; synthesized from the amino acid tryptophan	Pellagra (dermatitis, diarrhea, dementia, death), cheilosis, angular stomatitis, inflammation of mucous membranes, weakness	Dilation of the capillaries, vasomotor instability, "flushing" (utilization of muscle glycogen, serum lipids, mobilization of fatty acids during exercise)	Liver, meat, fish, poultry, peanuts, fortified cereal products, yeast, breast milk, infant formula

Table continued on following page

TABLE 1–14. Clinical Examination in Nutritional Deficiencies and Excesses *Continued*

	Major Physiologic Functions	Deficiency Signs	Excess Signs	Important Food Sources
Water-Soluble Vitamins *Continued*				
Pyridoxine (B₆)	Coenzyme component for many of the enzymes of amino acid metabolism	Convulsions, loss of weight, abdominal distress, vomiting, hyperirritability, depression, confusion, hypochromic and macrocytic anemia	None known	Fish, poultry, meat, wheat, breast milk, infant formula
Folacin	Utilized in carbon transfer and thus nucleotide synthesis	Megaloblastic anemia, stomatitis, glossitis	None known	Liver, leafy vegetables, fruit, yeast, breast milk, infant formula
Cobalamin (B₁₂; intrinsic factor required)	Cobalamin-containing coenzymes function in the degradation of certain odd-chain fatty acids and in the recycling of tetrahydrofolate	Megaloblastic anemia, neurologic deterioration	None known	Animal products, breast milk, infant formula
Biotin	Component of several carboxylating enzymes; plays an important role in the metabolism of fat and carbohydrate	Anorexia; nausea; vomiting; glossitis; depression; dry, scaly dermatitis; thin hair; loss of eyebrows	None known	Liver, kidney, egg yolk, breast milk, infant formula
Pantothenic Acid	Component of coenzyme A; plays a role in release of energy from carbohydrates and in synthesis and degradation of fatty acids	Infertility, abortion, slowed growth, depression	None known	Meat, fish, poultry, whole grains, legumes, breast milk, infant formula
Minerals				
Calcium	Essential for calcification of bone (matrix formation); assists in blood clotting; functions in normal muscle contraction and relaxation and in normal nerve transmission	Osteomalacia, osteoporosis	Hypercalcemia (vomiting anorexia)	Dairy products (i.e., milk, cheese) sardines, oysters, salmon, herring, greens, breast milk, infant formula
Phosphorus	Important intracellular anion; involved in many chemical reactions within the body; necessary for energy turnover (ATP)	Weakness, anorexia, malaise, bone pain, growth arrest	Hypocalcemia (when parathyroid gland not fully functioning)	Diary products, fish, legumes, pork, breast milk, infant formula

	Function	Deficiency	Excess	Food Sources
Magnesium	Essential part of many enzyme systems; important for maintaining electrical potential in nerves and muscle membranes and for energy turnover	Tremor, convulsions, hyperexcitability (hypocalcemia tetany)	Sedation	Widely distributed, especially in food of vegetable origin; breast milk, infant formula
Trace Elements				
Iron	Part of hemoglobin molecule; prevents nutritional anemia and fatigue; increases resistance to infection; functions as a part of enzymes involved in tissue respiration	Anemia, malabsorption, irritability, anorexia, pallor, lethargy	Hemosiderosis, hemochromatosis	Red meats, liver, dried beans and peas, enriched farina, breast milk, iron-fortified infant formula, infant cereal
Zinc	Constituent of enzymes involved in most major metabolic pathways (specifically nucleic acid synthesis for cellular growth and repair)	Growth failure, skin changes, delayed wound healing, hypogeusia, sexual immaturity, hair loss, diarrhea	Acute gastrointestinal upset, vomiting	Whole grains, legumes, beef, lamb, pork, poultry, nuts, seeds, shellfish, eggs, some cheeses, breast milk, infant formula
Iodine	Component of thyroid hormones triiodothyronine and thyroxine, important in regulation of cellular oxidation and growth	Goiter, depressed thyroid function, cretinism	Thyroid suppression (thyrotoxicosis)	Iodized table salt, salt water, fish, shellfish (content of most other foods geographically dependent), breast milk, infant formula
Copper	Constituent of proteins and enzymes, some of which are essential for the proper utilization of iron	Anemia (hemolytic), neutropenia, bone disease	Excess accumulation of the liver, brain, kidney, cornea	Oysters, nuts, liver, kidney, corn-oil margarine, dried legumes
Manganese	Essential part of several enzyme systems involved in protein and energy metabolism and in the formation of mucopolysaccharides	Impaired growth, skeletal abnormalities, lowered reproductive function, neonatal ataxia	In extremely high exposure of contamination: severe psychiatric and neurologic disorders	Nuts, whole grains, dried fruits, fruits, vegetables (nonleafy)
Fluoride	The main target organs of fluoride in man are the enamel of teeth and bones, where fluoride is incorporated into the crystalline structure of hydroxyapatite and produces increased caries resistance	Poor dentition, caries, osteoporosis	Mottling, brown staining of teeth (in excess of 4 ppm); fluorosis occurs after prolonged (10–20 yrs) ingestion of 20–80 mg/day	Fluoridated water; depends on the geochemical environment and therefore amount in foods varies widely
Chromium	Maintenance of normal glucose metabolism, cofactor for insulin	Disturbed glucose metabolism (lower glucose tolerance caused by insulin resistance)		Brewer's yeast, meat products, cheeses

Table continued on following page

TABLE 1–14. Clinical Examination in Nutritional Deficiencies and Excesses *Continued*

	Major Physiologic Functions	Deficiency Signs	Excess Signs	Important Food Sources
Trace Elements *Continued*				
Selenium	Functions as a part of the enzyme glutathione peroxidase, which protects cellular components from oxidative damage	Cardiomyopathy, probably secondary to oxidative damage	In animals, blindness, abdominal pain, lack of vitality	Seafoods, kidney, liver, meat, grains (depending on growing area)
Molybdenum	Essential for the function of flavin-dependent enzymes involved in the production of uric acid and in the oxidation of aldehydes and sulfites	Not described in man	Acts as an antagonist to the essential element copper; goutlike syndrome associated with elevated blood levels of molybdenum, uric acid, and xanthine oxidase	Varies considerably, depending on growing environment; main contributions come from meat, grains, and legumes

TABLE 1–15. Clinical Evaluation of Nutritional Status

	Clinical Findings	Deficiency	Differential Diagnosis
Skull	In infants: bossing of the skull over ossification centers, delayed closure of anterior fontanelle	Vitamin D, calcium	Syphilis, sickle-cell disease, positional deformity, hydrocephalus
	Decreased head circumference	Protein-calorie	
Hair	Dry, wirelike, easily pluckable, brittle, depigmented, sparse	Protein-calorie	
	Impaired keratinization (hair is "steely")	Copper	
	Hair loss	Zinc, biotin, protein, essential fatty acids	
Skin	Malar pigmentation (darkened pigment over malar eminences)	Calories, B complex, especially niacin	Melasma in pregnancy or from oral contraceptives, Addison's disease
	Nasolabial seborrhea	Niacin, riboflavin, B$_6$	
	Ecchymosis	Vitamin C	Hematologic disorders (thrombocytopenia), trauma, liver disease, anticoagulant overdose, orthostatic purpura, Fabry's disease, emboli, stasis, clotting factor deficiency
	Perifollicular petechiae	Vitamin K	
	Follicular hyperkeratosis (skin is rough, surrounding skin is dry)	Vitamin A	Fungus infection, perifolliculitis or scurvy, keratosis pilaris, Darier's disease
	Xerosis (skin is dry, with fine flaking)	Vitamin A, essential fatty acids	Aging, environmental drying, hypothyroidism, uremia, poor hygiene, ichthyosis
	Hyperpigmentation (seen more frequently on hands and face)	Niacin, folic acid, B$_{12}$	Addison's disease, environmental factors, trauma
	Scrotal dermatitis	Riboflavin, zinc	Fungus infection
	Pellagrous dermatitis (lesions are symmetric and in areas exposed to the sun)	Niacin	Chemical injury, sunburn, thermal burn
	Thickened skin at pressure points (predominantly in belt area)		
	Delayed wound healing	Zinc, vitamin C, protein	
Eyes	Circumcorneal injection (bilateral)	Riboflavin	
	Xerophthalmia (conjunctiva is dull, lusterless, exhibits a striated or rough surface)	Vitamin A	
	Bitot's spots (small circumscribed, dull, dry lesions usually seen on the lateral aspect of the bulbar conjunctiva)	Vitamin A	Pterygium
	Keratomalacia	Vitamin A	
	Night blindness	Vitamin A	
	Xanthomatosis, hyperlipidemia, and hypercholesterolemia leading to localized deposits of lipids	Excess intake of fat with elevated serum lipoproteins	

Table continued on following page

TABLE 1–15. Clinical Evaluation of Nutritional Status *Continued*

	Clinical Findings	Deficiency	Differential Diagnosis
Lips	Cheilosis (lips may be swollen)	Niacin, riboflavin	Herpes simplex, arid or arctic environmental exposure
	Angular fissures (corners of mouth broken or macerated)	Niacin, riboflavin, iron, B_6	Herpes, syphilis
Gums	Bleeding gums (spongy)	Vitamin C	Dilantin toxicity, periodontal disease
Teeth	Dental caries	Fluoride	Poor oral hygiene
	Mottled enamel	Excess fluoride	Staining from tetracyclines
Tongue	Glossitis (red, painful tongue—may be fissured)	Folic acid, niacin, riboflavin, B_{12}, B_6, iron	Uremia, antibiotics, malignancy, aphthous stomatitis, monilial infection
	Atrophy of filiform papillae (low or absent)	Niacin, folic acid, B_{12}, iron	Non-nutritional anemias
	Hypertrophy of fungiform papillae	General malnutrition	Dietary irritants
	Pale, atrophic tongue	Iron, folic acid, B_{12}, niacin, riboflavin, B_6	Non-nutritional anemias
Exocrine	Parotid enlargement	Protein (?)	Mumps
Endocrine	Goiter	Iodine	Thyroglossal duct cyst, bronchial cleft cysts and tumors, hyperthyroidism, thyroiditis, thyroid carcinoma
Oral	Dysgeusia (disordered taste)	Zinc	Cancer therapy
	Hypogeusia (loss of taste acuity)		
Nails	Koilonychia (spoon nails; nails are thin, concave)	Iron	Cardiac or pulmonary disease
Cardiac	Cardia enlargement, tachycardia	Thiamine, iron	

Table continued on opposite page

TABLE 1–15. Clinical Evaluation of Nutritional Status *Continued*

	Clinical Findings	Deficiency	Differential Diagnosis
Abdominal	Hepatomegaly	Chronic malnutrition	Liver disease
Skeletal	Rickets (bowed legs, deformities may also be seen in pelvic bones)	Calcium, phosphates, vitamin D	Renal rickets, malabsorption, congenital deformity
	Costochondral beading (?)	Calcium, vitamin D	
	Scorbutic rosary (costochondral junctions may have sharp edges caused by epiphyseal separation)	Vitamin C	
	Epiphyseal swelling secondary to epiphyseal hyperplasia (in rickets, secondary to tenderness and swelling caused by hemorrhage)	Vitamin D, calcium, vitamin C	Renal disease, malabsorption, congenital deformity
Neurologic	Absence of tendon reflexes (bilateral)	Thiamine, B_{12}	Peripheral neuropathy from other causes
	Absence of vibratory sense (bilateral)		
	Calf tenderness	Thiamine	
	Pseudoparalysis (movement restricted because of pain)	Vitamin C	Hypokalemia
Extremities	Calf tenderness	Thiamine	Muscle strain, trauma, other causes of peripheral neuropathy, deep venous thrombosis
	Bilateral edema of lower extremities	Protein (occurs late in deficiency)	Congestive heart failure, renal failure, protein-losing enteropathy
Growth	Nutritional dwarfism, subcutaneous fat loss	Calories, protein	
	Dwarfism, hypogonadism	Zinc	

TABLE 1–16. Laboratory Evaluation of Nutritional Status

Nutrient	Age of Subject	Status		
		Deficient	*Marginal*	*Acceptable*
Hemoglobin (g/100 ml)*	6–23 mo	Up to 9.0	9.0–9.9	10.0 +
	2–5 yr	Up to 10.0	10.0–10.9	11.0 +
	6–12	Up to 10.0	10.0–11.4	11.5 +
	13–16 (m)	Up to 12.0	12.0–12.9	13.0 +
	13–16 (f)	Up to 10.0	10.0–11.4	11.5 +
	16 + (m)	Up to 12.0	12.0–13.9	14.0 +
	16 + (f)	Up to 10.0	10.0–11.9	12.0 +
	Pregnant (after 6 + mo)	Up to 9.5	9.5–10.9	11.0 +
Hematocrit (packed cell volume, %)*	Up to 2 yr	Up to 28	28–30	31 +
	2–5	Up to 30	30–33	34 +
	6–12	Up to 30	30–35	36 +
	13–16 (m)	Up to 37	37–39	40 +
	13–16 (f)	Up to 31	31–35	36 +
	16 + (m)	Up to 37	37–43	44 +
	16 + (f)	Up to 31	31–37	38 +
	Pregnant	Up to 30	30–32	33 +
Serum albumin (g/100 ml)*	Up to 1 yr	—	Up to 2.5	2.5 +
	1–5	—	Up to 3.0	3.0 +
	6–16	—	Up to 3.5	3.5 +
	16 +	Up to 2.8	2.8–3.4	3.5 +
	Pregnant	Up to 3.0	3.0–3.4	3.5 +
Serum protein (g/100 ml)*	Up to 1 yr	—	Up to 5.0	5.0 +
	1–5	—	Up to 5.5	5.5 +
	6–16	—	Up to 6.0	6.0 +
	16 +	Up to 6.0	6.0–6.4	6.5 +
	Pregnant	Up to 5.5	5.5–5.9	6.0 +
Serum ascorbic acid (mg/100 ml)*	All ages	Up to 0.1	0.1–0.19	0.2 +
Plasma vitamin A (μg/100 ml)*	All ages	Up to 10	10–19	20 +
Plasma carotene (μg/100 ml)*	All ages	Up to 20	20–39	40 +
	Pregnant	—	40–79	80 +
Serum iron (μg/100 ml)*	Up to 2 yr	Up to 30	—	30 +
	2–5	Up to 40	—	40 +
	8–12	Up to 50	—	50 +
	12 + (m)	Up to 60	—	60 +
	12 + (f)	Up to 40	—	40 +
Transferrin saturation (percent)*	Up to 2 yr	Up to 15.0	—	15.0 +
	2–12	Up to 20.0	—	20.0 +
	12 + (m)	Up to 20.0	—	20.0 +
	12 + (f)	Up to 15.0	—	15.0 +
Serum folacin (ng/ml)†	All ages	Up to 2.0	2.1–5.9	6.0 +
Serum vitamin B$_{12}$ (pg/ml)†	All ages	Up to 100	—	100 +
Thiamine in urine (μg/g creatinine)*	1–3 yr	Up to 120	120–175	175 +
	4–5	Up to 85	85–120	120 +
	6–9	Up to 70	70–180	180 +
	10–15	Up to 55	55–150	150 +
	16 +	Up to 27	27–65	65 +
	Pregnant	Up to 21	21–49	50 +
Riboflavin in urine (μg/g creatinine)*	1–3 yr	Up to 150	150–499	500 +
	4–5	Up to 100	100–299	300 +
	6–9	Up to 85	85–269	270 +
	10–16	Up to 70	70–199	200 +
	16 +	Up to 27	27–79	80 +
	Pregnant	Up to 30	30–89	90 +
RBC transketolase-TPP-effect (ratio)† (Thiamine)	All ages	25 +	15–25	Up to 15
RBC glutathione reductase-FAD-effect (ratio)† (Riboflavin)	All ages	1.2 +	—	Up to 1.2

Table continued on opposite page

TABLE 1–16. Laboratory Evaluation of Nutritional Status *Continued*

Nutrient	Age of Subject	Status		
		Deficient	*Marginal*	*Acceptable*
Tryptophan load (mg xanthurenic acid excreted)† (Pyridoxine)	Adults (Dose: 100 mg/kg body weight)	25 + (6 hr) 75 + (24 hr)	— —	Up to 25 Up to 75
Urinary pyridoxine (μg/g creatinine)†	1–3 yr	Up to 90	—	90 +
	4–6	Up to 80	—	80 +
	7–9	Up to 60	—	60 +
	10–12	Up to 40	—	40 +
	13–15	Up to 30	—	30 +
	16 +	Up to 20	—	20 +
Urinary N′ methyl nicotinamide (mg/g creatinine)* (Niacin)	All ages Pregnant	Up to 0.2 Up to 0.8	0.2–5.59 0.8–2.49	0.6 + 2.5 +
Urinary pantothenic acid (μg)*	All ages	Up to 200	—	200 +
Plasma vitamin E (mg/100 ml)†	All ages	Up to 0.2	0.2–0.6	0.6 +
Transaminase index (ratio)†:				
EGOT‡	Adult	2.0 +	—	Up to 2.0
EGPT§	Adult	1.25 +	—	Up to 1.25

*Adapted from the Ten State Nutrition Survey; from Christakis G, ed.: Nutritional assessment in health programs. Am J Public Health 63:1, 1973.
†Criteria may vary with different methodology
‡Erythrocyte glutamic oxalacetic transaminase
§Erythrocyte glutamic pyruvic transaminase

LABORATORY EVALUATION

Laboratory studies may confirm nutrient deficiencies determined by anthropometric, clinical, or dietary evaluation, or they may define deficiencies that are clinically inapparent. The quantitative measurement of a nutrient concentration in blood or urine reflects body stores with varying degrees of precision and, therefore, may mislead the examiner. Useful laboratory determinants for the evaluation of nutrient status are shown in Table 1–16. In addition, various tests that may be helpful in the differential diagnosis of nutritional anemias are shown in Table 1–17.[5, 6, 8]

Severe nutritional deprivation often causes a deficient cellular immune response, whereas hormonal antibody activity is normal or enhanced.[41] This anergic response is reversible as nutritional status improves and, together with total lymphocyte count, can be used to determine the severity of malnutrition. Anergy also occurs in the presence of fever, sepsis, steroid therapy, tumor, and shock. For delayed hypersensitivity skin testing, the patient receives intradermally three common recall antigens (such as streptokinase-streptodornase, *Candida*, mumps, or *Trichophyton*[42]) in the forearm area. Skin-test reactions are read at 24 and 48 hours. Induration greater than 5 mm is considered normal, and the presence of one normal test indicates intact immunity. Total lymphocyte counts less than 1500/mm³ fall

TABLE 1–17. Laboratory Tests in the Differential Diagnosis of Anemias

Type of Anemia	Hb	Hct	MCV	Serum Iron	TIBC	Transferrin Saturation	Ferritin	Marrow Hemosiderin	Sideroblasts	RBC	Retic	Other
Iron deficiency	D	D	D	D	I	D	D	D	D	N	D	Hypochromic, microcytic, or normocytic
Vitamin B$_{12}$	D	D	I	I	D or N	I, D, or N	N	I	I	D	D or N	Macrocytic, megaloblastic, hypersegmented neutrophils, low-serum B$_{12}$, thrombocytopenia, leukopenia
Folic acid	D	D	I	I	D or N	I, D, or N	D	I	I	D	D or N	Macrocytic, megaloblastic, normal or slightly low B$_{12}$, decreased red cell folate
Vitamin E	D	D	I or N	I	D	N	N	I	I	D	I	Hemolytic anemia, low serum vitamin E, increased RBC, hemolysis, normochromic, normocytic
Anemia of chronic disease	D	D	N	D	D	D	N	N or I	D	D	D	Usually normocytic, normochromic, may be hypochromic, microcytic
Anemia of chronic infection	D	D	N or D	D	D	D or N	I or N	I, N, or D	D	D	D	Normochromic and normocytic, may be hypochromic and microcytic

D: decreased; N: normal; I: increased.

TABLE 1–18. Normal Values for 24-Hour Creatinine Excretion

Height (cm)	Both Sexes*	Males†	Females†
55	50.0		
60	65.2		
65	80.5		
70	97.5		
75	118.0		
80	139.6		
85	167.6		
90	199.9		
95	239.8		
100	278.7		
105	305.4		
110	349.8		
115	394.5		
120	456.0		
125	535.1		
130		448.1	525.2
135		480.1	589.2
140		556.3	653.1
145		684.3	717.2
150		812.2	780.9
155		940.3	844.8
160		1068.3	908.8
165		1196.3	
170		1324.3	
175		1452.3	
180		1580.3	

*Adapted from Viteri FE, Awarad J: The creatinine height index: its use in the estimation of the degree of protein depletion and repletion in protein calorie malnourished children. Pediatrics 96:696, 1970.
†Adapted from Cheek DB, ed.: Human Growth. Philadelphia: Lea & Febiger, 1968.
From Suskind RM, ed.: Textbook of Pediatric Nutrition. New York: Raven Press, 1981.

more than 2 standard deviations below the mean at any age,[43] and indicate impaired immune function. To calculate total lymphocyte count:

$$\text{total lymphocyte count} = \frac{\text{percent lymphocytes} \times \text{white blood cells}}{100}$$

$>1500/mm^3$ is acceptable

The creatinine–height index is a measure of lean body mass or muscle mass. In normal individuals, creatinine excretion correlates well with lean body mass, surface area, and body weight. In patients with muscle-wasting disease, creatinine excretion is reduced and no longer correlates with body weight. Presumably this change results from the distortions of body composition, especially the loss of body protein, produced by disease.[44] Since height remains essentially unaltered by acute malnutrition and creatinine excretion continues to correlate with body cell mass, a creatinine–height index affords a means of assessing the nutritional status of the metabolically active tissue by allowing a comparison between expected body cell mass for height and actual body cell mass. A 24-hour urinary creatinine level can be determined and compared with standards (Table 1–18).

$$\text{creatinine height index} = \frac{\text{actual urinary creatinine excretion}}{\text{ideal urinary creatinine excretion}}$$

normal = 1.0
acceptable = >0.8

Pediatric Diet History Form

Name _____   Date _____

Unit number _____   Dietitian _____

Birth Date _____   Doctor _____

Informant _____   Reliability _____

Main Caretaker _____

Current Problems: _____

_____

_____

_____

Past Problems & Medical History: _____

_____

_____

_____

_____

Age _____

Wt: _____ kg _____ % ile   Wt/Ht _____% ile

Ht: _____ cm _____ % ile

Head Circumference _____ cm _____% ile

Other Anthropometric Measurements: _____

_____

Hct: _____   Other Lab Data _____

Hbg: _____

Alb (Serum) _____

Activity pattern (include daily pattern, naps, etc.) _____

_____

Has the child ever been on a special diet?

    Diet _____

    Reason _____

Figure 1–18. Form for recording pediatric diet history.

Illustration continued on opposite page

Is the child presently on a special diet?

    Diet _____

    Reason _____

Do you think the child has a feeding problem?

    Describe _____

_____

Briefly describe the changes in child's feeding pattern since birth. Include formulas and all changes, addition of solids to the diet, changes in consistency. Note age at time of change or introduction.

_____

_____

_____

At Present:	*Yes*	*No*
Is the child breast-fed?	_____	_____
Also receiving milk or formula?	_____	_____

Specify type or amount _____

_____

	Yes	*No*
Does the child receive formula?	_____	_____

Specify type and method of preparation _____

_____

	Yes	*No*
Does the child drink milk?	_____	_____

Kind _____

Usual intake of milk or formula in a day is _____ ounces.

Dose the child usually take a bottle to bed? _____

Usual contents _____

Does the child take vitamin, fluoride, or iron drops? _____

    What kind? _____

    How often? _____

The child takes:
    Bottle/cup _____

    Strained/junior/finger foods _____

    Feeds self _____

Figure 1–18 *Continued*

Illustration continued on following page

Typical Pattern

Record all solids and liquids usually consumed daily. Indicate kind, amount, method of preparation, and anything added.

Time	Food	Amount	Cross Check
			Milk and milk products:
			Cheese:
			Eggs:
			Meat/Poultry:
			Fish:
			Pasta/Rice:
			Bread/Crackers:
			Cereal:
			Fruits:
			Fruit Juice:
			Vegetables (includes Salads):
			Fats:
			Desserts:
			Sweets:

ESTIMATED DAILY INTAKE: kcal _____; Pro _____ (g); Fat _____ (g); Cho _____

CALORIC DISTRIBUTION: % Pro _____: % Fat _____: % Cho _____

Fluid _____; _____ kcal/kg; _____ g pro/kg; _____ ml/kg

ASSESSMENT OF NUTRIENT INTAKE: Vit. A _____; Ca _____;

Vit. C _____; Iron _____; Vit. B-Complex _____; Vit. D _____; Fluoride _____

Figure 1–18 *Continued*

Food Records

To determine a person's intake accurately, it is important to keep a close record of everything he or she has to eat and drink. List each food and beverage. Record the size of servings in measurements such as teaspoons, tablespoons, ounces, or cups. Type of preparation (baked, fried) or any special note (low fat or skim milk, diet tonic, how formula is mixed) is important, so please be as specific as possible.

Date: Amount and Description of Food Eaten Time:	Date: Amount and Description of Food Eaten Time:	Date: Amount and Description of Food Eaten Time:

Figure 1–19. Form for recording food intake.

DIETARY EVALUATION

Accurate dietary evaluation plays an important role in the diagnosis and treatment of patients. It measures not only quality and quantity of food intake and the macro- and micronutrients provided, but also other factors that influence past and present food intake. Activity level, feeding history, food allergies, abnormal eating habits, developmental delay in feeding, and difficulties in chewing or swallowing are some of the factors. Currently, several methods are available for the collection of information about food consumption. Records can be based on 24-hour recall, 3 to 7 day feeding histories, or "usual patterns." Each methodology has certain weaknesses and limitations,[45–47] and difficulty in qualifying the actual intake is well documented. Normal-weight patients give the most accurate records, whereas underweight patients overestimate and obese patients underestimate the actual amounts consumed.[47] Similarly, dietary interviews conducted over long periods tend to overestimate actual intake, and those covering a short period tend to underestimate it. Because of the considerable differences between nutrient intakes obtained by different interviewing techniques, it is helpful in some cases to use two separate methods (24-hour recall or usual intake in combination with food records) to provide a more accurate dietary evaluation. Emphasis should be placed on careful questioning and recording of food intake. Examples of each are included

TABLE 1–19. Recommended Feeding Schedule—Birth to 12 Months*

	Birth to 4 Months	4 to 6 Months	6 to 8 Months	8 to 10 Months	10 to 12 Months
Milk	Breast milk or formula; 180 ml/kg provides 120 cal/kg	Breast milk or formula; 160–180 ml/kg	Breast milk or formula, about 32 oz; wait until infant is well established on table food to begin pasteurized whole milk	Breast milk, formula or whole milk; encourage use of cup (may be taking breast milk and formula or whole milk)	Breast milk, formula, whole milk (24 oz/day)
Fruit and Vegetable Group	None	None	Commercial baby food or mashed or milled table food without added sugar or salt; work toward 1 source of vitamin C/day and a dark green or yellow fruit or vegetable 3 times/week for vitamin A	Juices may be introduced one at a time, preferably from a cup; more than 8 oz/day, may replace other nutritious foods; be sure to use real juices, not canned fruit drinks	Aim for 3–4 servings/ day, including juice (3 oz juice or about 2 tbs/serving; include 1 good vitamin A source 3 times/week, 1 vitamin C source daily
Cereal and Bread Group	None	May begin iron-fortified rice cereal for baby, mixed with formula; gradually increase amount	Begin 1 new grain at a time	Good finger foods to try include crackers, bread, pasta, regular cereals; begin 1 new grain at a time	Grains provide B vitamins and iron; try to include 4 servings/day; a serving for this age would be ¼ slice bread, 2 tbs cereal or pasta, 2 small crackers; continue infant cereals
Meat and Other Protein Sources	None	None	None	Commercial baby food or finely milled meat; casseroles, eggs, fish, poultry, peanut butter, legumes, cheese are all good protein sources to try	Aim for 1–2 oz/day

*Schedules vary and overlap since each infant will progress at his or her own rate; it generally takes 1 to 1½ months from starting one food group to the next. In all instances: (1) start with small serving sizes of 1–2 tsp and increase gradually to 3–4 tbs/feeding; (2) introduce single-ingredient foods one at a time and continue for 4 to 5 days before introducing another food; (3) remember, do not overfeed—even though a food is nutritious, the amount given must not exceed the total caloric requirement.

Based on the recommendations of the Committee on Nutrition of the American Academy of Pediatrics, Pediatric Nutrition Handbook. Evanston, IL: American Academy of Pediatrics, 1979.

TABLE 1–20. Guidelines for Normal Infant Feeding

Food Group	2 to 3 Years	4 to 5 Years	Calcium Equivalents for the Child who will not Drink Milk
Milk, including fortified whole or skin milk, yogurt, cheese, ice cream, custard, pudding, buttermilk 3–4 servings/day	1 serving = 6 oz (¾ c) milk or equivalent	1 serving = 8 oz (1 c) milk or equivalent	⅔ c milk = 1 oz cheese, 1 c cooked collards, 3 oz sardines, 1 c cooked turnip greens, 1 c cottage cheese, 1 c oysters, or 1 c cooked rhubarb ½ c milk = 1 medium stalk broccoli, 1 c ice cream, 1 c cooked mustard greens, 1 c spinach, or 3 oz salmon ⅓ c milk = 1 c farina, 3 oz canned herring, 1 c cooked kale, 1 tbs blackstrap molasses, 1 c cooked soybeans, 5 tbs maple syrup
Meat, fish, poultry, legumes, nuts, eggs (recommended for eggs, 2–3/week) 2 or more servings/day	1 serving = 1–2 oz meat, poultry, or fish; 1 egg; 2 tbs peanut butter; ½ c legumes	1 serving = 2½–3 oz meat, fish, or poultry; 1 egg; 3 tbs peanut butter; ½–¾ c legumes	
Cereals and bread, whole grain or enriched bread, muffins, cereal, rice, noodles, rolls, pasta 3 or more servings/day	1 serving = ½ slice bread or roll; ⅓–½ c cereal, macaroni, spaghetti, noodles, or rice	1 serving = 1 slice bread or roll, ½–¾ c cereal or pasta	
Fruits and vegetables including: fresh, frozen, dried or canned fruits, vegetables or their juices 3 or more servings/day, including one good source of vitamin C* daily, one good source of vitamin A† three times a week	1 serving = ⅓–½ c juice; ¼ c fresh, frozen, or canned fruit or vegetable; 2 tbs dried fruit	1 serving = ½ c juice, ⅓ c fruit or vegetable	
Fats, oils, and simple sugars	Used as needed as an extra energy source	Used as needed as an extra energy source	

*Good sources of vitamin C: cantaloupe, orange, grapefruit, lemon, cabbage, sauerkraut, asparagus, broccoli, spinach, kale, turnip and other greens, white potato, tomato, green peppers, tangerines, strawberries
†Good sources of vitamin A: dairy products, cantaloupe, peach, apricots, plums, liver, asparagus, broccoli, carrots, green beans, spinach, kale, turnip and other greens, tomato, winter squash

(Figs. 1–18 and 1–19). Additional limitations to the establishment of intake include wide variations in food composition tables and difficulty in establishing actual nutrient needs.

A sample form used for gathering pertinent nutrition information, a recommended feeding schedule for addition of foods from birth to 12 months[48] (Table 1–19), and a pattern of normal intake in childhood (Table 1–20) are included for comparison.

ASSESSMENT OF FEEDING SKILLS

Feeding problems, such as the inability or refusal to eat normally for age, may have single or multiple causes. Such factors include neuromuscular abnormalities, psychosocial disorders, or obstructive lesions; often organic disease in combination with psychosocial factors interferes with feeding skills. In infancy, poor sucking reflexes or abnormal postural tone during feeding may point to nervous system dysfunction. However, the ease with which rooting, lip, and sucking reflexes are elicited varies greatly and its diagnostic significance is limited.[49] Observation of how well older infants and young children chew, swallow, suck through a straw, eat finger foods, and grasp feeding utensils, and what textures they prefer, can provide more helpful information. Development of normal feeding skills is outlined in Table 1–21 and evaluation of oral reflexes is found in Table 1–22.[51]

Spontaneous feeding behavior can be a measure of a child's level of motor, adaptive, and social maturation, since it determines not only the presence or absence of feeding reflexes but also their integration.[49] Psychosocial causes of delayed development of feeding skills may appear at any age but occur most

TABLE 1–21. Development of Feeding Skills

Age	Oral and Neuromuscular	Feeding Behavior
Birth	Rooting relfex Sucking reflex Swallowing reflex	Turns mouth toward nipple or any object brushing cheek; initial swallowing involves the posterior part of the tongue; by 9 to 12 weeks, anterior portion is increasingly involved, facilitating ingestion of semi-solid food
	Extrusion reflex	Pushes food out when placed on tongue; strong the first 9 weeks; by 6 to 10 weeks, recognizes feeding position and begins mouthing and sucking when placed in this position
3 to 6 Months	Beginning coordination between eyes and body movements	Explores world with eyes, fingers, hands, and mouth; starts reaching for objects at 4 months but overshoots; hands get in the way during feeding
	Learning to reach mouth with hands at 4 months	Finger sucking—by 6 months all objects go into the mouth
	Extrusion reflex present until 4 months	May continue to push out food placed on tongue
	Able to grasp objects voluntarily at 5 months	Grasps objects in mitten-like fashion
	Sucking reflex becomes voluntary and lateral motions of the jaw begin	Can approximate lips to the rim of cup by 5 months; chewing action begins; by 6 months begins drinking from cup
6 to 12 Months	Eyes and hands work together	Brings hand to mouth; at 7 months able to feed self biscuit
	Sits erect with support at 6 months	Bangs cup and objects on table at 7 months
	Sits erect without support at 9 months	
	Development of grasp (finger to thumb opposition)	Holds own bottle at 9 to 12 months; pincer approach to food; pokes at food with index finger at 10 months
	Relates to objects at 10 months	Reaches for food and utensils, including those beyond reach; pushes plate around with spoon; insists on holding spoon, not to put in mouth, but to return to plate or cup
1 to 3 Years	Development of manual dexterity	Increased desire to feed self: 15 months—begins to use spoon but turns it before reaching mouth; may hold cup, likely to tilt the cup rather than head, causing spilling
		18 months—eats with spoon, spills frequently, turns spoon in mouth; holds glass with both hands
		2 years—inserts spoon correctly occasionally with one hand; holds glass; plays with food; distinguishes between food and inedible materials
		2–3 years—self-feeding complete with occasional spilling; uses fork; pours from pitcher; obtains drink of water from faucet

From Getchell E, Howard R: Nutrition in development, in Scripien G, et al., eds.: Comprehensive Pediatric Nursing. New York: McGraw-Hill, 1975.

TABLE 1–22. Oral Reflexes in Normal Infants*

Rooting

Test position:	Supine
Stimulation:	Index finger on cheek or cardinal point
Reflex:	The immediate reaction to the touch is turning of the head to the side of the stimulation; also obtainable by touch on upper or lower lip
Development:	Birth onward

Sucking and Swallowing

Test position:	Supine
Stimulation:	Index finger in mouth
Reflex:	Strong, rhythmic sucking or swallowing movement (42–84/min in normal infant)
Development:	From birth onward, but irregular within the first 3 to 6 days; active up to month 3 to 4, possibly even to 6 or 7, depending on ways of feeding, but will lessen in intensity in any case

Bite

Test position:	Supine
Stimulation:	Index finger on gums
Reflex:	Rhythmic opening and closing of the jaw, which continues as long as the stimulation is present
Development:	From the first days after birth until months 2 to 4; seldom until month 6 or 7, depending on ways of feeding

Gag

Test position:	Supine
Stimulation:	Index finger on hard palate or tongue
Reflex:	Stimulation on posterior half of tongue or posterior third of hard palate causes head and jaw extension, and rhythmic protrusions of tongue and contraction of the pharynx, lasting as long as stimulation is present
Development:	From birth onward until month 7, from then on, reduced

*The oral reflexes are preferably tested between meal times, certainly not immediately after or before feeding.

frequently between birth and 4 years of age. Some clinicians feel there is a sensitive period that is optimal or application of a stimulus, and after that critical period, a particular behavior may be much more difficult to learn.[50] It is important, especially in hospitalized children who may be tube-fed for medical reasons (e.g., obstruction or other lesion, diarrhea), that development of feeding skills not be overlooked, as this may lead to difficulties in feeding after the primary disorder has been resolved. In all cases, education of the caretaker in normal feeding behavior may help prevent problems. If they do occur, and depending on their origin and scope, an interdisciplinary team (consisting of specialists in behavior management, nutrition, speech pathology, and physical therapy) may be beneficial in the resolution of these problems.

References

1. Blackburn GL, Bistrian BR, Maini BS, et al.: Nutritional and metabolic assessment of the hospitalized patient. JPEN 1:11, 1977.
2. Roberts SLW: Nutrition Assessment Manual. Iowa City: University of Iowa Hospitals and Clinics, 1977.
3. Grant A: Nutritional Assessment: Guidelines for Dieticians. Seattle: Northwest Kidney Center, 1977.
4. Baker JP, Detsky AS, Wesson DE, et al.: Nutritional assessment: comparison of clinical judgment and objective measurements. N Engl J Med 306:969, 1982.
5. Christakis G: Nutritional assessment in health programs. Am J Public Health (Suppl) 63:1, 1973.
6. American Dietetic Association: Handbook of Clinical Dietetics. New Haven: Yale University Press, 1980.
7. Laramee SH, Hendricks KM: Development and use of a pediatric nutrition and metabolic worksheet. Abstracts of the American Dietetic Association, 1979.

8. Lowrey GH: Growth and Development of Children, 7th ed. Chicago: Year Book Medical, 1978.
9. United States Department of Health, Education and Welfare: Nutritional disorders of children: prevention, screening and follow-up. Rockville, MD: DHEW Publication NA (HSA) 76–5612, 1976.
10. Hamill PVV, Drizd TA, Johnson CL, et al.: NCHS Growth Charts—1976. Rockville, MD: Monthly Vital Statistics Report (HBA) 76–1120 Vol. 25, No. 3 (Suppl), 1976.
11. Fomon, SJ: Infant Nutrition, 2nd ed. Philadelphia: WB Saunders, 1974.
12. Tanner JM, Whitehouse RH, Takaishi M: Standards from birth to maturity for height, weight, height velocity, and weight velocity: British children, 1965. Arch Dis Child 41:613, 1966.
13. Garn SM, Rothmann CG: Interaction of nutrition and genetics in the timing of growth and development. Pediatr Clin North Am 13:353, 1966.
14. Tanner JM, Healy MJR, Lockhart RO, et al.: Aberdeen growth study. I. The prediction of adult body measurements from measurements taken each year from birth to five years. Arch Dis Child 31:372, 1956.
15. Karlberg P, Engstrom I, Lichtenstein H, et al.: The development of children in a Swedish urban community: a prospective longitudinal study. III. Physical growth during the first three years of life. Acta Paediatr Scand (Suppl) 187:48,1968.
16. Frisancho AR: New norms of upper limb fat and muscle areas for assessment of nutritional status. Am J Clin Nutr 34:2540, 1981.
17. Owen GM: Measurement, recording and assessment of skinfold thickness in childhood and adolescence. Am J Clin Nutr 35:629, 1982.
18. Gurney JM, Jelliffe DB: Arm anthropometry in nutritional assessment: nomogram for rapid calculation of muscle circumference and cross-sectional muscle and fat areas. Am J Clin Nutr 26:912, 1973.
19. Cooper A, Heird NC: Nutritional assessment of the pediatric patient including the low birth weight infant. Am J Clin Nutr 35:1132, 1982.
20. Greulich WW, Pyle SI: Radiographic Atlas of Skeletal Development of the Hand and Wrist, 2nd ed. Stanford: Stanford University Press, 1959.
21. Gardner LI, ed.: Endocrine and Genetic Diseases of Childhood and Adolescence, 2nd ed. Philadelphia: WB Saunders, 1975.
22. Edelsten AD, Hughes IA, Oakes S, et al.: Height and skeletal maturity in children with newly diagnosed juvenile-onset diabetes. Arch Dis Child 56:40, 1981.
23. Cronk CE: Growth of children with Down's syndrome: birth to age 3 years. Pediatrics 61:564, 1978.
24. Morley D, Cutting W: Charts to help with malnutrition and overpopulation problems. Lancet 1:712, 1974.
25. Fine RN, Malekzadeh MH, Pennisi AJ, et al.: Long-term results of renal transplantation in children. Pediatrics 61:641, 1978.
26. Shull MW, Reed RB, Valadian I, et al.: Velocities of growth in vegetarian preschool children. Pediatrics 60:410, 1977.
27. Usher R, McLean F.: Intrauterine growth of live-born Caucasian infants at sea level. J Pediatr 74:901, 1969.
28. Lubchenco LO, Hansman C, Boyd E: Intrauterine growth in length and head circumference as estimated from live births at gestational ages from 26 to 42 weeks. Pediatrics 37:403, 1966.
29. Gomez F, Glavan R, Cravioto J, et al.: Malnutrition in infancy and childhood with special reference to kwashiorkor. Adv Pediatr 7:131, 1955.
30. McLaren DS, Read WWC: Weight/length classification of nutritional status. Lacet 2:219, 1975.
31. Forse RA, Shizgal HM: One assessment of malnutrition. Surgery 8:17, 1980.
32. Jelliffe D: The assessment of nutritional status of the community. Geneva, Switzerland: World Health Organization Monograph 53, 1966.
33. Garrow JS, Pike MC: The short-term prognosis of severe primary infantile malnutrition. Br J Nutr 21:155, 1967.
34. Galvan RR, Calderon JM: Death among children with third degree malnutrition. Am J Clin Nutr 16:351, 1965.
35. Sommer A, Loewenstein MS: Nutritional status and mortality. Am J Clin Nutr 28:287, 1975.
36. McLaren DS, Shirajian E, Loshkajian H, et al.: Short-term prognosis in protein-calorie malnutrition. Am J Clin Nutr 22:863, 1969.
37. Palmer S, Ekvall S: Pediatric Nutrition in Development Disorders. Springfield, IL: Charles C Thomas, 1978.
38. Goodhart RS, Shils ME: Modern Nutrition in Health and Disease, 6th ed. Philadelphia: Lea & Febiger, 1980.
39. Underwood EJ: Trace Elements in Human and Animal Nutrition, 4th ed. New York: Academic Press, 1977.
40. National Research Council, Food and Nutrition Board Dietary Allowances Committee: Recommended Dietary Allowances, 9th ed. Washington, DC: National Academy of Sciences, 1980.
41. Chandra RK, Scrimshaw NS: Immunocompetence in nutritional assessment. Am J Clin Nutr 33:2694, 1980.
42. Jensen TG, Englert DM, Dudrick SJ, et al.: Delayed hypersensitivity skin testing: response ratios in a surgical population. J Am Diet Assoc 82:17, 1983.

43. Merritt RJ, Blackburn GL: Nutritional assessment and metabolic response to illness of the hospitalized child. In: Suskind RM, ed.: Textbook of Pediatric Nutrition. New York: Raven Press, 1981.
44. Viteri FE, Alvarado J: The creatinine height index: its use in the estimation of the degree of protein depletion and repletion in protein calorie malnourished children. Pediatrics 96:696, 1970.
45. Carter RL, Sharbaugh CO, Stapell CA: Reliability and validity of the 24-hour recall. J Am Diet Assoc 79:542, 1981.
46. Karvetti RL, Knuts LR: Agreement between dietary interviews. J Am Diet Assoc 79:654, 1981.
47. Stunkard AJ, Waxman M: Accuracy of self-reports of food intake. J Am Diet Assoc 79:547, 1981.
48. American Academy of Pediatrics Committee on Nutrition: Pediatric Nutrition Handbook. Evanston, IL: American Academy of Pediatrics, 1979.
49. Ingram TTS: Clinical significance of infantile feeding reflexes. Dev Med Clin Neurol 4:159, 1962.
50. Illingworth RS, Lister J: The critical or sensitive period, with special reference to certain feeding problems in infants and children. J Pediatr 65:839, 1964.
51. Mueller H: Feeding. In: Finnie Nr, Haynes U, eds.: Handling the Young Cerebral Palsied Child at Home, 2nd ed. New York: EP Dutton, 1975.

2

ESTIMATION OF ENERGY NEEDS

Recommended Dietary Allowances are the most commonly used standard against which nutrient intake is evaluated. In certain instances, more precise calculations are needed for the assessment of caloric and nutrient needs. These methods for determining basal energy requirements include the use of the Mayo Clinic nomogram and the Benedict formula for basal energy expenditure and an estimation of energy metabolism based on weight. All three methods, indications for their use, and clinical applications are described in this chapter. In addition, calculation of energy requirements for activity and during periods of stress and disease are explained.

RECOMMENDED DIETARY ALLOWANCES

The Recommended Dietary Allowances (RDA), published by the Food and Nutrition Board of the National Academy of Sciences National Research Council, are designed for the maintenance of good nutrition for practically all healthy people in the United States. They are meant to be applied to population groups, not individuals, and to encourage patterns of food consumption that will promote health.[1] They are derived from knowledge of human requirements and, except for energy values, they exceed the actual requirements of the healthy individual and provide a margin of safety. In addition, allowances have not been established for all essential nutrients; many foods have not been analyzed for nutrient composition and the interaction between nutrients may effect the usefulness of certain information about food intake. However, the RDAs provide a basis upon which to evaluate nutrient intake and to compare it with what is recommended for metabolically normal children with normal body composition, normal activity, and normal growth.[1, 2]

Use of the Recommended Dietary Allowances to Estimate Energy Needs

Bob is a 12-year-old male newly diagnosed as having diabetes mellitus. His weight is 31.5 kg (70 lb) (10th percentile, Fig. 1–5), and his height is 142 cm (56 in) (10th percentile). Estimated energy needs, from Table 2–1, are 2700 calories per day with a range of 2000 to 3700 calories. From Table 2–2, Bob's estimated caloric needs based on his weight are calculated to be 1890 calories (31.5 kg ×

TABLE 2–1. Mean Heights and Weights and Recommended Energy Intake*

	Age (yr)	Weight (kg)	Weight (lb)	Height (cm)	Height (in)	Energy Needs (kcal)	Energy Needs (range)	Mega Joule (MJ)
Infants	0.0–0.5	6	13	60	24	kg × 115	(95–145)	kg × 0.48
	0.5–1.0	9	20	71	28	kg × 105	(80–135)	kg × 0.44
Children	1–3	13	29	90	35	1300	(900–1800)	5.5
	4–6	20	44	112	44	1700	(1300–2300)	7.1
	7–10	28	62	132	52	2400	(1650–3300)	10.1
Males	11–14	45	99	157	62	2700	(2000–3700)	11.3
	15–18	66	145	176	69	2800	(2100–3900)	11.8
	19–22	70	154	177	70	2900	(2500–3300)	12.2
	23–50	70	154	178	70	2700	(2300–3100)	11.3
	51–75	70	154	178	70	2400	(2000–2800)	10.1
	76 +	70	154	178	70	2050	(1650–2450)	8.6
Females	11–14	46	101	157	62	2200	(1500–3000)	9.2
	15–18	55	120	163	64	2100	(1200–3000)	8.8
	19–22	55	120	163	64	2100	(1700–2500)	8.8
	23–50	55	120	163	64	2000	(1600–2400)	8.4
	51–75	55	120	163	64	1800	(1400–2200)	7.6
	76 +	55	120	163	64	1600	(1200–2000)	6.7
Pregnant						> 300		
Lactating						> 500		

*The data in this table have been assembled from the observed median heights and weights of children and the mean heights of men (70 in) and women (64 in) between the ages of 18 and 34 years as surveyed in the U.S. population (HEW/NCHS data).

The energy allowances for the young adults are for men and women doing light work. The allowances for the two older age groups represent mean weight.

Energy needs over these age spans allows for a 2 percent decrease in basal (resting) metabolic rate per decade and a reduction in activity of 200 kcal/day for men and women between 51 and 75 years, 500 kcal for men over 75 years, and 400 kcal for women over 75 years. The customary range of daily energy output is shown in parentheses for adults; it is based on a variation in energy needs of 400 kcal at any one age and emphasizes the wide range of energy intakes appropriate for any group of people.

Energy allowances for children through age 18 are based on median energy intakes of children of these ages followed in longitudinal growth studies. The values in parentheses are 10th and 90th percentiles of energy intake, and they indicate the range of energy consumption among children of these ages.

60 cal/kg = 1890 cal). Weight for height is at the 25th percentile (Fig. 1–9), and parental midpoint height is 161 cm (Table 1–4); these values indicate that he is constitutionally small rather than undergrown because of chronic undernutrition and suggest that his needs might be closer to 1890 cal/day than to 2700 cal/day.

TABLE 2–2. Estimated Nutrient Needs per Kilogram*

Age (yr)	Calories (per kg)		Protein (per kg)
0–0.5		(115)	(2.2)
0.5–1.0		(105)	(2.0)
1–3	1300	(100)	23 (1.8)
4–6	1700	(85)	30 (1.5)
7–10	2400	(85)	34 (1.2)
Male			
11–14	2700	(60)	45 (1.0)
15–18	2800	(42)	56 (0.85)
Female			
11–14	2200	(48)	46 (1.0)
15–18	2100	(38)	46 (0.85)

*For women who are pregnant, an additional 30 g of protein are recommended. Lactating women require an additional 20 g of protein/day.

Adapted from the Recommended Dietary Allowances, 9th ed. Washington, DC: National Academy of Sciences, 1980.

54 ☐ NUTRITIONAL ASSESSMENT

TABLE 2–3. Recommended Dietary Allowances of Fat-Soluble Vitamins

	Age (yr)	Vitamin A (µg RE)*	Vitamin D (µg)†	Vitamin E (mg α-TE)‡
Infants	0.0–0.5	420	10	3
	0.5–1.0	400	10	4
Children	1–3	400	10	5
	4–6	500	10	6
	7–10	700	10	7
Males	11–14	1000	10	8
	15–18	1000	10	10
	19–22	1000	7.5	10
	23–50	1000	5	10
	51 +	1000	5	10
Females	11–14	800	10	8
	15–18	800	10	8
	19–22	800	7.5	8
	23–50	800	5	8
	51 +	800	5	8
Pregnant		>200	>5	>2
Lactating		>400	>5	>3

*Retinol equivalents. 1 retinol equivalent = 1 µg retinol or 6 µg carotene.
†As cholecalciferol. 10µg cholecalciferol = 400 IU of vitamin D.
‡α-Tocopherol Equivalents or α-TE. 1 mg D-α-tocopherol = 1 α-TE.
From National Research Council Food and Nutrition Board: Recommended Dietary Allowance, 9th ed. Washington, DC: National Academy of Sciences, 1980.

TABLE 2–4. Recommended Dietary Allowances for Water-Soluble Vitamins

	Age (yr)	Vitamin C (mg)	Thiamin (mg)	Riboflavin (mg)	Niacin (mg NE)*	Vitamin B$_6$ (mg)	Folacin (µg)	Vitamin B$_{12}$ (µg)
Infants	0.0–1.5	35	0.3	0.4	6	0.3	30	0.5†
	0.5–1.0	35	0.5	0.6	8	0.6	45	1.5
Children	1–3	45	0.7	0.8	9	0.9	100	2.0
	4–6	45	0.9	1.0	11	1.3	200	2.5
	7–10	45	1.2	1.4	16	1.6	300	3.0
Males	11–14	50	1.4	1.6	18	1.8	400	3.0
	15–18	60	1.4	1.7	18	2.0	400	3.0
	19–22	60	1.5	1.7	19	2.2	400	3.0
	23–50	60	1.4	1.6	18	2.2	400	3.0
	51+	60	1.2	1.4	16	2.2	400	3.0
Females	11–14	50	1.1	1.3	15	1.8	400	3.0
	15–18	60	1.1	1.3	14	2.0	400	3.0
	19–22	60	1.1	1.3	14	2.0	400	3.0
	23–50	60	1.0	1.2	13	2.0	400	3.0
	51+	60	1.0	1.2	13	2.0	400	3.0
Pregnant		>20	>0.4	>0.3	>2	>0.6	>400	>1.0
Lactating		>40	>0.5	>0.5	>5	>0.5	>100	>1.0

*One niacin equivalent (NE) is equal to 1 mg of niacin or 60 mg of dietary tryptophan
†The recommended dietary allowance for vitamin B$_{12}$ in infants is based on average concentration of the vitamin in human milk; the allowances after weaning are based on energy intake (as recommended by the American Academy of Pediatrics) and consideration of other factors, such as intestinal absorption.
From National Research Council Food and Nutrition Board: Recommended Dietary Allowance, 9th ed. Washington, DC: National Academy of Sciences, 1980.

TABLE 2–5. Recommended Dietary Allowances for Minerals

	Age (yr)	Calcium (mg)	Phosphorus (mg)	Magnesium (mg)	Iron (mg)	Zinc (mg)	Iodine (μg)
Infants	0.0–0.5	360	240	50	10	3	40
	0.5–1.0	540	360	70	15	5	50
Children	1–3	800	800	150	15	10	70
	4–6	800	800	200	10	10	90
	7–10	800	800	250	10	10	120
Males	11–14	1200	1200	350	18	15	150
	15–18	1200	1200	400	18	15	150
	19–22	800	800	350	10	15	150
	23–50	800	800	350	10	15	150
	51+	800	800	350	10	15	150
Females	11–14	1200	1200	300	18	15	150
	15–18	1200	1200	300	18	15	150
	19–22	800	800	300	18	15	150
	23–50	800	800	300	18	15	150
	51+	800	800	300	10	15	150
Pregnant		>400	>400	>150	*	>5	>25
Lactating		>400	>400	>150	*	>10	>50

*The increased requirement during pregnancy cannot be met by the iron content of habitual American diets or by the existing iron stores of many women; therefore, the use of 30 to 60 mg of supplemental elemental iron is recommended. Iron needs during lactation are not substantially different from those of nonpregnant women, but continued supplementation of the mother 2 to 3 months after parturition is advisable in order to replenish stores depleted by pregnancy.

From National Research Council Food and Nutrition Board: Recommended Dietary Allowance, 9th ed. Washington, DC: National Academy of Sciences, 1980.

TABLE 2–6. Estimated Safe and Adequate Daily Dietary Intake of Selected Vitamins*

	Age (yr)	Vitamin K (μg)	Biotin (μg)	Pantothenic Acid (mg)
Infants	0–0.5	12	35	2
	0.5–1	10–20	50	3
Children and	1–3	15–30	65	3
Adolescents	4–6	20–40	85	3–4
	7–10	30–60	120	4–5
	11+	50–100	100–200	4–7
Adults		70–140	100–200	4–7

*Because there is little information on which to base allowances, these figures are provided here in the form of ranges of recommended intakes.

From National Research Council Food and Nutrition Board: Recommended Dietary Allowance, 9th ed. Washington, DC: National Academy of Sciences, 1980.

TABLE 2–7. Estimated Safe and Adequate Daily Dietary Intake of Selected Trace Elements*

	Age (yr)	Copper (mg)	Manganese (mg)	Fluoride (mg)	Chromium (mg)	Selenium (mg)	Molybdenum (mg)
Infants	0–0.5	0.5–0.7	0.5–0.7	0.1–0.5	0.01–0.04	0.01–0.04	0.03–0.06
	0.5–1	0.7–1.0	0.7–1.0	0.2–1.0	0.02–0.06	0.02–0.06	0.04–0.08
Children and	1–3	1.0–1.5	1.0–1.5	0.5–1.5	0.02–0.08	0.02–0.08	0.05–0.1
Adolescents	4–6	1.5–2.0	1.5–2.0	1.0–2.5	0.03–0.12	0.03–0.12	0.06–0.15
	7–10	2.0–2.5	2.0–3.0	1.5–2.5	0.05–0.2	0.05–0.2	0.10–0.3
	11+	2.0–3.0	2.5–5.0	1.5–2.5	0.05–0.2	0.05–0.2	0.15–0.5
Adults		2.0–3.0	2.5–5.0	1.5–4.0	0.05–0.2	0.05–0.2	0.15–0.5

*Because there is little information on which to base allowances, these figures are provided here in the form of ranges of recommended intakes. Since the toxic levels for many trace elements may be only several times usual intakes, the upper levels for the trace elements given in this table should not be habitually exceeded.

From National Research Council Food and Nutrition Board: Recommended Dietary Allowance, 9th ed. Washington, DC: National Academy of Sciences, 1980.

TABLE 2–8. Estimated Safe and Adequate Daily Dietary Intake of Selected Electrolytes*

	Age (yr)	Sodium (mg)	Potassium (mg)	Chloride (mg)
Infants	0–0.5	115–350	350–925	275–700
	0.5–1	250–750	425–1275	400–1200
Children and	1–3	325–975	550–1650	500–1500
Adolescents	4–6	450–1350	775–2325	700–2100
	7–10	600–1800	1000–3000	925–2775
	11+	900–2700	1525–4575	1400–4200
Adults		1100–3300	1875–5625	1700–5100

*Because there is little information on which to base allowances, these figures are provided here in the form of ranges of recommended intakes.
From National Research Council Food and Nutrition Board: Recommended Dietary Allowance, 9th ed. Washington, DC: National Academy of Sciences, 1980.

ESTIMATION OF BASAL ENERGY REQUIREMENTS

Energy requirements are highly individualized and vary widely, particularly with disease. In some instances, as in the case of an infant or child with marked psychomotor retardation, requirements may be significantly less than the predicted RDA. Chronic conditions such as inflammatory bowel disease, which is accompanied by nutrient losses, may increase requirements substantially above the RDA predicted for age. The estimation of basal energy needs (caloric requirements postabsorptive, recumbent, and at room temperature) is the first step in the assessment of total caloric needs. The following methods provide a highly predictive estimate of basal needs and correlate well with actual requirements.[3, 4] Continued evaluation and adjustment of recommendations based on response (weight gain or loss) are always necessary.

In some instances, techniques such as open-circuit, indirect calorimetry may be available for measurement of energy expenditure. The respiratory quotient derived from the CO_2/O_2 volume ratio can be used to calculate more accurately energy needs of the sick, hospitalized child.

Use of the Mayo Clinic Nomogram

The Mayo Clinic nomogram relates basal metabolic rate to the surface area, age, sex of an individual. To calculate energy needs, one first determines surface area from the individual's weight and height (Fig. 2–1).[5] This is multiplied by the estimated calories used per square meter per hour (cal/m²/hr), as shown in Table 2–9; these figures are based on an individual's sex and age and take into account the additional needs for growth. Therefore, this method is appropriate for calculating the caloric needs of children (over 15 kg in weight and 60 cm in height) as well as adults.

Since Bob weighs 31.5 kg and is 142 cm tall, his surface area (determined from the nomogram) is 1.1 m². Since he is 12 years old, his mean for cal/m²/hr is 46.75. His basal energy requirements, calculated for calories per day, is therefore:

$$46.75 \text{ cal/m}^2 \times 1.1 \text{ m}^2 \times 24 \text{ hr} = 1234 \text{ cal/day}$$

As another example, Jill is a 6-year-old with severe developmental delay. She is very inactive and requires tube feedings for nutritional support. Her height is 114 cm (45 in) (50th percentile, Fig. 1–4), and she weighs 20 kg (43 lb) (50th percentile). With the nomogram, Jill's surface area is estimated to be 0.8 m². Table 2–9 shows

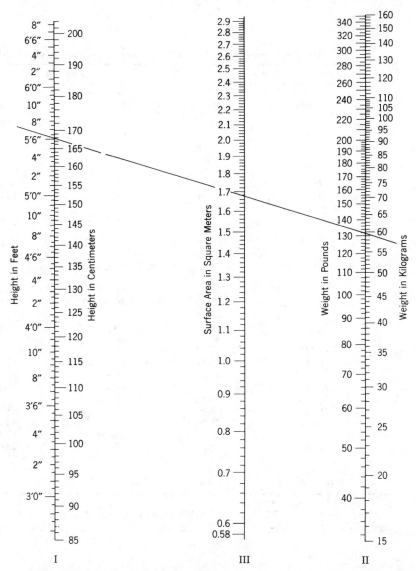

Figure 2–1. Mayo Clinic Nomogram for calculating surface area. (From Pike RL, Brown ML: Nutrition: An Integrated Approach, 2nd ed. New York: John Wiley & Sons, 1975.)

that the estimate for cal/m²/hr for a 6-year-old female is 50.62. Therefore, Jill's daily caloric requirement for basal energy expenditure is:

$$50.62 \text{ cal/m}^2 \times 0.8 \text{ m}^2 \times 24 \text{ hr} = 972 \text{ cal/day}$$

The RDA for Jill, as calculated from Tables 2–1 and 2–2, would be 1700 cal/day, in a range from 1300 to 2300 cal/day.

Basal Energy Expenditure (BEE)

As defined by Harris and Benedict,[6] basal energy expenditure takes into account body weight, stature, sex, and age in the determination of calories expended. Their studies showed changes in metabolism with age and a decrease in heat production by an individual throughout the range of adulthood (7.15 cal/yr

TABLE 2–9. The Mayo Foundation Normal Standards (cal/m²/hr)

Males		Females	
Age at Last Birthday	*Mean*	*Age at Last Birthday*	*Mean*
6	53.00	6	50.62
7	52.45	6½	50.23
8	51.78	7	49.12
8½	51.20	7½	47.84
9	50.54	8	47.00
9½	49.42	8½	46.50
10	48.50	9–10	45.90
10½	47.71	11	45.26
11	47.18	11½	44.80
12	46.75	12	44.28
13–15	46.35	12½	43.58
16	45.72	13	42.90
16½	45.30	13½	42.10
17	44.80	14	41.25
17½	44.03	14½	40.74
18	43.25	15	40.10
18½	42.70	15½	39.40
19	42.32	16	38.85
19½	42.00	16½	38.30
20–21	41.43	17	37.82
22–23	40.82	17½	37.40
24–27	40.24	18–19	36.74
28–29	39.81	20–24	36.18
30–34	39.34	25–44	35.70
35–39	38.68	45–49	34.94
40–44	38.00	50–54	33.96
45–49	37.37	55–59	33.18
50–54	36.73	60–64	32.61
55–59	36.10	65–69	32.30
60–64	35.48	*	
65–69	34.80		

*Obtained by extrapolation
From Pike R, Brown M: Nutrition: An Integrated Approach, 2nd ed. New York: John Wiley & Sons, 1975.

TABLE 2–10. Suggested Desirable Weights for Heights and Ranges for Adult Males and Females

Height		Weight, Men				Weight, Women			
(in)	(cm)	(lb)		(kg)		(lb)		(kg)	
58	147		—		—	102	(92–119)	46	(42–54)
60	152		—		—	107	(96–125)	49	(44–57)
62	158	123	(112–141)	56	(51–64)	113	(102–131)	51	(46–59)
64	163	130	(118–148)	59	(54–67)	120	(108–138)	55	(49–63)
66	168	136	(124–156)	62	(56–71)	128	(114–146)	58	(52–66)
68	173	145	(132–166)	66	(60–75)	136	(122–154)	62	(55–70)
70	178	154	(140–174)	70	(64–79)	144	(130–163)	65	(59–74)
72	183	162	(148–184)	74	(67–84)	152	(138–173)	69	(63–79)
74	188	171	(156–194)	78	(71–88)		—		—
76	193	181	(164–204)	82	(74–93)		—		—

From Bray GA, ed.: Obesity in Perspective, Vol. 2, Part 1, Fogarty International Center Series on Preventive Medicine. Washington, DC: DHEW Publication No. (NIH) 75–708, US Dept HEW, 1975.

in men, 2.29 cal/yr in women). The basal energy requirements of women were found to be lower than those of men by 1.2 cal/kg or 77 cal/m²/24 hr. This difference is not evident in newborns, and this method is therefore appropriate for use only in adolescents and adults.

Basal energy expenditure can be calculated by the following equations:

$$\text{For men: } 66 + (13.7 \times \text{ideal weight in kg}) + (5 \times \text{height in cm}) - (6.8 \times \text{age in yrs})$$

$$\text{For women: } 655 + (9.6 \times \text{ideal weight in kg}) + (1.7 \times \text{height in cm}) - (4.7 \times \text{age in yr})$$

In the case of Bob, who was found to be at the ideal weight for his height (although constitutionally small), his BEE would be:

$$66 + (13.7 \times 31.5 \text{ kg}) + (5 \times 142 \text{ cm}) - (6.8 \times 12 \text{ years}) = 1126 \text{ cal/day}$$

Since The BEE is appropriate only for adolescents and adults, it cannot be used to calculate the requirements for 6-year-old Jill.

A third example, John, is a 25-year-old construction worker who requires a back brace and bed rest for the next 6 weeks because of a sprained back muscle. His height is 178 cm (71 in) and his weight is 75 kg (167 lb); his ideal weight for height is 70 kg (156 lb) (see Table 2–10). With the Harris-Benedict formula, his BEE can be calculated.

$$66 + (13.7 \times 70 \text{ kg}) + (5 \times 178 \text{ cm}) - (6.8 \times 25 \text{ yr}) = 1745 \text{ cal/day}$$

in John's case, the Mayo Clinic nomogram (Fig. 2–1, Table 2–9) makes an estimation of his basal needs to be:

$$40.24 \text{ cal/m}^2 \times 1.9 \text{ m}^2 \times 24 \text{ hr} = 1835 \text{ cal/day}$$

The RDA (Tables 2–1 and 2–2) for a healthy, active, 25-year-old male is 2700 cal/day (range: 2300–3100 cal/day).

Estimation of Energy Metabolism by Weight

Estimation of basal metabolic rate (BMR) based on surface area tends to correlate most closely with actual requirements. However, calculation of surface area is not possible on small infants and children, and Table 2–9 is recommended in such instances. Its use for older children should be limited to those close to ideal body weight.

For example, Tim is a 23-month-old infant with Down's syndrome who weighs 12 kg (26.5 lb) (25th to 50th percentile, Fig. 1–3); his length is 82 cm (32.5 in) (10th percentile). The RDA for his age (see Table 2–1) is 900–1800 cal/day. To estimate calories needed to ensure adequate intake but slow rate of weight gain, begin by estimating the BMR (see Table 2–11). At Tim's weight, his metabolic rate is 26.8 kcal/hr. For one day, his basal metabolic rate would be:

$$26.8 \text{ kcal/hr} \times 24 \text{ hr} = 643 \text{ kcal}$$

An increase in needs above these would be estimated 50 to 75 per cent, depending on activity and growth rate. Therefore, the range would be from 965 kcal (643 × 1.5) to 1125 kcal (643 × 1.75).

Use of other methods to estimate BMR is inappropriate at this age and weight.

TABLE 2–11. Basal Metabolic Rates: Infants and Children*

Age 1 wk to 10 mo		Age 11 to 36 mo			Age 3 to 16 yr		
	Metabolic Rate†		Metabolic Rate			Metabolic Rate	
Weight (kg)	(kcal/hr) Male or Female	Weight (kg)	(kcal/hr) Male	Female	Weight (kg)	(kcal/hr) Male	Female
3.5	8.4	9.0	22.0	21.2	15	35.8	33.3
4.0	9.5	9.5	22.8	22.0	20	39.7	37.4
4.5	10.5	10.0	23.6	22.8	25	43.6	41.5
5.0	11.6	10.5	24.4	23.6	30	47.5	45.5
5.5	12.7	11.0	25.2	24.4	35	51.3	49.6
6.0	13.8	11.5	26.0	25.2	40	55.2	53.7
6.5	14.9	12.0	26.8	26.0	45	59.1	57.8
7.0	16.0	12.5	27.6	26.9	50	63.0	61.9
7.5	17.1	13.0	28.4	27.7	55	66.9	66.0
8.0	18.2	13.5	29.2	28.5	50	70.8	70.0
8.5	19.3	14.0	30.0	29.3	65	74.7	74.0
9.0	20.4	14.5	30.8	30.1	70	78.6	78.1
9.5	21.4	15.0	31.6	30.9	75	82.5	82.2
10.0	22.5	15.5	32.4	31.7			
10.5	23.6	16.0	33.2	32.6			
11.0	24.7	16.5	34.0	33.4			

*To calculate BMR: (1) determine age of patient and locate appropriate column on table, (2) find weight in kg of child and read across to appropriate sex, (3) read kcal/hr and multiply by 24 to determine daily BMR.

†There is only one basal metabolic rate (BMR) for children of either sex at ages 1 week to 10 months.

From Altman PL, Dittmer DS, eds.: Metabolism. Bethesda, MD: Federation of American Societies for Experimental Biology, 1968.

ADJUSTMENT OF BASAL ENERGY NEEDS

In the preceding paragraphs we have described methods for estimating basal energy requirements. Caloric and nutrient requirements are higher than basal allowances, since they are adjusted for the activity and health of an individual.

Activity is a major factor that determines total energy needs. The BMR can be taken as a measure of metabolic rate only when the subject is in bed asleep or is awake and inactive. Recommended increases above the BMR for activity are shown in Table 2–12.[7]

Adjustment of Basal Energy Needs for Activity

Two examples of estimating increase in basal energy needs can be taken from the cases of Jill and John. Jill, the 6-year-old with severe developmental delay, has basal energy needs calculated to be 972 cal/day. Because her activity level is bed rest, her energy requirements would be appropriately 10 per cent above basal.

972 cal/day × 1.1 = 1069 cal/day

TABLE 2–12. Increase in Caloric Needs for Activity

Activity	Increase
Bed rest	+ 10% (e.g., caused by procedures)
Light activity	+ 30% (sitting, playing, or working with hands)
Moderate activity	+ 50% (standing, playing)
Heavy activity	+ 75% or greater (vigorous playing or working)

In the case of John, even though he is resting in bed, he is probably doing light activity and increasing his energy needs by 30 per cent above basal (see Table 2–12). Therefore, he requires:

$$1745 \text{ cal/day} \times 1.3 = 2269 \text{ cal/day}$$

When John recovers and returns to construction work, his energy requirements will be approximately 75% above basal:

$$1745 \text{ cal/day} \times 1.75 = 3054 \text{ cal/day}$$

Adjustment of Needs in Stress and Disease

Energy allowances must be adjusted to match the requirements imposed by such factors as metabolic disorders, chronic disease, prematurity, and surgical complications. Infections, even mild ones, cause a loss of nitrogen, vitamins, and minerals in the body. At the same time a decrease in appetite may lead to inadequate intake and may compound the depletion of body stores in such patients. Identification of a patient at risk and close monitoring of the patient's progress can alleviate many of these problems. Estimated increases above the BMR that can be anticipated in patients with general or specific conditions are noted in Figure 2–2. In addition, an increase in body temperature increases the BMR—7 per cent degree rise on the Farenheit Scale, 13 per cent per degree rise Centigrade.

Adjustment of basal energy requirement with the changes shown in Figure 2–2 can be found in the following examples. A 2-month-old infant is admitted to the hospital with third-degree burns over 40 per cent of her body. Total caloric

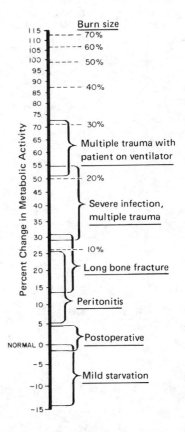

Figure 2–2. Increased energy needs with stress. (From Dialogues in Nutrition 3:1–12, 1979; adapted from Wilmore D: The Metabolic Management of the Critically Ill. New York: Plenum, 1977.)

requirements for age under normal conditions are 115 cal/kg (see Table 2–2). From Figure 2–2, increase in energy needs caused by stress are etimated at 90 per cent above normal.

$$115 \text{ cal/kg} \times 1.9 = 219 \text{ cal/kg}$$

If preburn weight was 4.5 kg, total daily energy requirements would be:

$$219 \text{ cal/kg} \times 4.5 = 985 \text{ cal}$$

In a second example, a 16-year-old female with anorexia nervosa has been consuming between 500 and 600 cal/day for the past month. She is now willing to begin a slow, controlled weight gain. Her height is 163 cm (64 in) and her weight is 43 kg (95 lb). With the Mayo Clinic nomogram (Fig. 2–1) and Table 2–9, her surface area is calculated to be 1.42 m^2 and her caloric needs to be 38.3 cal/m^2/hr. Therefore, her basal requirements are:

$$1.42 \text{ m}^2 \times 38.3 \text{ cal/m}^2\text{/hr} \times 24 \text{ hr} = 1305 \text{ cal/day}$$

Mild starvation creates a decrease in energy needs of about 10 per cent (see Fig. 2–2). Therefore, actual total energy requirements for this patient are:

$$1305 \text{ cal/day} \times 0.9 = 1175 \text{ cal/day}$$

References

1. National Research Council Food and Nutrition Board: Recommended Dietary Allowance, 9th ed. Washington, DC: National Academy of Sciences, 1980.
2. Lowrey GII: Growth and Development of Children, 7th ed. Chicago: Year Book Medical, 1978.
3. Mahalko JR, Johnson LK: Accuracy of long term energy needs. J Am Diet Assoc 77:557, 1980.
4. Sowers MF, Litzinger L, Stumbo P, et al: Development and critical evaluation of the Food Nomogram. J Am Diet Assoc 79:536, 1981.
5. Boothy WM, Babson J, Dunn HL: Studies of the energy of metabolism of normal individuals: a standard for basal metabolism, with a nomogram for clinical application. J Physiol 116:468, 1936.
6. Harris JA, Benedict FG: A Biometric Study of Basal Metabolism in Man. Washington, DC: Carnegie Institute, 1919.
7. Wilmore D: The Metabolic Management of the Critically Ill. New York: Plenum Press, 1977.

3

ENTERAL NUTRITION: SUPPORT OF THE PEDIATRIC PATIENT

Patients who fail to achieve spontaneously an oral intake adequate to meet nutritional needs require certain modifications in feeding. Technical advances in enteral nutrition include the development of specialized formulations and methods for the delivery of enteral alimentation.[1, 2] In addition to being more physiologic than parenteral solutions, enteral feedings are more nutritionally complete, since more is known about enteral requirements and utilization of nutrients. Enteral nutrition is generally safer, less expensive, and easier to continue at home than is parenteral nutrition.[3]

There are many clinical indications for specialized enteral alimentation; they include malnutrition, malabsorption, hypermetabolism, growth failure, prematurity, and a wide range of disorders of absorption, digestion, excretion, utilization, and storage of nutrients.[4, 5] In any instance, the clinical problem is the main factor influencing the type of feeding chosen and the method used to deliver the enteral product. The composition of the formula should be determined by the patient's particular needs. Delivery, volume, and rate are influenced by the formula chosen as well as by the clinical status of the patient.

In this chapter, formula selection, methods of administration, and a practical approach to enteral nutrition are discussed.

ENTERAL FEEDING PRODUCTS

A variety of formulas are available as alternatives to breast feeding in infants younger than 6 to 12 months of age. These formulas vary in caloric density, nutrient composition and source, digestibility, osmolality, viscosity, taste, and cost. The American Academy of Pediatrics provides specific guidelines for infant formulas (Table 3–1) and standards for normal infant feeding based on human breast milk (Table 3–2). Specific formulations available include those that are modified cow's milk formulas (Table 3–2), soy-protein formulas (Table 3–3), and "special" formulas (Table 3–4). The composition of breast milk of mothers delivering preterm infants

TABLE 3–1. Nutrient Levels of Infant Formulas

Nutrient (per 100 Kcal)	FDA 1971 Regulations: Minimum	CON 1976 Recommendations:	
		Minimum	**Maximum**
Protein (g)	1.8	1.8	4.5
Fat			
(g)	1.7	3.3	6.0
(% cal)	15.0	30.0	54.0
Essential Fatty Acids (linoleate)			
(% cal)	2.0	3.0	—
(g)	222.0	300.0	—
Vitamins			
A (IU)	250.0	250.0 (75µg)*	750.0 (225µg)*
D (IU)	40.0	40.0	100.0
K (µg)	—	4.0	—
E (IU)	0.3	3.0 (with 0.7 IU/g linoleic acid)	—
C (ascorbic acid) (mg)	7.8	8.0	—
B$_1$ (thiamine) (µg)	25.0	40.0	—
B$_2$ (riboflavin) (µg)	60.0	60.0	—
B$_6$ (pyridoxine) (µg)	35.0	35.0 (with 15µg/gm of protein in formula)	—
B$_{12}$ (µg)	0.15	0.15	—
Niacin			
(mg)	—	250.0	—
(mg equiv)	800.0	—	—
Folic acid (µg)	4.0	4.0	—
Pantothenic acid (µg)	300.0	300.0	—
Biotin (µg)	—	1.5	—
Choline (mg)	—	7.0	—
Inositol (mg)	—	4.0	—
Minerals			
Calcium (mg)	50.0†	50.0†	—
Phosphorus (mg)	25.0†	25.0†	—
Magnesium (mg)	6.0	6.0	—
Iron (mg)	1.0	0.15	—
Iodine (µg)	5.0	5.0	—
Zinc (mg)	—	0.5	—
Copper (µg)	60.0	60.0	—
Manganese (µg)	—	5.0	—
Sodium (mg)	—	20.0 (6 mEq)‡	60.0 (17 mEq)‡
Potassium (mg)	—	80.0 (14 mEq)‡	200.0 (34 mEq)‡
Chloride (mg)	—	55.0 (11 mEq)‡	150.0 (29 mEq)‡

*Retinol equivalents.
†Calcium to phosphorus ratio must be no less than 1.1 nor more than 2.0.
‡Milliequivalent for 670 kcal/L of formula.
From American Academy of Pediatrics Committee on Nutrition: Commentary on breast feeding and infant formulas, including proposed standards for formulas. Pediatrics 57:278, 1976.

TABLE 3–2. Human Milk– and Standard Cow's Milk–Based Formulas*

	Human Milk (mature)	Enfamil (Mead Johnson)	PM 60/40 (Ross)	SMA (Wyeth)	Similac (Ross)	Whole Cow's Milk
Protein g/dL	1.2	1.5	1.58	1.5	1.55	3.3
Source	Human	Skim milk, whey, casein	Whey, casein	Whey, casein	Skim milk	
% Cal	7	9	9	9	9	20
Fat g/dL	4.0	3.8	3.76	3.6	3.6	3.7
Source	Human	55% soy, 45% coconut oil	Coconut, corn oil	Coconut, corn, soy oil	Coconut, soy oil	Butter fat
% Cal	54	50	50	48	48	50
Carbohydrate g/dL	6.8	6.9	6.9	7.2	7.2	4.9
Source	Lactose	Lactose	Lactose	Lactose	Lactose	Lactose
% Cal	41	41	41	43	43	30
Osmolality	300	278	260	295	290	288
Renal Solute Load/L	81	100	90	80	108	226
Na (mEq/L)	7	9	7	6.5	11	24
K (mEq/L)	13	18	15	13.6	20	35
Ca (mg/L)	340	440	400	440	510	1150
P (mg/L)	140	300	200	330	390	920
Ca/P Ratio	2.2:1	1.5:1	2:1	1.3:1	1.3:1	1.3:1
Features/Indications	Normal infant feeding	Normal infant feeding	Normal infant feeding, renal conditions	Normal infant feeding, cardiac conditions	Normal infant feeding	Normal infant feeding after 6–12 mo of age; depends on intake of solids

*All values for concentrations of 0.67 cal/ml or 20 cal/oz.
These formulas contain cow's milk protein, long-chain fats, and lactose, and are recommended for normal infant feeding. Mineral and electrolyte content varies.

TABLE 3–3. Soy-Protein Formulas*

	Isomil (Ross)	Isomil SF (Ross)	Prosobee (Mead Johnson)	Ross Carbohydrate Free (Ross)	Nursoy (Wyeth)
Protein g/dL	2.0	2.0	2	2	2.1
Source	Soy protein isolate	Soy protein isolate	Soy protein isolate	Soy protein isolate	
% Cal	12	12	12	21	
Fat g/dL	3.6	3.6	3.6	3.6	3.7
Source	Coconut, soy oil	Coconut, soy oil	55% coconut oil, 45% corn or soy oil	Coconut and soy oil	
% Cal	48	48	48	79	
Carbohydrate g/dL	6.8	6.8	6.9		6.6
Source	Corn syrup, sucrose	Glucose polymers	Corn syrup solids		Sucrose, tapioca dextrose
% Cal	40	40	40		
Osmolality	250	250	200		
Renal Solute Load/L	130	130	122	126	
Na (mEq/L)	13	13	12	13	9
K (mEq/L)	18	18	19	18	20
Ca (mg/L)	700	700	500	700	630
P (mg/L)	500	500	420	500	420
Ca/P Ratio	1.4:1	1.4:1	1.2:1	1.4:1	1.5:1
Features/Indications	Lactose intolerance, galactosemia; 20 cal/oz	Lactose intolerance, galactosemia; 20 cal/oz	Sucrose or lactose intolerance, galactosemia; 20 cal/oz	Carbohydrate intolerance; 12 cal/oz without added carbohydrate	20 cal/oz

*These formulas contain soy protein isolate, long-chain fats, and either sucrose or glucose polymers. They are recommended for use in feeding infants with lactose intolerance or galactosemia, and for those in vegetarian families who desire a vegetable protein source.

TABLE 3—4. Special Formulas*

	Nutramigen (Mead Johnson)	Portagen (Mead Johnson)	Pregestimil (Mead Johnson)	Product 3232A (Mead Johnson)
Protein g/dL	2.6	2.4	1.9	2.1
Source	Hydrolyzed casein	Sodium caseinate	Hydrolyzed casein	Casein hydrolysate
% Cal	13	14	11	—
Fat g/dL	2.6	3.2	2.7	2.7
Source	Corn oil	Medium-chain triglycerides 85%, corn oil 15%	Medium-chain triglycerides 40%, corn oil 60%	Medium-chain triglycerides, corn oil
% Cal	35	40	35	—
Carbohydrate g/dL	8.8	7.8	9.1	Dependent on preparation
Source	Sucrose	Corn syrup solids, sucrose	Glucose polymers	—
% Cal	52	46	54	—
Osmolality	479	158	348	—
Renal Solute Load/L	126	140	118	—
Na (mEq/L)	13	13	13	13
K (mEq/L)	17	21	18	17
Ca (mg/L)	600	600	600	600
P (mg/L)	480	480	420	400
Ca/P Ratio	1.3:1	1.3:1	1.5:1	1.3:1
Features/Indications	Hypoallergenicity	Fat malabsorption	Malabsorption, maldigestion	Mono- and disaccharide free; see manufacturer's information for preparation

*All values for concentrations of 0.67 cal/ml or 20 cal/oz
These formulas are modified for use in infants with specific problems of digestion and absorption.

and formulas for premature infants are shown in Tables 3–5 to 3–7. Formulas for infants with inborn errors of amino acid metabolism are presented in Tables 3–8 to 3–10 and those for oral rehydration, in Table 3–11. Infants requiring specialized feedings should be assessed for metabolic and gastrointestinal factors, and any formula choice should be based on a logical evaluation of the specific problem of the patient;[6] general guidelines are shown in Table 3–12.[6, 8–16] Guidelines for formula dilutions appear in Tables 3–13 and 3–14. In general, it is best to use formula concentrate to achieve optimal intakes of protein, vitamins, and minerals; additional calories may then be added by using equal amounts of carbohydrate or fat in small quantities. Stool characteristics depend to some extent on the formula being fed—most specifically, the protein source. Stool characteristics and frequency appear in Tables 3–15 and 3–16.

Formulas available for use in older pediatric patients are generally made for adults and vary significantly in content of vitamins, minerals, and trace elements.[7] The three general categories include meal replacement formulas, which are about 30 per cent fat, are generally low in lactose and residue, and provide 1 cal/ml (Table 3–17); chemically defined or elemental formulas, which contain amino acids and oligosaccharides with little or no fat (Table 3–18); and feeding modules, which provide one component that is generally added to other formulations (Table 3–19). Long-term use of chemically defined diets in children and adolescents should be evaluated periodically to establish nutritional adequacy.

Text continued on page 77

TABLE 3–5. Nutritional Composition of Milk from Mothers Delivering Preterm (PT) and at Term (T)*

Nutrient		Days Postpartum				
		3	7	14	21	28
Lactose (g/dl)	PT†	5.96 ± 0.20 (26)	6.05 ± 0.18 (29)	6.21 ± 0.18 (22)	6.49 ± 0.21 (15)	6.95 ± 0.27 (13)
	T	6.16 ± 0.10 (10)	6.52 ± 0.20 (13)	6.78 ± 0.19 (13)	7.12 ± 0.19 (12)	7.26 ± 0.17 (11)
Fat (g/dl)	PT	1.63 ± 0.23 (25)	3.81 ± 0.21 (27)	4.40 ± 0.31 (21)	3.68 ± 0.40 (15)	4.00 ± 0.33 (13)
	T	1.71 ± 0.24 (10)	3.06 ± 0.46 (12)	3.48 ± 0.40 (12)	3.89 ± 0.49 (12)	4.01 ± 0.30 (11)
Protein (g/dl)	PT‡	3.24 ± 0.31 (26)	2.44 ± 0.15 (29)	2.17 ± 0.12 (22)	1.83 ± 0.14 (15)	1.81 ± 0.11 (13)
	T	2.29 ± 0.07 (12)	1.87 ± 0.08 (14)	1.57 ± 0.05 (13)	1.52 ± 0.06 (12)	1.42 ± 0.05 (11)
Energy (kcal/dL)	PT	51.4 ± 2.4 (25)	67.4 ± 1.7 (27)	72.3 ± 3.0 (21)	65.6 ± 4.3 (15)	70.1 ± 3.3 (13)
	T	48.7 ± 2.0 (10)	60.6 ± 4.3 (12)	64.2 ± 3.7 (12)	68.6 ± 4.0 (12)	69.7 ± 2.9 (11)
Sodium (mEq/L)	PT†	26.6 ± 3.0 (26)	21.8 ± 2.7 (29)	19.7 ± 2.3 (22)	13.4 ± 1.8 (15)	12.6 ± 2.5 (13)
	T	22.3 ± 2.4 (10)	16.9 ± 2.8 (13)	11.0 ± 1.7 (13)	10.8 ± 1.6 (12)	8.5 ± 1.8 (11)
Chloride (mEq/L)	PT†	31.6 ± 2.4 (26)	25.3 ± 2.2 (29)	22.8 ± 2.2 (22)	17.0 ± 1.7 (15)	16.8 ± 2.8 (13)
	T	26.9 ± 2.4 (10)	21.3 ± 2.7 (13)	14.5 ± 1.5 (13)	15.2 ± 1.9 (12)	13.1 ± 2.3 (11)
Potassium (mEq/L)	PT	17.4 ± 0.7 (26)	17.6 ± 0.5 (29)	16.2 ± 0.5 (22)	16.3 ± 0.9 (15)	15.5 ± 0.6 (13)
	T	18.5 ± 1.0 (10)	16.5 ± 0.5 (13)	15.4 ± 0.8 (13)	15.8 ± 0.6 (12)	15.0 ± 0.7 (11)
Calcium (mg/L)	PT	208 ± 17 (25)	247 ± 16 (27)	219 ± 12 (20)	204 ± 15 (13)	216 ± 15 (11)
	T	214 ± 38 (6)	254 ± 11 (8)	258 ± 17 (9)	266 ± 25 (8)	249 ± 18 (7)
Phosphorus (mg/L)	PT	95 ± 7 (25)	142 ± 10 (27)	144 ± 8 (20)	149 ± 13 (13)	143 ± 11 (11)
	T	110 ± 12 (6)	151 ± 18 (8)	168 ± 6 (9)	153 ± 14 (8)	158 ± 13 (7)
Magnesium (mg/L)	PT	28 ± 1 (25)	31 ± 1 (27)	30 ± 1 (20)	24 ± 1 (13)	25 ± 1 (11)
	T	25 ± 4 (6)	29 ± 2 (8)	26 ± 2 (9)	29 ± 3 (8)	25 ± 2 (7)

*Results are expressed as mean ± SEM with the number of subjects at each period in parentheses.
†$P < 0.05$ for PT milk against T milk
‡$P < 0.005$ for PT milk against T milk
From Gross SJ, et al.: Nutritional composition of milk produced by mothers delivering preterm. J Pediatr 96:643, 1980.

TABLE 3–6. Formulas for Premature Infants*

	Enfamil Premature Formula (Mead Johnson)	Premie SMA (Wyeth)	Similac LBW (Ross)	Similac Special Care (Ross)
Protein g/dL	2.4	2.0	2.2	2.2
Source	Skim milk, whey	Whey, casein	Skim milk	Whey, casein
% Cal	12	10	11	11
Fat g/dL	4.1	4.4	4.5	4.4
Source	Medium-chain triglycerides 40%, corn oil, coconut oil	Medium-chain triglycerides, oleo, oleic, coconut, soy	Medium-chain triglycerides 50%, corn 30%, coconut 20%	Medium-chain triglycerides 50%, corn 30%, coconut 20%
% Cal	44	48	47	46
Carbohydrate g/dl	8.9	8.6	8.5	8.6
Source	Glucose polymers, lactose	Glucose polymers, lactose	Lactose 50%, polycose 50%	Lactose 50%, polycose 50%
% Cal	44	42	42	42
Osmolality	300	268	300	300
Renal Solute Load/L	220	175	160	150
Na (mEq/L)	13	14	16	15
K (mEq/L)	22	19	31	26
Ca (mg/L)	900	750	730	1440
P (mg/L)	450	400	560	720
Ca/P Ratio	2:1	1.9:1	1.3:1	2:1
Features/Indications	Premature infants	Low birth-weight infants	Very low birth-weight infants	Premature infants

*All values for concentration of 24 cal/oz. These formulas contain cow's milk protein, a mix of long- and medium-chain fats, and glucose polymers and lactose to meet more closely the needs of the premature infant. Some are also available in 20 cal/oz concentration for the premature infant who is able to take adequate fluid intake to meet caloric needs.

TABLE 3–7. Nutrients in One Package of Human Milk Fortifier*

Nutrient	Amount
Calories	3.5 kcal
Protein	0.13 g (whey, casein)
Fat	0.01 g
Carbohydrate	0.7 g (corn syrup solids)
Calcium	15 mg
Phosphorus	8 mg
Sodium	1.8 mg
Potassium	4 mg
Chloride	4.4 mg
Magnesium	1 mg
Copper	10 μg
Zinc	0.2 mg

*This powdered supplement is added to human milk to help meet the needs of the preterm infant. Recommended amount to add to 100 ml of human milk is 4 packages.

TABLE 3–8. Special Formulas for Infants and Children with Metabolic Disorders*

	PKU 1 (Milupa)	PKU 2 (Milupa)	Lys 1 (Milupa)	Lys 2 (Milupa)	MSUD 1 (Milupa)	MSUD 2 (Milupa)	OS 1 (Milupa)
Protein (g/100 g)	50.3	66.7	58.2	77.3	49.1	65.2	50.7
Source	L-amino acids, low phenylalanine	L-amino acids, low phenylalanine	L-amino acids, free of lysine	L-amino acids, free of lysine	L-amino acids, free of isoleucine, leucine, valine	L-amino acids, free of isoleucine, leucine, valine	L-amino acids, free of isoleucine, methionine, threonine, valine
Carbohydrate (g/100 g)	17.6	7.1	20.9	11.4	28.8	22	27.2
Source	Sucrose	Sucrose	Sucrose	Sucrose	Sucrose	Sucrose	Sucrose
Calories	272	295	278	303	279	305	278
Na (mg)	1067	640	1067	640	1067	640	1067
K (mg)	2332	1329	2332	1329	2332	1329	2332
Ca (mg)	2400	1312	2400	1312	2400	1312	2400
P (mg)	1860	1014	1860	1014	1860	1014	1860
Features/Indications	For use in infants with phenylketonuria	For use in children with phenylketonuria	For infants with hyperlysinemia caused by lysine ketoglutarate reductase deficiency; hyperlysinemia with saccharopinuria	For children with hypertysinemia caused by lysine ketoglutarate reductase deficiency; hypertysinemia with saccharopinuria	For infants with Maple-syrup urine disease	For children with Maple-syrup urine disease	For infants with propionic acidemia, methylmalonic aciduria (B_{12}-independent form)

	OS 2 (Milupa)	Tyr 1 (Milupa)	Tyr 2 (Milupa)	Hist 1 (Milupa)	Hist 2 (Milupa)	Hom 1 (Milupa)	Hom 2 (Milupa)
Protein (g/100g)	67.4	56.9	75.6	60.8	80.9	61.9	82.5
Source	L-amino acids, free of isoleucine, methionine, threonine, valine	L-amino acids, free of phenylalanine, tyrosine	L-amino acids, free of phenylalanine, tryosine	L-amino acids, free of histidine	L-amino acids, free of histidine	L-amino acids, free of methionine, enriched with cystine	L-amino acids, free of methionine, enriched with cystine
Carbohydrate (g/100g)	19.8	21	11.6	17.1	6.3	16	4.7
Source	Sucrose	Sucrose	Sucrose	Sucrose	Sucrose	Sucrose	Sucrose
Calories	304	274	298	271	295	270	294
Na (mg)	640	1067	640	1067	640	1067	640
K (mg)	1329	2332	1329	2332	1329	2332	1329
Ca (mg)	1312	2400	1312	2400	1312	2400	1312
P (mg)	1014	1860	1014	1860	1014	1860	1014
Features/Indications	For children with propionic acidemia, methylmalonic aciduria (B_{12}-independent form)	For infants with tyrosinemia, hypertyrosinemia due to tyrosine amino-transferase deficiency (Richner-Hanhart syndrome)	For children with tryosinemia, hypertyrosinemia due to tyrosine amino-transferase deficiency (Richner-Hanhart syndrome)	For treatment of special cases of histidinemia in infants	For treatment of special cases of histidinemia in children	For infants with homocystinurea caused by cystathionine synthase deficiency (B_6-independent form); homocystinurea caused by methylenetetrahydrofolate reductase deficiency	For children with homocystinurea caused by cystathionine synthase deficiency (B_6-independent form); homocystinurea caused by methylenetetrahydrofolate reductase deficiency

*These formulas are intended for use in specific metabolic disorders; therefore, certain nutrients may be low or absent. Some are intended to be taken with calculated amounts of food. Specific information is available from the manufacturer.

TABLE 3–9. Special Formulas For Metabolic Disorders*

	Lofenalac (Mead Johnson)	MSUD Diet (Mead Johnson)	Phenyl-Free (Mead Johnson)	Low Phe/Tyr Powder Product 3200AB (Mead Johnson)	Low Methionine Powder Product 3200K (Mead Johnson)	Protein-Free Powder Product 8005.6 (Mead Johnson)
Protein Equivalent (g/dL)	2.2	1.2	4.2	2.2	2.1	—
Source	Casein hydrolysate with removal of most phenylalanine	—	—	—	—	—
% Cal	13	8	20	13	12	—
Fat (g/dL)	2.7	2.8	1.4	2.7	3.7	2.3
Source	—	—	—	—	—	—
% Cal	35	38	15	35	49	—
Carbohydrate (g/dL)	8.8	8.8	14	8.8	6.7	7.2
Source	—	—	—	—	—	—
% Cal	52	54	65	52	39	—
Osmolality	—	—	—	—	—	—
Renal Solute Load	—	—	—	—	—	—
Na (mg/L)	300	250	500	300	250	375
K (mg/L)	650	660	1400	650	550	600
Ca (mg/L)	600	660	1200	660	550	600
P (mg/L)	450	360	900	450	400	330
Ca/P Ratio	1.3:1	1.8:1	1.3:1	1.5:1	1.4:1	1.8:1
Features/Indications	11 mg phenylalanine/dL; for infants with phenylketonuria	For maple-syrup urine disease	25 cal/oz; not for use in infants; should be as a supplement on a phenylalanine-restricted diet	Low phenylalanine, low tyrosine powder; for use with hereditary tyrosinemia (6 mg tyrosine/dL; 11 mg phenyl-alanine/dL)	Does not have added methi-onine (22 mg/dL); for use with homocystinuria	Protein-free formula base for special diets needed in amino acid disorders; amino acids must be added.

*These formulas are intended for specific metabolic disorders; therefore, certain nutrients may be low or absent from the formulation. Specific information on exact composition is available from the manufacturer.

TABLE 3–10. Amino Acid Distribution of Special Formulas for Metabolic Disorders

	Lofenalac (g/dL formula) (20 kcal/oz)	Phenyl-Free (g/16 oz formula) (25 kcal/oz)	MSUD Diet Powder (g/dL formula) (20 kcal/oz)	MSUD Product 3200AB (g/dL formula) (20 kcal/oz)	MSUD Product 3200K (g/dL formula) (20 kcal/oz)	MSUD Product 3232A* (g/dL formula) (20 kcal/oz)
Essential Amino Acids						
Histidine	0.065	0.46	0.034	0.056	0.047	0.058
Isoleucine	0.121	1.08	0.0	0.12	0.094	0.119
Leucine	0.231	1.70	0.0	0.25	0.162	0.194
Lysine	0.231	1.86	0.108	0.26	0.121	0.174
L-Methionine	0.072	0.62	0.034	0.078	0.022	0.057
Cystine	0.008	0.34	0.034	0.006	0.014	0.0063
(methionine and cystine)	(0.08)	(0.96)	(0.068)	(0.084)	(0.036)	(0.063)
Phenylalanine	0.011	0.0	0.074	0.011	0.106	0.099
Tyrosine	0.111	0.93	0.087	<0.006	0.068	0.038
(phenylalanine and tyrosine)	(0.122)	(0.93)	(0.161)	(<0.107)	(0.174)	(0.137)
Threonine	0.108	0.93	0.074	0.09	0.073	0.09
Tryptophan	0.028	0.28	0.027	0.028	0.022	0.02
Valine	0.19	1.24	0.0	0.192	0.099	0.149
Nonessential Amino Acids						
Arginine	0.076	0.68	0.067	0.054	0.133	0.071
Alanine	0.095	0.0	0.061	0.106	0.084	0.068
Aspartic acid	0.195	5.12	0.153	0.22	0.246	0.16
Glutamic acid	0.553	1.85	0.281	0.59	0.385	0.46
Glycine	0.053	3.30	0.081	0.056	0.083	0.046
Proline	0.197	0.0	0.121	0.152	0.095	0.213
Serine	0.131	0.0	0.081	0.152	0.1	0.109

*Amino acid values for a quart of 3232A formula reflect the addition of 59 g carbohydrate plus 83.5 g 3232A powder; it is recommended for use in intractable diarrhea.

TABLE 3–11. Oral Rehydration Solutions

	Lytren (Mead Johnson)	Pedialyte (Ross)	Pedialyte RS (Ross)	WHO (World Health Organization)
Carbohydrate g/DL	7.5	4.5	2.5	1.8
Source	Corn syrup solids, dextrose	Dextrose	Dextrose	Dextrose
% Cal	100	100	100	100
Osmolality	290	388	—	333
Na (mEq/L)	30	30	60	90
K (mEq/L)	25	20	20	20
Ca (mEq/L)	4	4	—	—
Cl (mEq/L)	25	30	50	80
Bicarbonate (mmol/L)	—	—	—	30
Features/Indications	9 cal/oz oral electrolyte solution; rehydration	6 cal/oz oral electrolyte solution; rehydration		2–3 cal/oz oral rehydration solution

TABLE 3–12. Indications for Use of Infant Formulas

Problem in Infancy	Suggested Formula	Rationale
Allergy, to cow's milk protein or soy protein	Protein hydrolysate (Nutramigen or Pregestimil)	Protein sensitivity
Biliary atresia	Portagen	Impaired intraluminal digestion and absorption of long-chain fats
Cardiac disease	SMA, Enfamil	Low electrolyte content
Celiac disease	Pregestimil, followed by soy-based formula, followed by cow's milk formula	Advance to more complete formula as intestinal epithelium returns to normal
Constipation	Routine formula, increase sugar	Mild laxative effect
Cystic fibrosis	Portagen	Impaired intraluminal digestion and absorption of long-chain fats
	Pregestimil	Whey protein and disaccharide digestion and absorption impaired
Diarrhea—Chronic Nonspecific	Routine formula	Appropriate distribution of calories
—Intractable	Pregestimil	Impaired digestion of intact protein, long-chain fats, and disaccharides
Failure to thrive (when intestinal damage is suspected)	Pregestimil	Advance to more complete formula as intestinal epithelium returns to normal
Gastroesophageal reflux	Routine formula	Thicken with 1 tbs. cereal/oz; small, frequent feeds
GI bleeding	Consider soy– (?) or cow's milk–free formula	Milk toxicity in infants
Hepatitis—without failure	Routine formula	Impaired intraluminal digestion and absorption of long-chain fats
—with failure	Portagen	
Lactose intolerance	Soy-based formula (e.g., Isomil, Prosobee)	Impaired digestion or utilization of lactose
Necrotizing enterocolitis (after resection)	Pregestimil (when feeding is resumed)	Impaired digestion
Renal insufficiency	PM 60/40	Low phosphate content, low renal solution load

Modified from Gryboski J, Walker, WA: Gastrointestinal Problems in the Infant, 2nd ed. Philadelphia: WB Saunders, 1983.

TABLE 3–13. Concentration and Dilution of Formula Concentrates*

Desired Caloric Concentration (cal/oz)	Liquid Formula Concentrate (oz)	Water (oz)
10	1	3
15	1.5	2.5
20	1	1
24	3	2
26–27	3	1.5
28–29	5	2
30	3	1
32	2	0.5

*Currently marketed formula concentrates that require only the addition of water are forty calories per fluid ounce.

TABLE 3–14. Concentration and Dilution of Powdered Infant Formulas*

Desired Caloric Concentration (cal/oz)	Powdered Formula Concentrate (tbs)†	Water (oz)
10	1	4
15	3	8
20	1	2
24	3	5
28	7	10
30	3	4
32	4	5

*Powdered infant formulas are 40 cal/tbs (level, packed). For large volumes of formula, because the powder displaces the water and makes the volume larger and the formula more dilute, water should be added to the powder to equal the volume expected. For example, to make 32 oz of formula at 24 cal/oz, mix 19 tbs with enough water (29 oz) to equal 32 oz.
†1 tablespoon (tbs) = 1 scoop

TABLE 3–15. Stool Characteristics

Protein Source	Stool Characteristics
Breast milk	Pasty, yellow, soft
Modified skim milk (Enfamil, Similac)	Formed, greenish brown, very little free water
Whey, casein (PM 60/40, SMA)	Small volume, pasty yellow, some free water (similar to breast-milk stool)
Soy protein isolate (Isomil, Prosobee, RCF)	Soft, yellowish green
Sodium caseinate (Portagen)	Formed, greenish brown, little free water
Casein hydrolysate (Pregestimil, Nutramigen)	Green, some mucus, small volume

TABLE 3–16. Stool Frequency and Weight in Normal Infants

	1 Week	8–28 Days	1–12 Months	13–24 Months
No. stools/24 hr	4	2.2	1.8	1.7
Weight (g)	4.3	11	17	35
Water content (%)	72	73	75	73.8

From Gryboski J, Walker WA: Gastrointestinal Problems in the Infant, 2nd ed. Philadelphia: WB Saunders, 1983.

TABLE 3–17. Meal-Replacement Feedings for Older Children and Adolescents

	Meal Replacement—Formula Requires Digestion										Specialty	
	Precision Isotonic (Doyle)	Precision HN (Doyle)	Compleat Modified Formula (Doyle)	Portagen (Mead Johnson)	Osmolite HN (Ross)	Isocal (Mead Johnson)	Osmolite (Ross)	Ensure (Ross)	Enrish (Ross)	Ensure Plus (Ross)	Amin Aid (McGaw)	Hepatic Aid (McGaw)
kcal/ml	0.96	1	1	1	1	1	1	1	1.1	1.5	1.9	1.65
Protein source	Egg-white solids	Egg-white solids	Beef puree, calcium caseinate	Sodium caseinate	Calcium and sodium caseinate, soy protein	Calcium and sodium caseinate, soy protein	Calcium and sodium caseinate, soy protein	Sodium and calcium caseinate, soy protein	Calcium and sodium caseinate, soy protein	Sodium and calcium caseinate, soy protein	Crystalline essential amino acids	Crystalline branched-chain amino acids
Fat source	Soy oil, mono-diglycerides	Mono- and diglycerides, soy oil, MCT	Corn oil, beef fat	MCT* 86%, corn oil 14%	MCT* 50%, corn oil 40%, soy oil 10%	Soy oil 80%, MCT* 20%	MCT* 50%, corn oil 40%, soy oil 10%	Corn oil	Corn oil	Corn oil	Soy oil	Soy oil
Carbohydrate source	Glucose oligo-saccharides, sucrose	Maltodextrin, sucrose	Sucrose, maltodextrin, fructose	Corn syrup, sucrose, lactose (0.15%)	Hydrolyzed corn starch	Maltodextrin	Glucose polymers	Corn-syrup solids, sucrose	Corn-syrup solids, sucrose	Corn-syrup solids, sucrose	Maltodextrins, sucrose	Maltodextrins, sucrose
Protein (g/L)	28.8	44	43	35	44	34	37	37	40	55	19	43
Fat (g/L)	30	0.5	37	48	37	44	38	37	37	53	46	36
Carbohydrate (g/L)	144	218	141	115	141	130	145	145	162	197	366	285
Osmolality (mOsm/kg H_2O)	300	557	300	158	310	300	300	450	480	600	1050	1100
Na/K ratio (mEq/L)	33:24	42:23	29:36	20:32	40:40	22:33	24:26	37:40	37:40	50:60	<15:<3	<15:<2
Ca/P ratio (mEq/L)	32:41	14:17	34:58	47:46	38:49	32:34	27:35	27:35	36:48	32:40	<6: negligible	negligible
Vitamin content	Yes	Yes	Yes	Yes	Yes	Yes	Yes	Yes	Yes	Yes	No	No
Volume to meet RDA (ml)	1560	3000	1500	1000	1400	1920	1920	1900	1530	2000	—	—
Nonprotein (kcal/g N)	185	125	125	155	126	165	155	155	153	145	635	235
Available flavors	Vanilla, orange	Citrus fruit, vanilla	Natural	Unflavored	Unflavored†	Unflavored	Unflavored†	Vanilla†, chocolate, black walnut	Vanilla	Vanilla†, chocolate	Orange, grape, lemon-lime, strawberry	Chocolate, eggnog, custard
pH	7.8	4.9	6.3	Not available	6.5	6.8	6.5	6.5	—	6.5	5.5–7.0	7.5–8.5
Form	Powder	Powder	Ready to use	Powder	Ready to use	Ready to use	Ready to use	Ready to use	Ready to use	Ready to use	Powder	Powder
Features/ Indications	Tube feeding; lactose-free; low K	Supplements tube feeding; lactose-free; high protein; low K	Blenderized tube feeding; lactose-free; thick solution	Tube feeding; lactose-free; MCT*; low Na	Supplements tube feeding; lactose-free	Supplements tube feeding; low Na; lactose-free	Supplements tube feeding; lactose-free; low Na; low K	Supplements tube feeding; lactose-free	14 g of dietary fiber per liter	Supplements tube feeding; lactose-free; high protein	Supplements tube feeding; low electrolytes, essential amino acids; lactose-free	Supplements high branched-chain amino acids; low aromatic amino acids; low electrolytes

*Medium-chain triglycerides
†Flavor packs: cherry, pecan, orange, lemon, strawberry
Compiled by Nancy Hsu, RD, MS

TABLE 3–18. Chemically Defined Formulas for Older Children and Adolescents

	Vivonex HN (Eaton)	Vital HN (Ross)	Criticare HN (Mead Johnson)
kcal/ml	1	1	1
Protein source	L-Amino acids	Whey, soy protein, meat, free amino acids	Hydrolyzed casein, L-Amino acids
Fat source	Safflower oil	Safflower oil, MCT*	Safflower oil
Carbohydrate source	Glucose oligosaccharides	Glucose, oligo- and polysaccharides, sucrose	Maltodextrin, corn starch
Protein (g/L)	42	41	38
Fat (g/L)	1	10	3
Carbohydrate (g/L)	210	185	222
Osmolality (mOsm/kg H_2O)	844	450	650
Na/K ratio (mEq/L)	23:30	17:30	27:34
Ca/P ratio (mEq/L)	14:17	33:42	27:35
Vitamin content	Yes	Yes	Yes
Volume to meet RDA (ml)	3000	1500	1900
Nonprotein (kcal/g N)	125	125	148
Available flavors	Unflavored†	Vanilla	Unflavored
pH	4.8	7.1	Not available
Form	Powder	Powder	Ready to use
Features/Indications	Supplements tube feeding; lactose-free; absorbed in upper gut	Supplements tube feeding; absorbed in upper gut; low Na	Tube feeding; absorbed in upper gut; high carbohydrate

*Medium-chain triglycerides
†Flavor packs: vanilla, strawberry, orange-pineapple, lemon-lime
Compiled by Nancy Hsu, RD, MS

TABLE 3–19. Modular Formulas

	Soybean & Corn Oil	MCT Oil (Mead Johnson)	Casec (Mead Johnson)	Egg White Solids (Kraft)	Whole Egg Solids (Kraft)	Polycose (Ross)	
kcal	9/ml	7.7/ml	370/100 g	370/100 g	600/100 g	400/100 g	2/ml
Protein source	—	—	Calcium caseinate	Egg albumin	Egg albumin	—	—
Fat source	Soy & corn oil	C$_8$ (octanoic) 67%, C$_{10}$ (decanoic) 23%	Milk, fat	—	—		
Carbohydrate source	—		—	—	—	Hydrolyzed corn starch	
Protein (g/100 g)	—	—	88	82	47	—	—
Fat (g/L)	1000	960	2 (g/100 g)	—	43 (g/100 g)	—	—
Carbohydrate (g/L)	—	—	—	6 (g/100 g)	—	44 (g/100 g)	500
Osmolality (mOsm/kg H_2O)	—	—	—	—	—	—	570
Na/K ratio (mEq/100 g)	—	—	6.5:—	48:26	24:14	5:—	24:1
Ca/P ratio (mEq/100 g)	—	—	80:52	3.9:11	11:50	<1:<1	8:3 (mEq/L)
Vitamin content	—	—	No	Yes	Yes	No	No
Available flavors	Natural	Natural	Natural	Natural	Natural	Natural	Natural
pH	—	—	—	6.5	—	—	—
Form	Liquid	Liquid	Powder	Powder	Powder	Powder	Liquid
Features/Indications	Essential fatty acids; concentrated calories	No essential fatty acids; MCT*, concentrated calories	Protein supplement; high Ca, (1.6g Ca/100 g)	Protein (HBV) supplement conc. form	Low Na; high P (0.8 g/100 g); 1.9 g/chol/100 g; HBV† protein	Caloric supplements; lactose-free; concentrated calories.	

*Medium-chain triglycerides
†High biologic value
Compiled by Nancy Hsu, RD, MS

Enteral Alimentation—Methods of Administration

Historically, many of the drawbacks of enteral feeding were caused by the methods used to administer nutrients (e.g., large-bore tubes, bolus feedings). Currently marketed products, such as small-bore, highly flexible catheters and infusion pumps for control of flow rate in continuous infusion, offer more flexibility in the use of enteral alimentation for nutritional support. Factors that are presented here for consideration include appropriate choice of delivery site (Table 3–20),[18–21] method of administration (Table 3–21),[22–26] and advancement of feedings. Products available for enteral feeding, such as tubes, containers, gavage sets, and pumps, are outlined in Tables 3–22 to 3–24. General guidelines for monitoring of enteral feedings (Table 3–25), management of complications (Table 3–26), and approach to enteral feeding (Fig. 3–1)[5] are included.[27–30]

Text continued on page 82

TABLE 3–20. Delivery Site of Enteral Alimentation

Delivery Site	Advantages	Disadvantages or Complications	Advancement*	Contraindications
Gastric				
Nasogastric	Surgery at Nasogastric: not required	Nasal, esophageal, or tracheal irritation	Increase concentration, then volume	Vomiting, delayed gastric emptying, reflux
Gastrostomy		Local skin care required		
	More stable	Risk of intra-abdominal leak with peritonitis		
	Allows patient more mobility			
Jejunal	Bypasses stomach and pylorus, helpful with delayed gastric emptying or gastroesophageal reflux	Requires continuous infusion	Increase volume daily until fluid requirements met, then increase concentration	Distention
		Requires "elemental" formula		
		Risk of perforation		
	Decreases risk of aspiration	Change in small-intestinal flora		
	Can be used immediately postoperative	Tube displacement		
Cervical esophagoscopy	Avoids abdominal surgery	Risk of stricture or esophagitis	As above	Obstruction esophagitis, stricture; after certain radiation treatments of esophagus
	Easily replaced if accidentally removed			

*Volume should be increased first if discontinuation of IV is desired.

TABLE 3–21. Methods of Enteral Alimentation

Method of Administration	Advantages	Disadvantages or Complications	Advancement*	Contraindications
Bolus (intermittent, gravity)	Physiologic, more closely mimics normal feeding	Aspiration; tube clogging; time-consuming	Increase concentration, then volume	Vomiting; delayed gastric emptying; severe reflux
Continuous	Able to deliver larger total volume; less active gastrocolic reflux; allows maximal nutrient absorption with limited capacity for digestion	Bacterial contamination of formula	Infuse constantly and evenly, using gravity or pump to control rate	
Gastric	Physiologic, more closely mimics normal feeding		Increase concentration, then volume	
Jejunal	Increases volume without risk of aspiration	Tube displacement; perforation; bacterial overgrowth	Increase volume, then concentration	Not for routine use, but in carefully selected patients can obviate the need for parenteral alimentation

*Volume should be increased first if discontinuation of IV is desired.

TABLE 3–22. Enteral Feeding Equipment—Containers

Trade Mark (Company)	Volume (ml)	Features
Bags		
Kangaroo bag (Chesebrough-Pond's)	500, 1000, 1200	Tubing attached to bag
Vivonix bag (Eaton Lab)	1000 (?)	Tubing attached with screw clamp
Keofeed bag (Health Development Corp)	500, 1500	Tubing with liner-slip adaptor
Travenol (Travenol)	1500	Tubing optimal with universal port
Vitafeed (Pharmaseal)	1200	Universal port
Dobbhoff (Biosearch)	1000	Optimal tubing; universal port
Ethox-Barron (Ethox Corp)	1000	Tubing attached
Monitor (Corpak)	1000	Tubing not attached

Table continued on opposite page

TABLE 3–22. Enteral Feeding Equipment—Containers Continued

Trade Mark (Company)	Volume (ml)	Features
Bottles		
Abbott	1000	With sterile water
Travenol	1000	With sterile water
Cutter	1000	With sterile water
McGaw	500, 1000	With sterile water
Flexitainer (Ross)	1000	No sterile water
Gavage Sets		
Doyle	40 mm	Screw cap with tubing
Mead Johnson	40 mm	Screw cap with tubing
Ross	40 mm	Screw cap with tubing

TABLE 3–23. Infusion Pumps Designed for Enteral Use Only*

Trademark	Company	PSI	Flow Rate ml/hr (increments)	Features
Kangaroo 200	Chesebrough-Pond's	12	5–295 (5 ml)	Alarms: low battery (3 hours battery life); rate change; occlusion/empty
Flexiflo I	Ross	15	75–200 (25 ml)	No alarm; no battery; (for non-ambulatory patients only)
Flexiflo II	Ross	17.5	20–60 (20) 75–125 (25) 150–250 (50)	Alarms: Empty, low battery, occlusion
Biosearch	Biosearch	6	20–250 (10 ml) 125–250 (25 ml) 5–300 (5 ml)	Alarms: Low battery (8 hours battery life); occlusion
Keofeed 500 (IVAC)	Hedeco	15	1–400 (1 ml)	Alarms: Occlusion/empty; low battery (5 hours battery life); door open
Harvard Pump	Harvard Apparatus Company			None
Barron	Ethox	28	21–140 (20 ml)	Alarms: Rate change
VTR 300	Corpale	12	1–299 (1 ml)	Alarms: Occlusion/empty; Low battery

*Compiled by Nancy Hsu, MS, RD, Nutritional Support Unit, Massachusetts General Hospital, Boston, MA.

TABLE 3–24. Enteral Feeding Tubes

Company	Trademark	French Size	Length Inches (cm)	Material	Other Features
BioSearch Medical Products	Dobbhoff	8	43 (109)	Radiopaque polyurethane with hydrometer	7 g mercury weight; stainless-steel stylet
	Entriflex	8	36 (91)		3 g mercury weight; stainless-steel stylet
		8	43 (109)		
		8	20 (50)		3 g stainless-steel weight; nylon stylet
		6	20 (50)		Nylon stylet
Health Development Corp.	Keofeed	5	20 (50)	Radiopaque silicone	0.8 g mercury weight
		6	36 (90)	With Keolube	3 g mercury weight; nylon stylet
		7.3	30 (75) 36 (90) 42 (105)		Preassembled into the feeding tube
		9.6	36 (90) 42 (105)		
		14.6	36 (90) 43 (105)		
		18.0	36 (90) 43 (105)		
	Surgifeed	7.3	36 (90)	Silicone	Needle catheter; jejunostomy
Sherwood Medical	Duo-Tube	5	40 (102)	Radiopaque silicone	14 Fr. silicone weight 15 Fr. mercury weight
		6	40 (102)		15 Fr. silicone weight 16 Fr. mercury weight
		8	40 (102)		16 Fr. silicone weight 17 Fr. silicone weight
Health Care Group, Inc.	Vitafeed	5	15 (38)	Radiopaque silicone	No mercury weight
		6	42 (105)		3 or 7 g mercury weight
		8	15 (38) 42 (105)		No mercury weight 3 or 7 g mercury weight
		10	42 (105)		3 or 7 g mercury weight
		14*	42 (105)		3 g mercury weight
Norwich-Eaton Pharmaceuticals	Vivonex Jejunostomy Kit	5	36 (90)	Radiopaque polyurethane	Needle catheter
Argyle*	Indurell	5	20	Polyurethane	
		5	36		
		8	42		
	Duotube	5	40	Silicone	Weighted tip
		6	40		
		8	40		

*These tubes are not suplied with preassembled, stainless-steel stylets; all others are.

Table continued on opposite page

TABLE 3–24. Enteral Feeding Tubes *Continued*

Company	Trademark	French Size	Length Inches (cm)	Material	Other Features
	PVC Feeding Tube	3.5	12	Polyvinyl chloride	
		5	16 (36)		
		8	16 (42)		
		10	42		
Corpak		5	15	Urethane	Weighted tip
		6	22 (36)		
		8	22 (36)		
Pharmaseal	Nutra-Feed	5	15	Silicone	Weighted tip in all but 5 French
		6	42		
		8	20 (42)		
		10	42		
Superior	Safe-T-Flex	6	18 and 42	Silicone	Weighted tip
		8	18 and 42		
		10	42		

TABLE 3–25. General Guidelines for Monitoring Patients on Enteral Tube Feedings

1. Confirm the *position* of the feeding tube in the stomach or duodenum: Listen with a stethoscope as air is instilled, aspirate gastric contents, or confirm radiologically.

2. Administer feeding at room temperature at a constant rate.

3. Check *aspirates* every 2 hours. If residual is more than one-half the volume infused over the previous 2 hours, recheck 1 hour later. If there is still over one-half volume, notify physician. Gastric emptying is delayed by increased caloric density of the feeding, CNS disturbance, drugs that cause gastric stasis, and muscular and motility abnormalities.

4. Check *daily intake and output, stool pattern,* volume, and consistency; abdominal pain or distention.

5. Check urine for glucose when high-carbohydrate feedings (e.g., Vivonex, Aminaide) are given.

6. For *infection control,* follow hospital guidelines for the length of time feedings may be stored at room temperature and the care of feeding tubes and administration sets.

TABLE 3–26. Management of Complications in Enteral Feeding

Symptoms	Management
Gastrointestinal	
Distention, vomiting	Reduce volume, consider continuous infusion; if on continuous infusion, reduce rate
Diarrhea, abdominal pain	Check stool pH and reducing substances, infuse feeding constantly and evenly, decrease rate, reduce concentration, consider other formula, add antidiarrheal medication, evaluate patient for enteric infections
Mechanical	
Tube clogged	Flush with water, replace tube
Aspiration	Infuse past the pylorus, consider continuous infusion
Residuals (slowed gastric emptying)	Reduce volume, consider continuous feedings, then transpyloric infusion
Perforation	Stop feeds
Metabolic	
Hyperglycemia	Reduce carbohydrate content of feeding, reduce flow rate, give insulin
Congestive heart failure (fluid overload)	Reduce sodium content, concentrate feeding, slow flow rate, give diuretics
Azotemia	Decrease the protein content of feeding

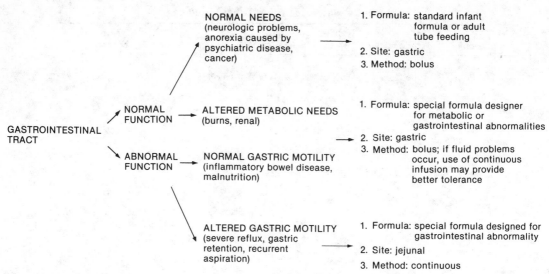

Figure 3–1. Guidelines for approach to enteral alimentation. (Modified from Rombeau JL, Barot LR: Enteral nutritional therapy. Surg Clin North Am 61:605, 1981.)

VITAMIN AND MINERAL SUPPLEMENTS

There are currently many popular misconceptions about the role of vitamins in the promotion of health and prevention of disease; these notions bring about the misuse of supplements and cause added expense for the patient. Recommendations

TABLE 3–27. Guidelines for Use of Supplements in Healthy Infants and Children*

Child	Multivitamin- Multimineral	Vitamins			Minerals
		D	E	Folate	Iron
Term infants					
Breast-fed	0	±	0	0	±†
Formula-fed	0	0	0	0	0
Preterm infants					
Breast-fed‡	+‡	+	±§	±‡	+
Formula-fed‡	+‡	+	±§	±‡	+†
Older infants (after 6 mo)					
Normal	0	0	0	0	±†
High-risk‖	+	0	0	0	±
Children					
Normal	0	0	0	0	0
High-risk	+	0	0	0	0
Pregnant teenager					
Normal	±	0	0	±	+
High-risk**	+	0	0	+	+

*Symbols indicate: +, that a supplement is usually indicated; ±, that it is possibly or sometimes indicated; 0, that it is not usually indicated. Vitamin K for newborn infants and fluoride in areas where there is insufficient fluoride in the water supply are not shown.

†Iron-fortified formula and/or infant cereal is a more convenient and reliable source of iron than a supplement.

‡Multivitamin supplement (plus added folate) is needed primarily when calorie intake is below approximately 300 kcal/day or when the infant weighs 2.5 kg or less; vitamin D should be supplied at least until 6 months of age in breast-fed infants. Iron should be started by 2 months of age.

§Vitamin E should be in a form that is well absorbed by small, premature infants. If this form of Vitamin E is approved for use in formulas, it need not be given separately to formula-fed infants. Infants fed breast milk are less susceptible to vitamin E deficiency.

‖Multivitamin-multimineral preparation (including iron) is preferred to use of iron alone.

**Multivitamin-multimineral preparation (including iron and folate) is preferred to use of iron alone or iron and folate alone.

From American Academy of Pediatrics Committee on Nutrition: Vitamin and mineral supplement needs in normal children in the United States. Pediatrics 66:1015, 1980.

TABLE 3–28. Supplemental Fluoride Dosage Schedule (mg/day*)

Age	Concentration of Fluoride in Drinking Water (ppm)		
	<0.3	0.3–0.7	>0.7
2 wk–2 yr	0.25	0	0
2–3 yr	0.50	0.25	0
3–16 yr	1.00	0.50	0

*2.2 mg sodium fluoride contains 1 mg fluoride
From American Academy of Pediatrics Committee on Nutrition: Fluoride supplementation: revised dosage schedule. Pediatrics 63:150, 1979.

for supplements for full-term and premature healthy infants and children are shown in Tables 3–27 and 3–28. The proper role of additional vitamin and mineral therapy depends upon overt nutritional deficiency (see Chap. 1), chronic disease (see Chap. 5 for specific disease), and drug-induced depletion (see Table 5–18).

Non–dietary induced vitamin deficiencies include alterations in absorption, storage, or excretion, and these are summarized in Table 3–29.

TABLE 3–29. Nondietary Causes of Vitamin Deficiencies

Vitamin	Cause of Deficiency
Fat-Soluble	
Vitamin A, D, E, K	Fat malabsorption (cystic fibrosis, inflammatory bowel disease, bacterial overgrowth, flat-villus lesion, intestinal resection, Whipple's disease)
	Liver disease (biliary atresia, obstruction, bile salt insufficiency, cirrhosis, fibrosis)
	Pancreatic insufficiency (cystic fibrosis, Zollinger-Ellison syndrome, protein-calorie malnutrition)
Vitamin A	Familial follicular hyperkeratosis, acanthocytosis, chronic nephritis
Vitamin D	Renal hydroxylase deficiency, familial hypophosphatemic rickets
Vitamin E	Deficient stores at birth
Vitamin K	Deficient stores at birth, prolonged antibiotic use
Water-Soluble	
Vitamin C	Burns, trauma, surgery
Niacin	Hartnup disease
Riboflavin	None known
Thiamine	Leigh's disease, branched-chain ketoaciduria (MSUD variant), Wernicke-Korsakoff syndrome, thiamine-responsive anemia, chronic lactic acidosis
Pyridoxine, Vitamin B_6	Cystathioninuria, homocystinuria, vitamin B_6–responsive anemia, vitamin B_6–dependent infantile convulsions
Folacin	Lesch-Nyhan syndrome, orotic aciduria, sickle-cell disease (?), trauma, short-gut or blind-loop syndrome, inflammatory bowel disease, celiac disease, homocystinuria, liver cirrhosis and fibrosis, chronic infection
Vitamin B_{12}	Methylmalonic aciduria, ileal resection, parasitic infestation, short-gut syndrome, liver cirrhosis and fibrosis, blind-loop syndrome, intrinsic factor deficiency, inflammatory bowel disease, hypothyroidism, gastric resection

References

1. American Academy of Pediatrics Committee on Nutrition: Commentary on breast feeding and infant formulas, including proposed standards for formulas. Pediatrics 57:278, 1976.
2. Heymsfield SB, Bethel RA, Ansley JD, et al.: Enteral hyperalimentation: an alternative to central venous hyperalimentation. Ann Intern Med 90:63, 1979.
3. Goodgame JI: A critical assessment of the indications for total parenteral nutrition. Surg Gynecol Obstet 151:433, 1980.
4. Koretz RN, Meyer JH: Elemental diets: facts and fantasies. Gastroenterology 78:393, 1980.

5. Rombeau JL, Barot LR: Enteral nutritional therapy. Surg Clin North Am 61:605, 1981.
6. Lake AM, Kleinman RE, Walker WA: Enteric alimentation in specialized gastrointestinal problems: an alternative to total parenteral nutrition. Adv Pediatr 28:319, 1981.
7. Michel L, Serrano A, Malt RA: Nutritional support of hospitalized patients. N Engl J Med 304:1147, 1981.
8. Gryboski J, Walker WA: Gastrointestinal Problems in the Infant, 2nd ed. Philadelphia: WB Saunders, 1983.
9. Hirai Y, Sanada Y, Nakagawa I: An enteral elemental diet for infants and children with surgical disorders. JPEN 4:460, 1980.
10. Iyngkaran N, Robinson MJ, Davis KA, et al.: Cow's milk protein sensitive enteropathy (CMPSE): an important cause of protracted diarrhoea in infancy. Aust Paediatr J 15:266, 1979.
11. Jonas IA, Avigad S, Tavier-Haber A, et al.: Disturbed fat absorption following infectious gastroenteritis in children. J Pediatr 95:366, 1979.
12. Kliegman RM, Fanaroff AA: Neonatal necrotizing enterocolitis: a nine year experience (outcome assessment). Am J Dis Child 135:6081, 1981.
13. MacLean WC, deRomana GL, Massa E, et al.: Nutritional management of diarrhea and malnutrition: primary reliance on oral feeding. J Pediatr 97:316, 1980.
14. Rossi TM, Lebenthal E, Nord KS, et al.: Extent and duration of small intestinal mucosal injury in intractable diarrhea of infancy. Pediatrics 66:730, 1980.
15. Sherman JO, Hamly CA, Khachadurina AK: Use of an oral elemental diet in infants with severe intractable diarrhea. J Pediatr 86:518, 1975.
16. Walker WA: Antigen absorption from the small intestine and gastrointestinal disease. Pediatr Clin North Am 22:731, 1975.
17. Jeans PC, Marriott WM: Infant Nutrition. St. Louis: CV Mosby, 1947.
18. Andrassay RJ, Mahour GH, Harrison MR, et al.: The role and safety of early postoperative feeding in the pediatric surgical patient. J Pediatr Surg 14:381, 1979.
19. Dryburg E: Transpyloric feeding in 49 infants undergoing intensive care. Arch Dis Child 55:879, 1980.
20. Hultén L, Andersson H, Bosaeus I, et al.: Enteral alimentation in the early postoperative course. JPEN 4:455, 1980.
21. Moss G: Maintenance of gastrointestinal function after bowel surgery and immediate enteral full nutrition. JPEN 5:215, 1981.
22. Greene HL, Helinen GL, Folk CC, et al.: Nasogastric tube feeding at home: A method for adjunctive nutritional support of malnourished patients. Am J Clin Nutr 34:1131, 1981.
23. Green HL, McCabe DR, Merenstein GB: Protracted diarrhea and malnutrition in infancy changes in intestinal morphology and disaccharidase activities during treatment with total intravenous nutrition or oral elemental diets. J Pediatr 87:695, 1975.
24. Hartline JV: Continuous intragastric infusion of elemental diet: experience with 10 infants having small intestinal disease. Clin Pediatr 16:1105, 1977.
25. Jones BJM, Payne S, Silk DBA: Indications for pump assisted enteral feeding. Lancet 2:1057, 1980.
26. Scammon RE, Doyle LO: Observations on the capacity of the stomach in the first ten days of postnatal life. Am J Dis Child 20:516, 1923.
27. Freed BA, Hsia B, Smith JP, et al.: Enteral nutrition: frequency of formula modification. JPEN 5:40, 1981.
28. Hunt LI, Antonson DL, Paxson CL Jr., et al.: Osmolality of carbohydrate solutions and gastric emptying in the newborn. Am J Dis Child 136:448, 1982.
29. Newmark SR, Simpson MS, Beskitt MP, et al.: Home tube feeding for long-term nutritional support. JPEN 5:76, 1981.
30. Page CP, Ryan JA, Haff RC: Continual catheter administration of an elemental diet. Surgery 142:184, 1976.
31. American Academy of Pediatrics Committee on Nutrition: Vitamin and mineral supplement needs in normal children in the United States. Report to the Food and Drug Administration, 1979.
32. National Research Council Food and Nutrition Board Committee on Dietary Allowances, ed.: Recommended Dietary Allowances, 9th ed. Washington, DC: National Academy of Sciences, 1980.
33. American Academy of Pediatrics Committee on Nutrition: Nutritional aspects of vegetarianism, health foods, and fad diets. Pediatrics 59:460, 1977.
34. American Academy of Pediatrics Committee on Nutrition: Megavitamin therapy for childhood psychoses and learning disabilities. Pediatrics 58:910, 1976.
35. American Academy of Pediatrics Committee on Nutrition: Iron supplementation for infants. J Pediatr 58:765, 1976.
36. American Academy of Pediatrics Committee on Nutrition: Fluoride supplementation: a revised dosage schedule. Pediatrics 57:278, 1976.
37. American Academy of Pediatrics Committee on Nutrition: Nutritional needs of low birth weight infants. Pediatrics 60:579, 1977.
38. National Nutrition Consortium Committee on Safety, Toxicity and Misuse of Vitamins and Trace Elements: Vitamin Mineral Safety Toxicity and Misuse. Chicago: American Dietetic Association, 1978.

4

PARENTERAL NUTRITION

In spite of the wide variety of enteral formulations available, certain conditions preclude or limit the use of the intestinal tract for nutritional support, and in these cases, parenteral solutions can provide infants and children with many of their nutrient requirements.[1] Examples of such infants and children are those who are premature or small for gestational age and who have limited tolerance for enteral nutrition and those who have congenital abnormalities of the gastrointestinal tract, inflammatory bowel disease, intractable diarrhea, short-gut syndrome, burns, malignancy, cardiac failure, or renal failure.[2–6]

Name
Unit —
Dr/Team
M/F
Birthdate
Gestational Age
Diagnosis

Date							
Wt (kg)							
Ht (cm)							
HC (cm)							
Skin Fold Thickness (mm)							
Parenteral Intake							
Enteral Intake							
Total calories							
Cal/kg							
Gms protein							
Gms fat							
Gm CHO							
Na/K	/	/	/	/	/	/	/
Cl/HCO$_3$	/	/	/	/	/	/	/
Bun/Creat	/	/	/	/	/	/	/
Ca/Phos	/	/	/	/	/	/	/
Mg							
Glucose							
SGOT							
Alkphos							
Bilirubin							
T Protein/Albumin	/	/	/	/	/	/	/
Protime							
HCT/Platelet Ct.	/	/	/	/	/	/	/
NH$_3$							
Vit D/Vit A	/	/	/	/	/	/	/
Copper/Zinc*	/	/	/	/	/	/	/
Folate/B$_{12}$	/	/	/	/	/	/	/
Triglycerides							

*Requires Zinc/Copper free tubes

Figure 4–1. Protocol for monitoring patients. (From Pediatric Parenteral Nutrition Manual. Boston: Children's Service, Massachusetts General Hospital, 1983.)

85

The purpose of this chapter is to provide recommendations and guidelines for the use of available solutions and a description of the techniques available for administration of parenteral nutrition in pediatric patients. The composition of standard pediatric solutions (Fig. 4–1, Tables 4–1 through 4–10), including allowable additives, recommended supplementation of vitamins, trace elements, and minerals, and protocols for monitoring patients, is described. Solutions are currently available that have concentrated mixtures of crystalline amino acids (3.5 to 10 percent), which are then diluted to meet varying requirements. Intakes of 2 to 3 g/kg/day of protein equivalents are recommended as adequate for growth in infancy.[1, 7] Higher levels may promote an increased incidence of azotemia and acidosis.[8] Dextrose is the most commonly used carbohydrate source in parenteral solutions. The quantity of carbohydrate that can be tolerated is variable, particularly in the premature infant, and concentrations therefore can be provided in increasing amounts each day to ensure tolerance.[9] A glucose infusion of 5 mg/kg/min that is increased to 15 mg/kg/min over a 2-day period optimizes insulin release and is usually tolerated well. A suggested protocol for gradually increasing the amount of glucose given an infant can be as follows:

1. A catheter is placed in a central vein and 5 percent dextrose in water is infused, pending x-ray confirmation that the catheter is in proper position.
2. The amount of glucose is gradually increased with the formulations shown in Table 4–11 (for a 3-kg infant).
3. If glucose intolerance develops at any point up to and including the 20 percent pediatric solution (central):
   a. The rate of infusion can be lowered and then increased slowly over several hours.
   b. An intravenous fat emulsion can be started. Begin at 0.5 g/kg/day over 20 hr and increase the volume over 9 hr to maximum of 4 g/kg/day or 45

Text continued on page 92

TABLE 4–1. Parenteral Nutrition Order Sheet*

1. Infuse "central" parenteral nutrition via sterile catheter terminating in a central vein. X-ray confirmation of placement of the catheter tip within the lumen of the vein is mandatory and should be documented on chart by the physician. Infuse 5% dextrose in water at a keep-open rate until x-ray confirmation and then begin infusion of pediatric 10% formulation.

2. Changes in electrolytes in solutions at other times may be made by ordering a dextrose/electrolyte solution in place of the parenteral nutrition solution. (Maintain same dextrose concentration.)

3. No additions may be made to any parenteral nutrition formulation except by the pharmacy staff.

4. Notify physician in event of blocked catheter or leakage from catheter site, and record it in the patient's chart. Blocked catheters should be repaired only by a physician properly trained in this procedure. Do not attempt to irrigate through an obstructed catheter.

5. Test urine every 6 hr for presence of sugar and acetone. For levels of glycosuria at 3+ or greater, obtain serum glucose level and notify physician.

6. Keep accurate measures of intake, output, daily calorie count, and weight. For neonates, include length and head circumference of child on day 1 and then once every 7 days.

7. Central line dressings are changed every 48 hr. IV administration sets, filters, and bottles with pediatric formulations are changed every 24 hr.

8. Infusion rate should be constant, checked every 30 min, and reset to the rate ordered. Do not change the rate of infusion to compensate for periods of increased or slowed infusion.

9. If parenteral nutrition solution is not available, notify physician for appropriate replacement.

10. Laboratory work should be ordered as indicated in Table 4–2.

11. If not added to the solution, vitamin K should be given, 1 mg every 2 weeks IM to patients receiving total parenteral nutrition for longer than 1 month.

*Keep in doctor's order book for duration of pareneral nutrition.
From Pediatric Parenteral Nutrition Manual. Boston: Children's Service, Massachusetts General Hospital, 1983.

TABLE 4–2. Metabolic Monitoring During Peripheral or Central Parenteral Nutrition

Variables to be Monitored	Initial Period*	Later Period†	Variables to be Monitored	Initial Period*	Later Period†
Growth			**Laboratory** Continued		
Weight	Daily	Daily	Platelet count	Weekly	Weekly
Height	Weekly	Weekly	Fe, TIBC, retic count	As indicated	As indicated
Head circumference	Weekly	Weekly	Serum folate and	Monthly	Monthly
Skin fold thickness/			vitamin B_{12}	Monthly	Monthly
mid–upper arm circumference‡	Every 2 weeks	Every 2 weeks	Serum copper and zinc	Daily	Daily
Laboratory			Serum turbidity‖ (or nephelometry level)		
Plasma electrolytes (Na, K, Cl, CO_2)	Weekly	3 ×/week	Serum triglyceride, cholesterol and	2 ×/week	Weekly
BUN	3 ×/week	2 ×/week	free fatty acids (or FA/SA)‖		
Plasma calcium, magnesium, phosphorus	2 ×/week	Weekly	Blood NH_3	2 ×/week	Weekly
Acid-base status	3–4 ×/week	Weekly			
Albumin	2 ×/week	Weekly	**Screening for Signs of Infection**		
Transferrin	Weekly	Weekly	WBC and differential	As indicated	As indicated
Nitrogen balance studies	Weekly	Weekly	Cultures	As indicated	As indicated
Urine glucose§	2–6 ×/day	2 ×/day	Clinical observations (activity, vital signs, etc.)	Daily	Daily
Liver function tests	Weekly	Weekly			
Hgb or Hct	2 ×/week	Weekly			

*The period before maximum doses of glucose, amino acids, or intravenous fat are achieved, or any period of metabolic stability

†The period during which the patient is in a metabolic steady state

‡ If you have access to a trained nutritionist

§If urine glucose is negative, it is safe to assume that serum glucose is not high enough to cause problems; although Dextrostix determinations are not sufficiently accurate to determine worrisome degrees of hyperglycemia, they are useful in monitoring for hypoglycemia (e.g., in the case of an infiltrated IV, or sudden cessation of a deep line, until a new line can be started)

‖When patient is receiving intravenous fat

From Kerner JA, ed.: Manual of Pediatric Parenteral Nutrition. New York: John Wiley & Sons, 1983.

TABLE 4–3. Parenteral Nutrition Solution: Standard Pediatric Formula Contents (per dL)

Component	Pediatric 5%	Pediatric 10%	Pediatric Central 15%	Pediatric Central 20%	Pediatric Central 25%
Amino Acids	2 g	2 g	2 g	2 g	2 g
Dextrose	5 g	10 g	15 g	20 g	25 g
Sodium*	0.2–5 mEq	0.2–5 mEq	0.2–5 mEq	0.2–5 mEq	0.2–5 mEq
Potassium*	0–5 mEq	0–5 mEq	1.1–5 mEq	1.8–5 mEq	1.8–5 MEq
Calcium	2 mEq	2 mEq	0.5 mEq	0.5 mEq	0.5 mEq
Magnesium	2 mEq	1 mEq	0.5 mEq	0.5 mEq	0.5 mEq
Chloride	0–4.8 mEq	0–4.8 mEq	0–4.8 mEq	0–4.8 mEq	0–4.8 mEq
Acetate	1–6 mEq	1–6 mEq	1–4.9 mEq	1–4.2 mEq	1–4.2 mEq
Phosphorus	0.2 mmol	0.2 mmol	1 mmol	1.5 mmol	1.5 mmol
Trace elements†	0.1 ml	0.1 ml	0.1 ml	0.1 ml	0.1 ml
Multiple Vitamins‡	2 ml	2 ml	2 ml	2 ml	2 ml
Osmolarity	700	825	980	1230	1485
Calories Protein	8.5	8.5	8.5	8.5	8.5
Calories carbohydrate	17	34	51	68	85

*Added in sufficient quantities by pharmacy in 1 mEq increments as whole integers up to 5 mEq; sodium added as sodium chloride and potassium added as potassium acetate.

†Trace elements—1 dL contains: zinc, 40 μg; copper, 20 μg; fluoride, 1 μg; iodide, 6 μg; manganese, 20 μg; chromium, 0.17 μg.

‡Multiple vitamins—MVI 12 added to the first bottle daily contains: vitamin A, 3300 IU; vitamin D, 200 IU (may be too low for the preterm infant); vitamin E, 10 IU; ascorbic acid, 100 mg; thiamine (B_1), 3 mg; riboflavin (B_2), 3.6 mg; pyridoxine (B_6), 4 mg; niacinamide, 40 mg; biotin, 60 μg; vitamin B_{12}, 5 μg; pantothenic acid, 15 mg; folic acid, 400 μg. Subsequent bottles do not contain vitamins.

From Pediatric Parenteral Nutrition Manual. Boston: Children's Service, Massachusetts General Hospital, 1983.

TABLE 4–4. Conversion Table

Element	To Convert mmol to mg or μmol to μg, Multiply by:	To Convert mmol to mEq, Multiply by:
Na	23	1
K	39	1
Cl	35.5	1
Ca	40	2
P	31	*
Mg	24	2
Zn	65	*
Cu	63.5	*
Mn	55	*
I	127	*
Fe	56	*
Cr	52	*
Se	79	*

*Valences of these elements vary. For nutritional purposes, it is most convenient to express quantities of these elements in moles.

TABLE 4–5. Maximum Allowable Electrolyte Additives

Electrolyte	Total per dL of Parenteral Solution	Additive	Explanation
Magnesium	1 mEq	Magnesium sulfate injection, 4 mEq/ml	Standard quantities may be omitted or additional quantities may be added up to maximum to the 15, 20, and 25% solution after consultation with nutritional support team
Sodium chloride*	Patient tolerance or need	Sodium chloride injection, 2.5 mEq/ml	0–5 mEq may be added without consultation
Potassium acetate	Patient tolerance or need	Potassium acetate injection, 2 mEq/ml	0–5 mEq may be added without consultation; additional quantities may be ordered after consultation with nutritional support team
Calcium, Phosphorus	2 mEq 2 mmoles	Calcium gluconate injection, 0.4 mEq/ml Potassium phosphate, 4.4 mEq K and 3 mM P/ml	Standard quantities may be omitted from all formulas or additional quantities may be added to maximum to the 15, 20, and 25% solution after consultation with nutritional support team; insoluble calcium phosphate will form if the ratio of these two ions is incorrect; known soluble Ca/P ratios per dL: 2.0 mEq/0.5 mmole; 1.0 mEq/1.0 mmole; 0.5 mEq/2.0 mmole

*Sodium acetate may be ordered for chloride-restricted patients
From Pediatric Parenteral Nutrition Manual. Boston: Children's Service, Massachusetts General Hospital, 1983.

TABLE 4–6. Formulations for Infants and Children Under 11 Years

Vitamins	RDA			AAP minimum/ 100 kcal orally*	Suggested Formulations	
	Range for Infants (/kg body wt, 0.0–0.5 and 0.5–1.0 yr)	Mean for Infants	Range for Children Under 11 yrs		Multivitamin for Intravenous Use for Children Under 11 yrs†	Water-Soluble Vitamins for Intramuscular Use
A (retinol), IU	233–222	227.0	2,000–3,300	250.0	2,300.0‡	
D, IU	66–44	55.0	400	40.0	400.0§	
E (α-tocopherol), IU	0.66–0.55	0.6	7–10	0.3	7.0	
K₁ (phylloquinone), mg					0.2	
Ascorbic acid, mg	6–4	5.0	40	8.0	80.0	80.0
Folacin, µg	8–6	7.0	100–300	4.0	140.0	140.0
Niacin, mg	0.9–0.8	0.85	9–16	0.25	17.0	17.0
Riboflavin, mg	0.07	0.07	0.8–1.2	0.06	1.4	1.4
Thiamin, mg	0.055–0.05	0.053	0.7–1.2	0.025	1.2	1.2
B₆ (pyridoxine), mg	0.05–0.04	0.045	0.6–1.2	0.035	1.0	1.0
B₁₂ (cyanocobalamin), µg	0.04–0.03	0.035	1–2	0.15	1.0	1.0
Panthothenic acid, mg				0.3	5.0‖	5.0
Biotin, µg					20.0‖	20.0

*American Academy of Pediatrics Committee on Nutrition: Proposed changes in Food and Drug Administration regulations concerning formula products and vitamin-mineral dietary supplements for infants. Pediatrics 40:916, 1967.
†May be provided in appropriate salt or ester form in equivalent potency.
‡700 µg of retinol.
§As ergocalciferol or cholecalciferol.
‖RDA not established; amount equals 20 × 100 kcal human milk.
From American Medical Association Department of Foods and Nutrition: Multivitamin preparations for parenteral use: a statement by the Nutrition Advisory Group. JPEN 3:258, 1979.

TABLE 4–7. Suggested Formulations for Children, Aged 11 yr and Above, and Adults*

Vitamins	RDA, Adult Range	Multivitamin Formulation for Intravenous Use	Water-Soluble Vitamin Formulation for Intramuscular Use
A, IU	4,000–5,000†	3,300	
D, IU	400	200	
E, IU	12–15	10.0	
Ascorbic acid, mg	45	100.0	100.0
Folacin, μg	400	400.0	400.0
Niacin, mg	12–20	40.0	40.0
Riboflavin, mg	1.1–1.8	3.6	3.6
Thiamin, mg	1.0–1.5	3.0	3.0
B_6 (pyridoxine), mg	1.6–2.0	4.0	4.0
B_{12} (cyanocobalamin), μg	3	5.0	5.0
Pantothenic acid, mg	5–10‡	15.0	15.0
Biotin, μg	150–300‡	60.0	60.0

*Results do not include requirements for pregnancy or lactation.
†Assumes 50% intake as carotene, which is less available than vitamin A.
‡RDA not established; amount considered adequate in usual dietary intake.
From American Medical Association Department of Foods and Nutrition: Multivitamin preparations for parenteral use: a statement by the Nutrition Advisory Group. JPEN 3:258, 1979.

TABLE 4–8. Suggested Daily Intravenous Intake of Essential Trace Elements

Component	Pediatric Patients, μg/kg*	Stable Adult	Adult in Acute Catabolic State†	Stable Adult With Intestinal Losses†
Zinc	300‡ 100§	2.5–4.0 mg	Additional 2.0 mg	Add 12.2 mg/L small-bowel fluid lost; 17.1 mg/kg of stool or ileostomy output‖
Copper	20	0.5–1.5 mg	—	—
Chromium	0.14–0.2	10–15 μg	—	20 μg**
Manganese	2–10	0.15–0.8 mg	—	—

*Limited data are available for infants weighing less than 1500 g. Their requirements may be more than the recommendations because of their low body reserves and increased requirements for growth.
†Frequent monitoring of blood levels in these patients is essential for proper dosage.
‡Premature infants (weight less than 1500 g) up to 3 kg of body weight; thereafter, the recommendations for full-term infants apply.
§Full-term infants and children up to 5 years old; thereafter, the recommendations for adults apply, up to a maximum dosage of 4 mg/day.
‖Values derived by mathematical fitting of balance data from a 71-patient–week study in 24 patients.
**Mean from balance study.
From American Medical Association Nutrition Advisory Group: Guidelines for essential trace-element preparations for parenteral use. JAMA 241:2051, 1979.

TABLE 4–9. Vitamin Content Per Package of Selected TPN Preparations

Product	A (Units)	D (Units)	E (Units)	B$_1$ (mg)	B$_2$ (mg)	Niacin (mg)	Pantothenic Acid (mg)	B$_6$ (mg)	C (mg)	Folic Acid (µg)	B$_{12}$ (µg)	Biotin (µg)
AMA/NAG*	3300	200	10	3	3.6	40	15	4	100	400	5	60
M.V.I.-12	3300	200	10	3	3.6	40	15	4	100	400	5	60
MVC 9 + 3†	3300	200	10	3	3.6	40	15	4	100	400	5	60
M.V.I.	10,000	1,000	5	50	10	100	25	15	500	—	—	—
Berocca-C	—	—	—	10	10	80	20	20	100	—	—	200
Betalin Complex F.C.	—	—	—	25	6	100	5	10	150	—	—	—
Folbesyn	—	—	—	10	10	75	10	15	300	1,000	15	—
Solu-B with Ascorbic Acid	—	—	—	10	10	250	50	5	500	—	—	—
Vi-Cert	—	—	—	25	10	100	20	20	500	—	—	—
Bejectal-C	—	—	—	200	30	750	50	50	1,000	—	20	—
Solu-B-forte	—	—	—	250	50	1,250	500	50	1,000	—	—	—

*Recommendations for children age 11 yr and above, and adults (American Medical Association Nutrition Advisory Group).
†Does not require refrigeration.
From Kerner JA, ed.: Manual of Pediatric Parenteral Nutrition. New York: John Wiley & Sons, 1983.

TABLE 4–10. Commercially Available IV Trace Element Preparations

Element	Concentration	Sizes Available (ml)	Manufacturer
Chromium (chromic chloride)	4 μg/ml	10	USV Laboratories
		10	Travenol Laboratories
		10, 30	American Quinine
		10, 30	Abbott Laboratories
Copper (sulfate)	0.4 mg/ml	10	Travenol Laboratories
		10, 30	American Quinine
Copper (cupric chloride)	0.4 mg/ml	10	USV Laboratories
		10, 30	Abbott Laboratories
Manganese (sulfate)	0.1 mg/ml	10	Travenol Laboratories
		10, 30	American Quinine
Manganese (chloride)	0.1 mg/ml	10, 50	Abbott Laboratories
		10	USV Laboratories
Zinc (sulfate)	1 mg/ml	10	Travenol Laboratories
		10, 30	American Quinine
Zinc (chloride)	1 mg/ml	10, 50	Abbott Laboratories
		10	USV Laboratories
Selenium (selenious acid)	40 μg/ml	10	Lympho-Med, Inc.
Multi trace elements			
Zinc	1.0 mg		
Copper	0.4 mg	per 10 ml	Travenol Laboratories
Chromium	4.0 μg		American Quinine
Manganese	0.1 mg		
Zinc	4.0 mg		
Copper	1.0 mg	per 5 ml	Abbott Laboratories
Chromium	10.0 μg		
Manganese	0.8 mg		

From Kerner JA, ed.: Manual of Pediatric Parenteral Nutrition. New York: John Wiley & Sons, 1983.

percent of total calories, whichever is reached first. Essential fatty acid requirements can be met by 0.5 to 1.0 g/kg/day. The intravenous fat emulsion will supply 1.1 cal/ml and will allow use of lower glucose loads but maintenance of adequate fluid volumes. It contains 87 percent wt/vol water and this amount should be counted in the total daily fluid intake.

c. Insulin can be administered either as bolus subcutaneous injections or as a continuous infusion in the parenteral nutrition solution.

In this protocol the volume of infusate is kept constant—between 120 and 150 ml/kg/day, depending on the infant's fluid requirements—and the concentration of glucose in the solution is slowly increased. Solutions containing more than 20 percent glucose at 150 ml/kg/day may not be beneficial[10] and may contribute to the hepatic steatosis seen with excessive carbohydrate loads.[1]

Vitamins, minerals, and trace elements must be supplied in parenteral solutions and are generally added to the glucose–amino acid infusate. Current recommendations are derived from oral requirements and are shown in Tables 4–6 to 4–8.[11, 12]

Parenteral lipid solutions, a concentrated source of energy, provide essential fatty acids and are iso-osmolar. The daily requirement of essential fatty acid (linoleic acid) can be supplied by 0.5 to 1 g/kg/day of intravenous lipids. The maximum

TABLE 4–11. Formulations for Gradually Increasing Glucose in a 3-kg Infant Receiving Central Parenteral Nutrition

Formulation	Volume	Cal/24 hr	Cal/kg/day
Pediatric 10% solution	100 ml/kg/day	127.5	42.5
Pediatric 10% solution	150 ml/kg/day	191	61
Pediatric solution 15% (central)	150 ml/kg/day	267	89
Pediatric solution 20% (central)	150 ml/kg/day	344	114.6
Pediatric solution 25% (central)	150 ml/kg/day	420	140

From Pediatric Parenteral Nutrition Manual. Boston: Children's Service, Massachusetts General Hospital, 1983.

TABLE 4–12. Metabolic Complications of Parenteral Nutrition

Metabolic Complications	Possible Cause	Management
Glucose Metabolism		
Hyperglycemia with glucosuria, osmotic diuresis, hyperosmolar dehydration, intracranial hemorrhage, coma, ketoacidosis	Excessive rate or amount of glucose infusion, inadequate endogenous insulin, glucocorticoids, sepsis, malnutrition, renal disease	Dilute the infusate or slow the rate of infusion, repair the fluid and electrolyte deficit by peripheral vein, and keep the glucose amounts at 7–10 g/kg/day
Hypoglycemia (postinfusion)	Increased insulin production, hepatic glycogenic enzyme immaturity, interrupted or too-rapid weaning of one dextrose solution	Carefully taper the infusion rate
Ketoacidosis in diabetes mellitus	Inadequate endogenous insulin response, inadequate exogenous insulin therapy	Add exogenous insulin
Amino Acid Metabolism		
Hyperchloremic acidosis	Excessive chloride and monohydrochloride content of crystalline amino acid solutions	Increase acetate content of solution; decrease chloride
Serum amino acid imbalance	Abnomal serum amino acid profiles have been reported in association with parenteral nutrition. The consequences of these imbalances are unknown, but the elevations of amino acids such as glutamine and glycine may be harmful to the developing central nervous system. In addition, lethargy and altered central nervous system function are seen in some infants who have marked elevations of serum amino acids caused by excessive protein intake (greater than 5 g/kg/d). Currently available solutions are formulated with crystalline amino acids. Protein hydrolysate solutions are no longer commercially available. Crystalline amino acid solutions may not contain all of the amino acids necessary (e.g., cysteine, tyrosine, taurine, and carnitine) for optimum growth in premature or small for gestational age infants. In spite of these deficiencies, the present crystalline amino acid solutions have been used successfully to promote the growth and development of newborn infants. Extensive research is under way to develop amino acid mixtures appropriate for children	
Hyperammonemia	Several investigators have reported hyperammonemia in infants receiving protein hydrolysate and crystalline amino acid solutions. Its presence is thought to be caused by the high loads of preformed ammonia and low levels of arginine found in the original amino acid formulations.	

Table continued on following page

TABLE 4–12. Metabolic Complications of Parenteral Nutrition *Continued*

Metabolic Complications	Possible Cause	Management
	These problems have been corrected in more recent solutions by an increase in the amount of arginine. Subclinical liver disease or hepatic immaturity may also produce hyperammonemia.	
Prerenal azotemia	Excessive nitrogen infusion, particularly in low birth-weight infants, when protein equivalent in excess of 5 g/kg/day is given	Lower protein
Lipid Metabolism		
Essential fatty acid deficiency (serum deficiencies of linoleic and/or arachidonic acids, serum elevations of 5,8,11-eicosatrienoic acid)	Inadequate essential fatty acid administration, inadequate vitamin E administration (Linolenic acid deficiency can occur if safflower oil mixtures such as Liposyn are used)	Essential fatty acid deficiency occurs commonly in patients on nutritional support without lipid supplementation. Requirements can be met by administering 0.5 g/kg twice a week, or 2–5% of total calories. Patients who require marked fluid restriction may be given a 20% intravenous fat emulsion.
Hypertriglyceridemia and high levels of free fatty acid	Rapid infusion of fat emulsion, malnutrition, stress, infection, diabetes, prematurity	Slow administration of fat emulsion
Kernicterus	Displacement of bilirubin from albumin by free fatty acids has been demonstrated *in vitro,* and, therefore, infants at risk for kernicterus with hyperbilirubinemia should not receive more than 0.5 g/kg/day of intravenous fat. Lipemic serum falsely elevates the spectrophotometric determination of bilirubin and also interferes with determination of serum calcium.	Limit lipid infusion to 0.5 g/kg/day
Fat overload syndrome, characterized by hyperlipemia, fever, lethargy, liver damage, and coagulation defects; problems with gas exchange and hypoxia	This has only rarely been described in infants and children who have had grossly lipemic sera. Therefore, triglyceride levels should be monitored weekly while the patient receives intravenous fat emulsion.	Stop infusion of intravenous fat emulsion
Platelet dysfunction and thrombocytopenia	Platelet dysfunction and thrombocytopenia have been associated with the use of cottonseed oil emulsions. Essential fatty acid deficiency as well as many of the underlying conditions of patients receiving parenteral nutrition is associated with thrombocytopenia. In a large series of patients who had thrombocytopenia before they received intravenous lipid, platelet counts were not affected by the fat emulsion.	

Table continued on opposite page

TABLE 4–12. Metabolic Complications of Parenteral Nutrition *Continued*

Metabolic Complications	Possible Cause	Management
	In several infants in this same series who had a malignancy and thrombocytopenia, platelet counts rose concomitantly with recovery from sepsis or the recovery of the bone marrow while the patient was receiving intravenous lipid infusion.	Use soybean oil emulsion
Deposition of fat pigment in reticuloendothelial cells in the liver, lungs, and spleen occurs in patients receiving intravenous fat emulsions	At the present time no known adverse clinical effect has been associated with this histologic finding in humans	
Hepatic dysfunction and hepatic failure. Elevation of alkaline phosphatase, bilirubin, and hepatic transaminases occurs in approximately 30% of infants and children on prolonged parenteral nutrition. Hepatomegaly occurs with accumulation of bilirubin in bile ductules and hepatocytes.		Although cholestasis and hepatocellular dysfunction are generally reversible even during continuation of parenteral nutrition, they may progress to hepatic failure. Initially there is no way to predict which patients will develop these changes or which will progress to hepatic failure. In the presence of hepatic dysfunction, parenteral nutrition solution should be discontinued if other means of nutritional support are available. In the absence of other means of nutritional support, parenteral nutrition solutions must be continued with close monitoring of hepatic function. With continued deterioration of hepatic function, the solution should be adjusted on an individual basis to fit the clinical situation until hepatic functions return toward normal.
Miscellaneous*		
Hypophosphatemia	High glucose infusions, inadequate phosphorus administration, malnutrition, or rapid growth	Increase phosphorus content of solution, especially with crystalline amino acid mixtures
Hypokalemia	Inadequate potassium relative to increased requirements for protein anabolism, diuresis	Increased potassium content of solution
Hyperkalemia	Excessive potassium administration, especially in metabolic acidosis, renal decompensation	Decrease potassium content of solution
Hypomagnesemia	Inadequate magnesium administration relative to increased requirements for protein anabolism and glucose metabolism	Increase magnesium content of solution
Hypermagnesemia	Excessive magnesium administration, renal decompensation	Decrease magnesium content of solution
Hypocalcemia	Inadequate intake may follow a previous increase in phosphorus intake	Increase calcium content of solution

*Fluid acid-base, electrolyte, calcium, phosphorus, trace element, and vitamin imbalances have all been seen with parenteral nutrition; close monitoring of these nutrients is important. For a complete review see references.[3,4,6,14–23]

Table continued on following page

dose of 4 g/kg/day (or 45 percent total calories) should be infused slowly over a 24-hour period to maximize tolerance.[1] In patients with infection or hyperbilirubinemia, the lowest dose that meets essential fatty acid requirements should be used. Recommendations for use in pulmonary disease are included in Chapter 6.

Lipid with a small amount of glucose and glucose alone appears to be equally effective in the restoration and maintenance of lean body mass. However, excessive substrate infusion can produce undesirable complications, such as hepatomegaly and liver dysfunction, respiratory insufficiency, and other metabolic complications.[13] Selection of the appropriate total parenteral nutrition regimen requires thorough medical evaluation of those patients at risk for complications secondary to infusions high in glucose or lipids.

TABLE 4–13. Mechanical Complications of Central Venous Catheters

Complication	Signs and Symptoms	Treatment	Prevention
Malposition of the catheter may produce subcutaneous collection of the parenteral solution. Extravasation of hypertonic solutions into the pleural or pericardial space may be life-threatening. Hemorrhage associated with erosion of a central vein or the right atrium has also been reported.	Swelling at the insertion site of the catheter; a rapid fall in serum glucose or the acute onset of circulatory compromise	Removal of catheter	Careful handling of catheter and secure typing of joints
Pneumothorax, hemorrhage, and *brachial plexus* injuries are possible complications of percutaneous subclavian line insertion.	Respiratory distress, decreased cardiac output, pain	Removal of catheter	Placement of central venous catheters in the neonate and small infant can be done by percutaneous insertion at the bedside or by incising the skin, exposing the vein, and inserting the catheter under general anesthesia in the operating room
Obstruction of the infusion is most commonly caused by inadvertent clamping of the line, an air leak in the filter, or kinking of the catheter or IV tubing	Pump occlusion alarm will sound; gravity flow of solution stops	If clotting of the line occurs, the physician may use sterile technique to attempt to dislodge the clot by carefully flushing with 1 ml normal saline from syringe directly attached to the catheter hub	Careful taping of catheter and dressings; use of pumps will detect obstructions immediately

Table continued on opposite page

Because these solutions are formulated to provide what is estimated to be the infant's nutrient requirements, they may be used for short or extended periods of time. Potential metabolic complications caused by the administration of the infusate and appropriate treatments for such problems are outlined in Table 4–12.[3, 4, 6, 14–23] Mechanical or catheter-related complications and treatment are listed in Table 4–13.[6, 9, 15, 16, 23–28]

The decision to choose central versus peripheral venous alimentation depends on the purpose of the parenteral nutrition program, the anticipated length of time parenteral nutrition will be necessary, and the strength of the solution. When possible, the use of peripheral veins for parenteral nutrition is preferred. Regimens employing the simultaneous administration of glucose–amino acid and lipid into

TABLE 4–13. Mechanical Complications of Central Venous Catheters Continued

Complication	Signs and Symptoms	Treatment	Prevention
Air embolus may occur during insertion of the catheter or when tubing is changed; also, if the system disconnects from the catheter, a sudden onset of respiratory distress may result.	Sudden onset respiratory distress, cyanosis	The patient is placed on the left side with head down, the infusion is stopped, and the physician is notified immediately	Use of a pump that prevents air from pumping into the system and clamping the catheter when the IV tubing is changed
Catheter embolus will occur if the tip of the catheter breaks off from its main body. Very high pressures will rupture silicone catheters, or the tip may be sheared off if the catheter is pulled back through the hub of the needle used to insert it.	Sudden onset respiratory distress, cyanosis	Same as above; removal of catheter	Careful handling of catheter and maintenance of normal pump pressure
Transient *arrhythmias* usually occur during catheter insertion, and heartbeat should be monitored carefully immediately after insertion.	Irregular heartbeats	May require repositioning of catheter	
Thrombosis of the central vein	Venous distention or edema of the part of the body drained by the vein; reduced flow under gravity of the parenteral nutrition solution	Removal of catheter	Use of a pump with obstruction alarm may provide early detection.
Accidental *uncoupling* of joints in the system	Leakage of the solution or blood return; hypoglycemia or infection may result; air may be introduced into the line	Clamp system, clean before reconnecting	Use of *Luer-lock* connectors and securing of connection points with adhesive tape
Insertion site infection or inflammation	Erythema and induration at the site of catheter insertion	Removal of catheter	

TABLE 4–14. Suggested Monitoring Schedule for Patients Receiving Peripheral Venous Alimentation (Glucose–Amino Acid)

Twice Daily	Daily	Weekly
Temperature	Intake	Length
Pulse	Output	Head circumference
Blood pressure	Weight	
	Urine glucose	
	Urine ketone	
	Serum Na, K, Cl, CO_2*	
	Blood glucose*	
	BUN*	

*Monitoring should be done daily for the first week, twice weekly thereafter.

the same vein have greatly improved the effectiveness of peripheral alimentation.[14, 15, 24–26, 29, 30] Peripheral alimentation is isotonic, is safe, and has few special technical requirements; thus it avoids many of the risks and complications of central venous catheters.

If the goal of therapy is nutritional support for 1 to 2 weeks, after which time enteral feeding will be initiated, peripheral venous alimentation with the standard pediatric 5 or 10 percent formulas (see Table 4–3) will probably be adequate. If significant catch-up growth or long-term intravenous nutritional support is required, it is best accomplished with central venous alimentation, since peripheral alimentation is most successful in adequately nourished patients who are not under major metabolic stress. A patient's failure to receive adequate energy requires use of central venous alimentation. If the patient's volume is limited (and thus requires a very hypertonic solution), a central line must also be used.

The advantages of higher intakes of calories and nitrogen must be balanced against the increased risk of infection and metabolic complications. In all cases, risk factors can be minimized if an assessment plan is outlined and implemented; protocols for administration and monitoring must be followed closely.

TABLE 4–15. Composition of Intravenous Lipid Emulsions*

	Intralipid 10% (Cutter)	Intralipid 20% (Cutter)	Liposyn 10% (Abbott)	Liposyn 20% (Abbott)	Travemulsion 10% (Travenol)	Travemulsion 20% (Travenol)
Base	Soybean oil 100 g/L	Soybean oil 200 g/L	Safflower oil 100 g/L	Safflower oil 200 g/L	Soybean oil 100 g/L	Soybean oil 200 g/L
Egg phospholipids (%)	1.2	1.2	1.2	1.2	1.2	1.2
Glycerin (%)	2.25	2.25	2.25	2.25	2.25	2.25
Linoleic acid (%)	54	54	77	77	56	56
Oleic acid (%)	26	26	13	13	23	23
Palmitic acid (%)	9	9	7	7	11	11
Linolenic acid (%)	8	8	<0.5	<0.5	6	6
Stearic acid (%)	—	—	2.5	2.5	—	—
Osmolality (mOsm/L)	280	330	300	—	270	330
Calorie content (cal/ml)	1.1	2.0	1.1	2.0	1.1	2.0
Vitamin E (IU)	71	71	—	—	—	—
Cholesterol (mg/L)	400–600	400–600	Trace	Trace	Trace	—
Water/liter (ml)	870	770	870	770	870	770
Supplied (ml)	100	100	50	50	500	770
	500	500	100	100		
			200	200		
			500	500		

*Intravenous fat emulsions should be started after maintenance glucose concentration is reached, since lipids may impair tolerance of large glucose loads and confuse the treatment of glucosuria. Begin fat emulsion at 0.5 g/kg/day, given over 20 to 24 hr, and increase the volume over 96 hr to a maximum of 4 g/kg/day.

TABLE 4–16. Complications and Management of Peripheral Venous Alimentation

Complication	Clinical Signs and Symptoms	Treatment	Prevention
Skin Slough (a rare but serious complication of extravasation of the parenteral solution into the interstitial space)	Swelling at the peripheral IV site and discoloration of the skin around the site	Remove IV immediately and cover skin sloughs with sterile dressing and antibiotic ointment	Observe IV site hourly for infiltration and change peripheral sites every 48 hr. An infusion pump is not recommended for peripheral IV administration unless the rate is very low.
Local Inflammatory Reaction	Erythema and induration at IV site	Remove line	Strict aseptic technique during insertion; frequent inspection of site
Phlebitis	Pain, tenderness, inflammation	Remove IV	Careful catheter insertion maintenance

Metabolic complications may be similar to those seen in central alimentation (see Table 4–12).

General guidelines for peripheral administration of amino acids and glucose are as follows:
1. Infuse via peripheral IV site.
2. If possible, the peripheral nutrition site should not be used for other IVs, medications, or blood sampling.
3. Infusion rate should be constant.
4. If peripheral formulation is not available, infuse 5 percent dextrose in water at the same rate.

Peripheral venous alimentation should be monitored as carefully as central alimentation, and a suggested schedule is shown in Table 4–14. A nutritional support team that assumes responsibility for patient care significantly decreases the number of complications seen and smoothes the transition to enteral feedings.

The composition of lipid emulsions is presented in Table 4–15. The following are guidelines for peripheral lipid administration:
1. IV fat emulsion may be infused simultaneously with amino acids and glucose through a Y connector near the infusion site and beyond the filter of the peripheral line. The fat emulsion contains particles of 0.4 to 0.5 μm and should not be filtered. Lipid is infused into the site closest to the catheter. The flow rates of each solution should be controlled by separate pumps.
2. A suggested monitoring schedule calls for daily serum turbidity checks and serum triglycerides as indicated.
3. In cases of decreased lipid tolerance, infuse the lowest dose necessary to meet essential fatty acid requirements (0.5 g/kg/day).

An outline of the complications of peripheral venous alimentation (and their management) are provided in Table 4–16. In addition, Table 4–17 shows a suggested protocol for advancing from peripheral alimentation to enteral feeding.

ENTERAL FEEDING

The transition from parenteral to enteral feedings requires selection of an appropriate composition and method of feeding that are based on individual requirements (see Chaps. 3 and 5). The transition should be gradual, and those patients who experience no complications can complete the transition to full enteral feedings over a 1-week period. In many instances the transition will require a slower advancement of enteral feedings; in addition, some patients experience feeding problems on resumption of oral intake after prolonged hyperalimentation (see Chaps. 5 and 6). Table 4–17 is one case example of advancement from peripheral alimentation to oral feedings. Basically, dilute, small-volume feedings are advanced to full strength; once full-strength concentration is reached, the volume of the enteral feedings is gradually increased and the parenteral feedings decreased.

TABLE 4–17. Advancement from Peripheral Alimentation to Enteral Feedings of a 3-kg Infant

Solution per 24 hr	Volume, ml (per kg)	Protein, g (per kg)	Glucose, g (per kg)	Lipid, g (per kg)	Calories (per kg)	Nonprotein Calories
Peripheral Alimentation						
10% lipid	120 (40)	—	—	12 (4)	108 (36)	108
2% amino acid/ 10% dextrose	360 (120)	7.5 (2.5)	36 (12)	—	152 (51)	122
TOTAL	480 (160)	7.5 (2.5)	36 (12)	12 (4)	260 (87)	230
Day 1: Initiation of Enteral Feedings						
10% lipid	120 (40)	—	—	12 (4)	108 (36)	108
2% amino acid/ 10% dextrose	300 (100)	6 (2)	30 (10)	—	126 (42)	102
Half-strength formula given by continuous infusion, 3 ml/hr (Pregestimil)	72 (24)	0.5 (0.16)	3.3 (1.1)	1 (0.3)	24 (8)	22
TOTAL	492 (164)	6.5 (2.16)	33.3 (11.1)	13 (4.3)	258 (86)	232
Day 2						
10% lipid	120 (40)	—	—	12 (4)	108 (36)	108
2% amino acid/ 10% dextrose	240 (80)	4.8 (1.6)	24 (8)	—	105 (35)	82
Half-strength formula given by continuous infusion, 5 ml/hr	120 (40)	0.8 (0.3)	5.5 (1.8)	1.6 (0.5)	40 (13)	36
TOTAL	480 (160)	5.6 (1.9)	29.5 (9.8)	13.6 (4.5)	253 (84)	226
Day 3						
10% lipid	120 (40)	—	—	12 (4)	108 (36)	108
2% amino acid/ 10% dextrose	240 (80)	4.8 (1.6)	24 (8)	—	106 (35)	82
Full-strength formula given by continuous infusion, 5 ml/hr	120 (40)	1.6 (0.5)	11 (3.6)	3.6 (1.2)	80 (27)	74
TOTAL	480 (160)	6.4 (2.1)	35 (11.6)	15.6 (5.2)	294 (98)	264
Day 4						
10% lipid	120 (40)	—	—	12 (4)	108 (36)	108
2% amino acid/ 10% dextrose	180 (60)	3.8 (1.25)	18 (6)	—	75 (25)	61
Full-strength formula given by continuous infusion, 7–8 ml/hr	180 (60)	2.5 (0.8)	16 (5.4)	4.9 (1.6)	119 (40)	109
TOTAL	480 (160)	6.3 (2.1)	34 (11.4)	16.9 (5.6)	302 (101)	278
Day 5						
10% lipid	120 (40)	—	—	12 (4)	108 (36)	108
2% amino acid/ 10% dextrose	120 (40)	2.4 (0.8)	12 (4)	—	51 (17)	41
Full-strength formula given by continuous infusion, 10 ml/hr	240 (80)	3.4 (1.1)	22 (7.3)	6.5 (2.2)	161 (54)	147
TOTAL	480 (160)	5.8 (1.9)	34 (11.3)	18.5 (6.2)	320 (107)	296
Day 6						
2% amino acid/ 10% dextrose	120 (40)	2.4 (0.8)	12 (4)	—	48 (16)	41
Full-strength formula given by continuous infusion, 15 ml/hr	360 (120)	5.1 (1.7)	33 (11)	9.9 (3.3)	240 (80)	221
TOTAL	480 (160)	7.5 (2.5)	45 (15)	9.9 (3.3)	288 (96)	262
Day 7: Enteral Alimentation						
Full-strength formula given by continuous infusion, 20 ml/hr	480 (160)	6.8 (2.25)	43.5 (14.5)	13.5 (4.5)	324 (108)	296

Increase Fluid or Concentrate Formula, Proceed to Bolus Feedings

References

1. American Academy of Pediatrics Committee on Nutrition: Commentary on parenteral nutrition Pediatrics 71:547, 1983.
2. Driscoll RH, Rosenberg IH: Total parenteral nutrition in inflammatory bowel disease. Med Clin North Am 62:185, 1978.
3. Winters RW, Hasselmeyer EG: Intravenous Nutrition in the High Risk Infant. New York: John Wiley & Sons, 1975.
4. Fisher JE: Total Parenteral Nutrition. Boston: Little, Brown, 1976.
5. Shenkin A, Wretlind A: Parenteral nutrition. World Rev Nutr Diet 28:1, 1978.
6. Duke JH Jr, Dudrick SJ: Parenteral feeding. In: Committee on Pre- and Postoperative Care, American College of Surgeons: Manual of Surgical Nutrition. Philadelphia: WB Saunders, 1975.
7. Seashore JH, Seashore MR: Protein requirements of infants receiving total parenteral nutrition. J Pediatr Surg 11:645, 1976.
8. Heird WD, Dell RB, Driscoll JM Jr, et al.: Metabolic acidosis resulting from intravenous alimentation mixtures containing synthetic amino acids. N Engl J Med 287:943, 1972.
9. Pediatric Parenteral Nutrition Manual. Boston: Children's Service, Massachusetts General Hospital, 1983.
10. Wolfe RR, Allsop JR, Burke JF: Glucose metabolism in man: responses to intravenous glucose infusion. Metabolism 28:210, 1979.
11. American Medical Association Department of Foods and Nutrition: Multivitamin preparations for parenteral use: a statement by the Nutrition Advisory Group. JPEN 3:258, 1979.
12. American Medical Association Nutrition Advisory Group: Guidelines for essential trace-element preparations for parenteral use. JPEN 3:263, 1979.
13. American Academy of Pediatrics Committee on Nutrition: Use of intravenous fat emulsions in pediatric patients. Pediatrics 68:738, 1981.
14. Cohen IT, Dahms B, Hays DM.: Peripheral total parenteral nutrition employing a lipid emulsion (Intralipid): complications encountered in pediatric patients. J Pediatr Surg 12:837, 1977.
15. Kerner JA, ed.: Manual of Pediatric Parenteral Nutrition. New York: John Wiley & Sons, 1983.
16. Borrensen HC, Bjordal R, Knutrud O: Total balanced intravenous feeding by peripheral veins in paediatric surgery. Ann Chir Gynaecol Fenn 62:319, 1973.
17. Goodgame JT: A critical assessment of the indications for total parenteral nutrition. Surg Gynecol Obstet 151:433, 1980.
18. Wretlind A: Parenteral nutrition. Nutr Rev 39:257, 1981.
19. Schiff D, Chan G, Seccombe D, et al.: Plasma carnitine levels during intravenous feeding of the neonate. J Pediatr 95:1043, 1979.
20. Sondheimer JM, Bryan H, Andrews W, et al.: Cholestatic tendencies in premature infants on and off parenteral nutrition. Pediatrics 62:984, 1978.
21. Stasinski R, Shafrir E: Displacement of albumin-bound bilirubin by free fatty acids. Implications for neonatal hyperbilirubinemia. Clin Chim Acta 29:311, 1970.
22. Sturman JA, Gaull G, Raiha NC: Absence of cystathionase in human fetal liver: is cystine essential? Science 169:74, 1970.
23. TPN Handbook. Boston: Nutrition Support Service, Children's Hospital Medical Center, 1981.
24. Batton DG, Maisels J, Appelbaum P: Use of peripheral intravenous cannulas in premature infants: a controlled study. Pediatrics 70:487, 1982.
25. Coran AG: Total intravenous feeding of infants and children without the risk of a central venous catheter. Ann Surg 179:445, 1974.
26. Fox HA, Krasna IH: Total intravenous nutrition by peripheral vein in neonatal surgical patients. Pediatrics 52:14, 1973.
27. Kosloshe AM, Klein MD: Techniques of central venous access for long term parenteral nutrition in infants. Surg Gynecol Obstet 154:395, 1982.
28. Ladefoged K, Efsen F, Kragh Christoffersen J, et al.: Long-term parenteral nutrition. II. Catheter-related complications. Scand J Gastroenterol 16:913, 1981.
29. Van Landingham S, Newmark SR: Peripheral vein nutrition. Nutr Support Ser 2:26, 1982.
30. Gunn T, Reaman G, Outerbridge EW, et al.: Peripheral total parenteral nutrition for premature infants with the respiratory distress syndrome: a continued study. J Pediatr 92:608, 1978.

5

NUTRITIONAL SUPPORT IN PATIENTS WITH ALTERED INTESTINAL FUNCTION

The nutritional support of patients with gastrointestinal disorders can best be accomplished when the functional limitations of each particular disorder are understood. If known impairments of intestinal function secondary to disease, infection, or immaturity are not respected and if the infant is fed inappropriately, continued deterioration of nutritional status, compromised intestinal healing, and further impairment of gastrointestinal function will result. Trials of irrational nutritional regimes may lead to a dangerous cycle of diarrhea and malnutrition. Included in this chapter on the nutritional management of patients with maldigestion is a brief overview of normal intestinal development and function (Table 5–1, Fig. 5–1).[1-7] The chapter is then divided into four major categories, namely, carbohydrate, fat, protein, and generalized maldigestion or malabsorption. In each particular

TABLE 5–1. Normal Digestion and Absorption

Site	Digestion	Enzyme/Function/Secretion	Absorption
Mouth	Starch, glycogen	Salivary amylase	
	Fat	Lingual lipase	
Stomach	Protein	Gastric pepsin, gastric HCl, regulated release of peptides to upper bowel, intrinsic factor	
Duodenum	Starch, glycogen	Pancreatic amylase	Hexoses, pentoses
	Fat	Pancreatic lipase	Glycerol
	Protein	Pancreatic trypsin	Fatty acids
		Chymotrypsin	Iron
		Polypeptidases	Minerals
		Carboxypeptidase A and B	
Jejunum	Oligopeptides	Brush border hydrolysis	Dipeptides, amino acids
	Disaccharides	Disaccharidases	Glucose, fructose, galactose
	Sucrose	Sucrase	Vitamins
	Maltose	Maltase	
	Lactose	Lactase	
	1:6 glucosides	Isomaltase or 1:6 glucosidase	Fatty acids, glycerol
Ileum	Starch	Amylase	Sugars, fatty acids
	Fat	Bile salts	Glycerol
		Cholecystokinin	Cholesterol
		Cholesterol esterase	Bile salts
	Dipeptides	Enterokinase	Amino acids, vitamin B_{12}, phosphate
Colon			Water, electrolytes

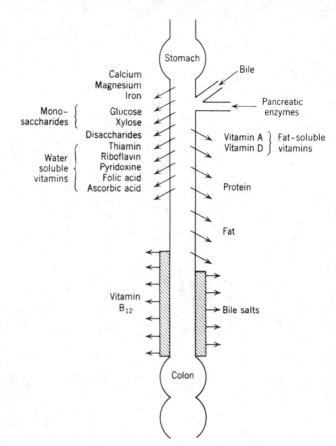

Figure 5–1. Known sites of absorption in the small intestine. (From Booth CC: Handbook of Physiology, vol. 3, sec. 6, ed. CF Code. Washington, DC: American Physiological Society, 1968.)

category many diseases may result, and they are listed together with suggested dietary therapy. An example of the approach to a representative problem is given.

In many instances, more than one mechanism may cause altered gastrointestinal function. This often results in generalized malabsorption. In such cases initial treatment should be directed toward generalized malabsorption. The treatment will change, however, as intestinal repair occurs. The treatment strategies for infants with severe gastroenteritis and for premature infants are examples in which nutritional management evolves as the infant recovers or matures. Detailed protocols for each of these examples are provided.

At the end of this chapter, a summary of suggested formulas to use for common gastrointestinal problems of infancy and a brief overview of drug-nutrient interactions and gastrointestinal side effects are outlined.

NUTRITIONAL SUPPORT IN DISORDERS OF CARBOHYDRATE DIGESTION AND ABSORPTION

Dietary carbohydrates, which supply a metabolized energy of 4 cal/g, are classified as monosaccharides, disaccharides, oligosaccharides, or polysaccharides; they account for 40 to 50 percent of the average infant's caloric intake. Carbohydrate digestion is significantly influenced by gastrointestinal maturity as well as by specific intestinal disorders. The development and physiology of intestinal digestion of carbohydrates are depicted in Table 5–2.[2, 4, 7] Briefly, carbohydrate digestion begins when salivary α-amylase causes the hydrolysis of α-(1,4) linkages of starch molecules. This action is inhibited by the acidic pH of the stomach. In the small

Text continued on page 108

TABLE 5–2. Development of Normal Digestion and Absorption of Carbohydrates

Substrate	Enzyme	Age of Development	Mechanism of Action	Products
Glucose		18 weeks' gestation	Glucose transport	
Sucrose	Sucrase (mucosal)	20 weeks' gestation	Hydrolysis of α-(1,4) linkage	Glucose, fructose
Maltose, maltotriose	Maltase, glucoamylase (mucosal)	20 weeks' gestation	Sequential removal of glucosyl residue from nonreducing end	Glucose
Lactose	Lactase (mucosal)	30 weeks' gestation	Hydrolysis of β-(1,4) linkage	Glucose, galactose
Starch	Salivary amylase	Unknown		Dextrans, maltotriose, maltose
	Pancreatic amylase (luminal)	4 to 6 months postnatally (inefficient until then)	Hydrolysis of α-(1,4) linkages	Maltose, maltotrioses, or dextrins
Dextrins	Glucoamylase or α-dextrinase (mucosal)		Initial removal of α-(1→4) linked glucose residues from nonreducing end	Oligosaccharides with terminal α-(1→6) linked glucose residue, glucose
	α-dextrinase (mucosal)	Unknown	Cleavage of α-(1→6) linked glucose	Maltose, oligosaccharides, glucose
	Sucrase or glucoamylase (mucosal)		Hydrolysis of release saccharides	Glucose
	Trehalase (mucosal)			Glucose

TABLE 5–3. Common Carbohydrates in Foods (g/100 g Edible Portion)

| Food | Mono-saccharides | | Disaccharides | | | | Polysaccharides | | | | | |
	Fructose	Glucose	Reducing Sugars*	Lactose	Maltose	Sucrose	Cellulose	Dextrins	Hemicellulose	Pectin	Pentosans	Starch
FRUITS												
Agave juice	17.0		19.0	†		3.1						
Apple	5.0	1.7	8.3			3.1	0.4		0.7	0.6		0.6
Apple juice			8.0			4.2						
Apricots	0.4	1.9				5.5	0.8		1.2	1.0		
Banana												
Yellow green			5.0			5.1						8.8
Yellow			8.4			8.9						1.9
Flecked	3.5	4.5				11.9						1.2
Powder			32.6			33.2		9.6				7.8
Blackberries	2.9	3.2				0.2						
Blueberry juice, commercial			9.6			0.2						
Boysenberries			5.3			1.1				0.3		
Breadfruit												
Hawaiian			1.8			7.7						
Samoan			4.9			9.7						
Cherries												
Eating	7.2	4.7	12.5			0.1				0.3		
Cooking	6.1	5.5	11.6			0.1						
Cranberries	0.7	2.7				0.1						
Currants												
Black	3.7	2.4				0.6						
Red	1.9	2.3				0.2						
White	2.6	3.0										
Dates												
Invert sugar, seedling type	23.9	24.9				0.3						
Deglet Noor			16.2			45.4						
Egyptian			35.8			48.5						3.0
Figs, Kadota												
Fresh	8.2	9.6				0.9						0.1
Dried	30.9	42.0				0.1						0.3
Gooseberries	4.1	4.4				0.7						
Grapes												
Black	7.3	8.2										
Concord	4.3	4.8	9.5			0.2						
Malaga			22.2			0.2						
White	8.0	8.1										
Grapefruit	1.2	2.0				2.9					1.3	
Guava			4.4			1.9						
Lemon												
Edible portion			1.3			0.2				3.0	0.7	
Whole	1.4	1.4				0.4						
Juice	0.9	0.5				0.1						
Peel			3.4			0.1						
Loganberries	1.3	1.9				0.2						
Loquat												
Champagne		12.0				0.8						
Thales		9.0				0.9						
Mango			3.4			11.6						0.3
Melon												
Cantaloupe	0.9	1.2	2.3			4.4				0.3		
Casaba,												
Vine ripened			2.8			6.2						
Picked green			3.2			3.9						
Honeydew												
Vine ripened			3.3			7.4						
Picked green			3.6			3.3						
Yellow	1.5	2.1				1.4						
Mulberries	3.6	4.4										
Orange												
Valencia (Calif.)	2.3	2.4	4.7			4.2						
Composite values	1.8	2.5	5.0			4.6	0.3		0.3	1.3	0.3	
Juice												
Fresh	2.4	2.4	5.1			4.7						
Frozen, reconstituted			4.6			3.2						
Palmyra palm, tender kernel	1.5	3.2				0.4						
Papaw (*Asimina triloba*)												
(North America)			5.9			2.7						
Papaya (*Carica papaya*)												
(tropics)			9.0			0.5						
Passion fruit juice	3.6	3.6				3.8						1.8
Peaches	1.6	1.5	3.1			6.6	0.7			0.7		
Pears												
Anjou			7.6			1.9				0.7		
Bartlett	5.0	2.5	8.0			1.5				0.6		
Bosc	6.5	2.6				1.7				0.6		
Persimmon			17.7									
Pineapple												
Ripened on plant	1.4	2.3	4.2			7.9						
Picked green			1.3			2.4						

Table continued on following page

TABLE 5–3. Common Carbohydrates in Foods (g/100 g Edible Portion) Continued

Food	Mono-saccharides Fructose	Glucose	Reducing Sugars*	Disaccharides Lactose	Maltose	Sucrose	Cellulose	Dextrins	Polysaccharides Hemicellulose	Pectin	Pentosans	Starch
FRUITS Continued												
Plums												
Damson	3.4	5.2	8.4			1.0						
Greengage	4.0	5.5				2.9						
Italian prunes			4.6			5.4				0.9		
Sweet	2.9	4.5	7.4			4.4		0.5		1.0	0.1	
Sour	1.3	3.5				1.5				1.0		
Pomegranate			12.0			0.6				1.0		
Prunes, uncooked	15.0	30.0	47.0			2.0	2.8		10.7	0.9	2.0	0.7
Raisins, Thompson seedless			70.0							1.0		
Raspberries	2.4	2.3	5.0			1.0				0.8		
Sapote	3.8	4.2		0.7								
Strawberries												
Ripe	2.3	2.6				1.4						
Medium ripe			3.8			0.3						
Tangerine			4.8			9.0						
Tomatoes	1.2	1.6	3.4				0.2			0.3		
Canned			3.0			0.3						
Seedless pulp			6.5			0.4	0.4			0.5		
Watermelon												
Flesh red and firm, ripe			3.8			4.0					0.1	
Red, mealy, overripe			3.0			4.9					0.1	
VEGETABLES												
Asparagus, raw			1.2						0.3			
Bamboo shoots			0.5			0.2	1.2					
Beans												
Lima												
Canned						1.4						
Fresh						1.4						
Snap, fresh			1.7			0.5	0.5	0.3	1.0	0.5	1.2	2.0
Beets, sugar						12.9	0.9		0.8			
Broccoli						0.9			0.9		0.9	1.3
Brussels sprouts							1.1		1.5			
Cabbage, raw			3.4			0.3	0.8		1.0			
Carrots, raw			5.8			1.7	1.0		1.7	0.9		
Cauliflower		2.8				0.3	0.7		0.6			
Celery												
Fresh			0.3			0.3						
Hearts			1.7			0.2						
Corn												
Fresh		0.5				0.3	0.6	0.1	0.9		1.3	14.5
Bran									77.1		4.0	
Cucumber			2.5			0.1						
Eggplant			2.1			0.6			0.5			
Lettuce			1.4			0.2	0.4		0.6			
Licorice root		1.4				3.2						22.0
Mushrooms, fresh			0.1				0.9		0.7			2.5
Onions, raw			5.4			2.9			0.3	0.6		
Parsnips, fresh						3.5						7.0
Peas, green						5.5	1.1		2.2			4.1
Potatoes, white	0.1	0.1	0.8			0.1	0.4		0.3			17.0
Pumpkin			2.2			0.6			0.5			0.1
Radishes			3.1			0.3			0.3	0.4		
Rutabagas		5.0				1.3					0.8	
Spinach			0.2				0.4		0.8			
Squash												
Butternut	0.2	0.1				0.4						2.6
Blue Hubbard	1.2	1.1				0.4	0.7					4.8
Golden Crookneck			2.8			1.0						
Sweet potato												
Raw	0.3	0.4	0.8		1.6	4.1	0.6		1.4	2.2		16.5
Baked			14.5			7.2						4.0
MATURE DRY LEGUMES												
Beans												
Mung												
Black gram						1.6						
Green gram						1.8						
Navy						3.1		3.7	6.4		8.2	35.2
Soy			1.6			7.2		2.6	6.6		4.0	1.9
Cow pea						1.5		1.4	4.8			
Garbanzo (chick peas)						2.4						
Garden pea (*Pisum sativum*)‡						6.7	5.0		5.1			38.0
Horse gram (*Dolichos biplorus*)						2.7						
Lentils						2.1						28.5
Pigeon pea (red gram)						1.6						
Soybean												
Flour						6.8						
Meal						6.8						

Table continued on opposite page

TABLE 5–3. Common Carbohydrates in Foods (g/100 g Edible Portion) *Continued*

Food	Mono-saccharides		Reducing Sugars*	Disaccharides			Cellulose	Polysaccharides				
	Fructose	Glucose		Lactose	Maltose	Sucrose		Dextrins	Hemicellulose	Pectin	Pentosans	Starch
MILK AND MILK PRODUCTS												
Buttermilk												
Dry				39.9								
Fluid, genuine and cultured				5.0								
Casein		0.1		4.9								
Ice cream (14.5% cream)				3.6		16.6						
Milk												
Ass				6.0								
Cow				4.9								
Dried												
Skim				52.0								
Whole				38.1								
Fluid												
Skim				5.0								
Whole				4.9								
Sweetened, condensed				14.1		43.5						
Ewe				4.9								
Goat				4.7								
Human												
Colostrum				5.3								
Mature				6.9								
Whey				4.9								
Yogurt				3.8								
NUTS AND NUT PRODUCTS												
Almonds, blanched			0.2			2.3					2.1	
Chestnuts			2.2			3.6					1.2	18.0
Virginia			1.2			8.1		0.3			2.8	18.6
French			3.3			3.6					2.5	33.1
Coconut milk, ripe						2.6						
Copra meal, dried	1.2	1.2				14.3	15.6	0.6			2.2	0.9
Macadamia nut			0.3			5.5						
Peanuts			0.2			4.5	2.4	2.5	3.8			4.0
Peanut butter			0.9									5.9
Pecans						1.1					0.2	
CEREALS AND CEREAL PRODUCTS												
Barley												
Grain, hulled							2.6		6.0		8.5	62.0
Flour						3.1					1.2	69.0
Corn, yellow						4.5			4.9		6.2	62.0
Flaxseed							1.8		5.2			
Millet grain									0.9		6.5	56.0
Oats, hulled											6.4	56.4
Rice												
Bran			1.4			10.6	11.4		7.0		7.4	
Brown, raw			0.1			0.8		2.1			2.1	69.7
Polished, raw		2.0	Trace[b]			0.4	0.3	0.9			1.8	72.9
Polish			0.7								3.8	
Rye												
Grain							3.8		5.6		6.8	57.0
Flour											4.1	71.4
Sorghum grain											2.5	70.2
Soya-wheat (cereal)											3.3	46.4
Wheat												
Germ, defatted						8.3					6.2	
Grain			2.0			1.5	2.0	2.5	5.8		6.6	59.0
Flour, patent			2.0		0.1	0.2		5.5			2.1	68.8
SPICES AND CONDIMENTS												
Allspice (pimenta)			18.0			3.0						
Cassia			23.3									
Cinnamon			19.3									
Cloves			9.0									2.7
Nutmeg			17.2									14.6
Pepper, black			38.6									34.2
SYRUPS AND OTHER SWEETS												
Corn syrup		21.2			26.4			34.7				
High conversion		33.0			23.0			19.0				
Medium conversion		26.0			21.0			23.0				
Corn sugar		87.5			3.5			0.5				
Chocolate, sweet dry						56.4						
Golden syrup			37.5			31.0						
Honey	40.5	34.2				1.9		1.5				
Invert sugar			74.0			6.0						
Jellies, pectin						40–65						
Royal jelly	11.3	9.8				0.9						
Jellies, starch						25–60						7–12

Table continued on following page

TABLE 5–3. Common Carbohydrates in Foods (g/100 g Edible Portion) *Continued*

	Mono-saccharides			Disaccharides			Polysaccharides					
Food	Fructose	Glucose	Reduc-ing Sugars*	Lactose	Maltose	Sucrose	Cellu-lose	Dextrins	Hemi-cellu-lose	Pectin	Pento-sans	Starch
Syrups and Other Sweets *Continued*												
Maple syrup			1.5			62.9						
Milk chocolate				8.1		43.0						
Molasses	8.0	8.8				53.6						
Blackstrap	6.8	6.8	26.9			36.9						
Sorghum syrup			27.0			36.0						
Miscellaneous												
Beer			1.5						2.8		0.3	
Cacao beans, raw, Arriba	0.6	0.5	1.1			1.9						
Carob bean												
Pod			11.2			23.2				1.4		
Pod and seeds			11.1			19.4						
Soy sauce	0.9											

*Mainly monosaccharides plus the disaccharides, maltose and lactose
†Blanks indicate lack of acceptable data
‡Also known as Alaska pea, field pea, and common pea
bTrace = less than 0.05 g
From Hardinge MG, Swarner JB, Crooks H: Carbohydrates in foods. Copyright The American Dietetic Association. Reprinted by permission from Journal of the American Dietetic Association 46:197, 1965.

intestine, pancreatic amylase also hydrolyzes the α-(1,4) linkages and leaves as products oligosaccharides, disaccharides, and dextrins. These products are further digested by specific enzymes located in the brush border on the surface of the mucosal cells, principally in the jejunum. Most of the glucose molecules formed enter the mucosal cells, although some remain in the intestinal lumen to be absorbed further along.[1-3] If dietary carbohydrates are not completely digested and absorbed, the patient may manifest the following symptoms:

1. Fermentative diarrhea with lowered stool pH
2. Watery stools with an acrid odor that contain increased lactic and other organic acids and the nonabsorbed sugar
3. Abdominal distention, increased flatulence, and cramping abdominal pain following ingestion of the specific carbohydrate
4. Increase in breath hydrogen after sugar ingestion
5. Recovery upon removal of the offending sugar

Common carbohydrates in foods are listed in Table 5–3. The various disorders of carbohydrate digestion and absorption and recommended dietary management plans are outlined in Table 5–4.[1, 5, 8–12] Since disaccharidases are formed in the brush border, many kinds of injury to the mucosa of the small intestine may lead to transient (secondary) carbohydrate intolerance. Lactase is distributed mostly in the upper small bowel, and injury can result in a significant decrease of this critical enzyme. Sucrase is more diffusely distributed, and injury is therefore less likely to cause malabsorption unless there is extensive damage. Also, lactose is the preferred carbohydrate source in the diet of healthy infants. Since lactose intolerance is the most frequently encountered disorder of carbohydrate absorption, a lactose-free diet and a clinical example of secondary lactose intolerance follow.

Lactose-Free Diet

This diet (Table 5–5) is for the patient who must eliminate *all* sources of lactose. Lactose is the sugar found in milk, so all foods containing milk are to be excluded from the diet.

Read the labels of prepared foods carefully. Avoid any foods that contain milk, nonfat milk solids, skim milk, butter, cream, lactose, casein, caseinate or sodium caseinate, or whey.

TABLE 5–4. Disorders of Altered Carbohydrate Digestion and Absorption

Enzyme Deficiency	Manifestation	Cause	Dietary Therapy
Lactase deficiency	Primary lactose intolerance	Absence of disaccharidase (lactase) from birth throughout life	Infancy: lactose-free formula (soy or casein-based) Childhood and adolescence: lactose-free diet (correction of secondary nutritional disturbances)
	Secondary lactose intolerance (acquired lactose intolerance is generally secondary to infection, inflammation, or reduced surface area)	Reduced brush border enzyme activity (infectious enteritis, gluten-sensitive enteropathy, radiation enteritis, giardiasis, malnutrition, inflammatory bowel disease, milk- or soy-protein allergy, hypoxia, antibiotics)	Treatment of primary disorder; lactose restriction until intestinal recovery (may take days or several months) and return of lactase activity
Sucrase deficiency	Primary sucrose intolerance	Absence of sucrase from birth throughout life	Infancy: sucrose-free formula During the recovery phase a lactose-free, sucrose-free feeding will probably be necessary; once intestinal epithelium recovers, a formula based on cow's milk is recommended.
	Secondary sucrose intolerance (acquired sucrose intolerance)	More severe intestinal damage (as listed under causes of secondary lactose intolerance)	The same treatment is recommended; once the intestine has recovered, no restrictions are necessary. In childhood and adolescence, a sucrose-free diet
Sucrase isomaltase deficiency	Sucrase isomaltose intolerance	Congenital enzyme deficiency	Sucrose- and isomaltose-free diet (formula containing lactose is well tolerated in infancy); as children mature they are able to tolerate increasing amounts of dietary sucrose and starch.
Trehalase deficiency	Trehalose intolerance		Elimination of trehalose (the major source of this sugar is the young mushroom)
	Congenital glucose and galactose malabsorption	Inability of the intestinal mucosal sites to transport glucose and galactose	In infancy: a carbohydrate-free formula with fructose added; absorption does not improve with age but many children tolerate small amounts as body size increases.
Fructose-1-phosphate aldolase deficiency	Hereditary fructose intolerance	Congenital lack of hepatic enzyme necessary to metabolize fructose-1-phosphate	Fructose-free diet
—	Glucose malabsorption	The cause at birth is unknown; in older infants, intolerance may develop after severe infections, gastroenteritis.	Intravenous glucose may be required initially; advancement to oral glucose and electrolyte solutions (glucose transport is coupled with sodium), then elemental formula

TABLE 5–5. Lactose-Free Diet

Foods Allowed	Foods Avoided
Lactose-free infant formulas; Milk—An enzymatic preparation such as Lact-Aid may be added to milk to convert lactose into digestible sugars; instructions are for conversion of 70 to 95% of the lactose to glucose and galactose; check with your nutritionist or physician before beginning use of Lact-Aid	All milk, milk drinks—whole, skim, low fat, dried, evaporated, and condensed milk, human breast milk Yogurt—any type Cream—sweet or sour Infant formulas other than those permitted Frappes, ice cream sodas
Beverages—powdered, fruit-flavored drinks; ginger ale; tonics	Any made with milk—frappes, eggnog, hot chocolate
Eggs—as desired	Eggs made with milk—use specific formula; do not prepare with butter
Meats—any except those to be avoided	Creamed or breaded meat, fish, or poultry; prepared meats that contain dried milk solids—bologna and cold cuts, frankfurters, salami, commercially prepared fish sticks, some sausages; kosher products are milk-free
Cheese—although made from milk, some cheeses are lactose-free and may be permitted; these are Camembert, brick, cheddar, Edam, Provolone, Swiss, pasteurized process American, Blue, and Colby	All types of cheeses and cheese dishes not listed as allowed
Breads—only breads made without milk, such as French bread, Italian bread, water bagels, and "parve" breads	Baked products made with milk or any form of milk—muffins, biscuits, waffles, pancakes, donuts, sweet rolls, commercial mixes
Cereal—any made without milk (cooked or ready-to-eat); all macaroni, spaghetti, pasta, and rice prepared without milk	Any prepared cereal that contains dry milk solids
Vegetables and Potatoes—all cooked, canned, frozen, or fresh	Any vegetable prepared with milk, butter, milk solids, bread or bread crumbs; no cheese or cream sauces
Fruits—all	
Desserts—any made without milk or milk products, such as gelatin desserts, fruit crisp, snow puddings, fruit and water sherbets, pie with fruit filling, angel cake	All commercial cake and cookie mixes, ice cream, custard puddings, junket, ice milk or sherbets that contain milk; frosting made with milk or butter; dessert sauces; cheesecakes
Soup—any prepared without milk or milk products; homemade or canned (e.g., chicken rice)	All creamed soups, chowders; no cheese
Fats—milk-free margarine or "parve" margarine; oils, nuts, peanut butter	Butter, margarine, some commercial salad dressings (check labels)
Sugar and Seasonings—sugar, honey, molasses, maple syrup, corn syrup, jelly and jam, hard candy, gum drops, marshmallow, hard peppermints, fondant; salt, pepper, spices, herbs, condiments, vinegar, catsup, relish, pickles, olives, tomato sauce, coconut, wheat germ; artificial flavoring or extracts	Any product made from milk, butter, cream—chocolate, toffee, cream mints, caramel candy, candy with cream centers
Miscellaneous	Medications that use lactose as filler or bulk agents; party dips, nonprescription vitamins; spice blends; Easter egg dyes; dietetic foods and foods advertised as "high protein" sometimes contain lactose or dry milk solids; *check all labels carefully*

This diet is for the patient who must eliminate *all* sources of lactose from the diet. Lactose is the sugar found in milk, so all foods containing milk are to be excluded from the diet.

Read the label carefully. Avoid any food containing *milk, nonfat milk solids, skim milk, butter, cream, lactose, casein, caseinate* or *sodium caseinate, or whey.*

Lactase capsules (containing lactase enzyme) may be used occasionally but should not be a substitute for the diet (Kremers-Urban Company, Milwaukee, Wisconsin).

Secondary Lactose Intolerance

Insufficient intestinal lactase in infancy is usually a self-limited process induced by an acute infectious enteritis or ischemic episode. In many cases, continuation of a lactose-containing formula is compatible with recovery; alternatively, a soy-based formula that is lactose-free may be used. In more severely ill infants or those with a previous illness such as chronic intestinal inflammation, an elemental formula should be administered. Patients who do well clinically (normal stools, weight gain) can generally be switched to a soy-based formula in 2 to 3 weeks. Gradual reintroducton of lactose into the diet should begin after an additional 2 to 4 weeks.

NUTRITIONAL SUPPORT IN DISORDERS OF FAT DIGESTION AND ABSORPTION

Dietary fat is the most calorically dense macronutrient; it has an average metabolizable energy of 9 cal/g. Fat provides the essential fatty acids, linoleic and linolenic acids, and accounts for 40 to 50 percent of an infant's caloric intake. Fat digestion and absorption are influenced significantly by gastrointestinal maturity as well as by specific disorders of fat metabolism. An overview of the development of normal fat digestion and absorption is outlined in Table 5–6.[1, 4, 7, 13] Briefly, dietary triglycerides enter the small intestinal lumen, where they are converted to free fatty acids by pancreatic lipase and emulsified by bile salts. Long-chain fatty acids (> C12) are formed into micellar structures, absorbed through the intestinal wall, converted to chylomicrons, and transported via the lymphatics to the blood stream. Medium-chain fatty acids are absorbed through the intestinal wall, are combined

TABLE 5–6. Development of Normal Digestion and Absorption of Fats

Substrate	Enzyme	Age of Development	Mechanism of Action	Product
Breast milk	Human milk lipase	Present in breast milk	Bile salt stimulates lipase and lipoprotein lipase	Micelles
Fat	Lingual lipase	Present at 25 weeks, increased significantly by 34 weeks' gestation	Secreted by and active in mouth and stomach	Glycerides
Glycerides, free fatty acids	Pancreatic lipase	Present at 20 weeks' gestation, decreased in neonate	Cleaves (1,3) glycerol bonds	Monoglycerides, free fatty acids
Free fatty acids	Bile salts	Decreased in neonate	Emulsification	Micelles
Micelles	Intestinal mucosal lipase	Decreased bile salt pool in the neonate	Transported into mucosal cell, esterified, transported out of mucosal cell	Fatty acids
Cholesterol esters	Pancreatic esterase			Cholesterol
Lecithin	Phospholipase A		Activated by trypsin	Lysolecithin

TABLE 5–7. Disorders of Altered Fat Digestion and Absorption

General Disorders	Specific Disease	Dietary Therapy
Pancreatic insufficiency	Cystic fibrosis, Shwachman syndrome, hereditary fibrosing pancreatitis	In infancy, Portagen or Pregestimil is the formula of choice (medium-chain triglyceride [MCT] oil-based formulas or standard infant formula with supplemental pancreatic enzymes). Supplemental foods may be begun earlier than usual to supply additional calories.
	Pancreatic resection; tumors (neuroblastoma, Zollinger-Ellison syndrome, carcinoid tumor)	Supplemental fat-soluble vitamins should be given
	Protein-energy malnutrition	In children and adolescents, dietary therapy should be individualized with emphasis on a high protein and calorie intake. Fat needs to be restricted only in patients with symptoms of fat malabsorption, despite pancreatic replacement.
Liver disease (The liver performs many varied activities, and disorders of liver function will exhibit many pathologic conditions; the type of dietary treatment required is directly related to the liver's malfunction.)	Hepatitis	Without liver failure, a routine formula is used; with failure, use Portagen. Most patients suffer a marked reduction in appetite and smaller, frequent feeding may help provide nutritional support. With marked jaundice, a decrease in fat may be helpful in the older patient.
	Cirrhosis with failure	In infancy, Portagen is used; in older children, lowered protein and fat; low sodium with ascites
Hepatobiliary dysfunction	Neonatal cholestasis, portal hypertension, bacterial deconjugation of bile salts, intestinal lymphangiectasia, biliary atresia, extrahepatic biliary obstruction, insufficient intraluminal bile acid activity	In infancy, MCT formula (Portagen) with supplemental fat-soluble vitamins and calcium; if the patient remains cholestatic, keep on the Portagen as long as possible or begin a low-fat diet supplemented with MCT oil. If the patient appears to be doing well clinically, a regular diet is advised.
Toxic diarrhea	Antibiotics, chemotherapy, radiation	A lowered fat intake until intestine has recovered; in infancy, Portagen or Pregestimil; in older children, a moderate fat intake or tube feeding with some MCT oil
Immune defects	Defective cellular immunity and combined immune deficiency (with and without mucosal damage), acquired agamma-globulinemia and isolated IgA deficiency (occurs with and without mucosal damage)	With decreased mucosal surface area, Pregestimil; without mucosal damage, no restrictions

Table continued on opposite page

TABLE 5–7. Disorders of Altered Fat Digestion and Absorption *Continued*

General Disorders	Specific Disease	Dietary Therapy
Miscellaneous	Short-bowel syndrome, blind- or stagnant-loop syndrome, inflammatory bowel disease, intractable diarrhea, eosinophilic gastroenteritis	Lowered fat intake until underlying disorder is in remission; MCT formula as needed, depending on severity of disease; in infancy, Portagen or Pregestimil initially, advancing to soy and then cow's milk formula; in children and adolescents, elemental formula advancing to lactose-free tube feeding and then a regular diet
Inborn errors of metabolism	Abetalipoproteinemia, hypobetalipoproteinemia	In infancy, an MCT-based formula (Portagen); in older children, a longer-chain fat intake may be tolerated
	Wolman's disease	MCT supplement may be used to supplement calories
	Primary bile acid malabsorption	See therapy for hepatobiliary dysfunction
Isolated conditions	Lipase, enterokinase, amylase, or trypsinogen deficiency	Pregestimil in infancy

with albumin in the blood, and are transported directly to the liver by the portal veins.[7] Patients with fat malabsorption generally present with the following symptoms:

1. Failure to thrive
2. Mild to severe diarrhea with bulky, foul-smelling stools
3. Signs of fat-soluble vitamin deficiency
4. Decreased coefficient of fat absorption on 72-hour fecal fat analysis (< 90 percent)

Various disorders of altered fat digestion and absorption and recommended dietary therapy are outlined in Table 5–7.[1, 7, 10, 14, 15] A case example of the nutritional management of a patient with cystic fibrosis, one component of which is fat malabsorption, follows.

Dietary Therapy in Cystic Fibrosis

Cystic fibrosis is the most frequently lethal genetic disease in childhood; it has an incidence in the United States Caucasian population of 1 in every 2000 live births.[16] It is a complex disorder with widespread dysfunction of all exocrine glands, including those that secrete mucus. The clinical manifestations are characterized by obstructive lesions throughout multiple organ systems and disturbances in mucous and electrolyte secretions.[17] The most prominent complications are pancreatic insufficiency and pulmonary compromise. Pancreatic insufficiency occurs in varying degrees but is eventually present in 85 to 90 percent of patients.[17] Chymotrypsin, lipase, amylase, bicarbonate, and electrolytes are not excreted in normal amounts by the pancreas; this results in malabsorption of fat, protein, minerals, and fat-soluble vitamins. Chronic obstructive pulmonary disease is eventually present in all cases and accounts for much of the morbidity and almost all the mortality in cystic fibrosis patients who survive beyond the neonatal period.[17] As the disease progresses there is increased pulmonary involvement, characterized by diffuse and progressive obstructive processes.

Cystic fibrosis was once largely limited to infants and children, but improved medical care has greatly increased life expectancy, and many patients now survive beyond adolescence. Malnutrition is often a prominent component of the progressive disease, and growth failure and nutritional deficiencies commonly occur. Children with cystic fibrosis show significant growth retardation at all ages,[18] but it is most pronounced in preadolescent and adolescent age groups. Growth failure increases in severity with advancing age.[18] Relative underweight is a major factor affecting survival, and some investigators suggest that achieving optimal nutrition may influence the clinical complications of the disease.[19, 20] The pathogenesis of malnutrition and its management remain an enigma; inadequate intake, increased losses caused by malabsorption, and increased requirements caused by pulmonary disease have been expounded as possible causes.

Cystic fibrosis patients have historically been considered to have voracious appetites, but a few recent studies have shown their caloric intake to be significantly lower than that of healthy children of the same age and sex.[19] In reality, the appetites of children with cystic fibrosis are often decreased secondary to bloating, cramps, and pulmonary disease,[21, 22] and one study estimates intake to be 67 percent of the recommended dietary allowances for age.[19] The goal of nutritional therapy is to achieve ideal height and weight and to prevent clinical compromise. Supplemental fat-soluble vitamins and zinc are routinely given, and increased caloric intake is encouraged. Despite the many benefits of supplemental nutritional support, acutal clinical experience has shown that this is rarely adequate to prevent nutritional deficiencies, and growth failure continues to be a common complication.

In the absence of a defined chemical lesion, treatment of the disease remains empirical.[21] For pancreatic insufficiency, the goal of pancreatic enzyme replacement is to deliver adequate concentrations of enzymes into the duodenum to optimize nutrient absorption and maintain adequate nutrition. Replacement therapy affects but does not resolve malabsorption.[17] However, most children with cystic fibrosis are able to tolerate a diet similar to that of healthy children at the same age. If the patient is severely affected by fat malabsorption, the diet should be adjusted to reflect individual tolerance. Elimination of high-fat foods and use of low-fat dairy products should be limited to those patients with more severe symptoms, as the restriction will decrease overall caloric intake.

The goal of nutritional support should be a normal, well-balanced diet with an energy intake 130 percent of the RDA for age (Table 5–8).[22] Guidelines for increasing calorie, protein, and nutrient density of the diet are outlined in Chapter 6 and Table 6–5. Recommended routine supplements of vitamins, minerals, and

TABLE 5–8. Recommended Increased Energy Intake in Cystic Fibrosis

	Age (yr)	Energy Needs (cal, 130% of RDA)
Infants	0.0–0.5	kg × 150
	0.5–1.0	kg × 137
Children	1–3	1690
	4–6	2210
	7–10	3120
Males	11–14	3510
	15–18	3640
	19–22	3770
Females	11–14	2860
	15–18	2730
	19–22	2730

Modified from Roy CC, Weber AM: Nutrition of the child with cystic fibrosis. In: Walker WA, Watkins J, eds.: Nutrition in Pediatrics: Basic Science and Clinical Application. Boston: Little, Brown, 1985.

TABLE 5–9. Recommended Supplements of Vitamins, Minerals, and Trace Elements for Patients with Cystic Fibrosis

Nutrient	Indications	Dosage
Vitamin A	All patients	5000–10,000 IU
Vitamin D	All patients	800 Units
Vitamin E	All patients	200 IU
Vitamin K	Antibiotic therapy or liver disease	5 mg every 3 days
Vitamin B group	Antibiotic therapy or liver disease	RDA
Vitamin C and folic acid	Antibiotic therapy or liver disease	RDA
Vitamin B_{12}	Ileal resection	100 μg IM per month
Sodium	First year of life	23–35 mEq
Zinc	All patients	15 mg elemental Zn (75 mg $ZnSO_4$)

From Roy CC, Weber AM: Nutrition of the child with cystic fibrosis. In: Walker WA, Watkins J, eds.: Nutrition in Pediatrics: Basic Science and Clinical Application. Boston: Little, Brown, 1985.

trace elements are shown in Table 5–9.[22–24] Since excessive sodium chloride is lost in sweat, the liberal use of salt and salty foods should be encouraged.

NUTRITIONAL SUPPORT IN DISORDERS OF PROTEIN DIGESTION AND ABSORPTION

Dietary proteins, which supply an average metabolizable energy of 4 cal/g, may be in the form of amino acids, dipeptides, tripeptides, or oligopeptides; they account for 8 to 15 percent of calories in the average infant's diet. Protein digestion begins in the stomach, where pepsin cleaves some peptide linkages. In the small intestine, smaller peptides are formed by the action of trypsin, chymotrypsin, and elastase; their enzymatic precursors are secreted by the pancreas. Pancreatic carboxypeptidases and intestinal peptidases split these fragments into smaller peptides and amino acids. Some di- and tripeptides are actively transported into the intestinal cells and hydrolyzed intracellularly, and these amino acids enter the blood stream directly. There are at least three separate transport systems for absorption of amino acids from the intestinal lumen. Absorption is rapid in the duodenum and jejunum but slow in the ileum. The development and physiology of intestinal digestion of protein are depicted in Table 5–10.[1, 4, 6, 7]

Alterations of protein digestion are most commonly caused by a decrease or disruption of proteolytic enzyme activity, as in pancreatic disease. Disorders of protein absorption occur when uptake of protein is either enhanced, as in gastrointestinal allergy, or decreased, as in protein-losing enteropathy.

The gastrointestinal tract plays a prominent role in the metabolism of plasma proteins. The gut synthesizes serum protein, including immunoglobulins and lipoproteins, and degrades plasma proteins. Serum proteins normally lost into the gastrointestinal tract are rapidly degraded, resorbed as amino acids, and resynthesized into protein.

Protein-losing enteropathy occurs most commonly in mucosal ulceration, lymphatic obstruction, and disorders of metabolism or turnover of epithelial cells.[10] In addition to decreased absorption, excess proteins are secreted, and patients present with hypoproteinemia and edema secondary to enteric loss of plasma proteins. Most plasma proteins are synthesized by the liver, and decreased synthesis may occur in liver disease. Synthesis of plasma proteins produced in the intestinal mucosa and necessary for lipid transport may be decreased in mucosal disease.

TABLE 5–10. Development of Normal Digestion and Absorption of Protein

Substrate	Enzyme	Age of Development	Mechanism or Site of Action	End Product of Digestion
Protein and polypeptides	Gastric pepsin	Decreased in infancy	Cleaves peptide bonds adjacent to aromatic amino acids	Peptides
	Duodenal enterokinase	Full term	Activates trypsin	
	Pancreatic trypsin	Full term	Peptides with carboxyl-terminal arginine or lysine; activates chymotrypsin, elastase, carboxypeptidases	Peptides
	Pancreatic chymotrypsin	Full term	Peptides with aromatic side chains	Peptides
	Elastase	Low in neonate	Peptides with aliphatic side chains	Small peptides, neutral amino acids
Peptides	Carboxypeptidase A	Full term	Cleaves carboxyl-terminal amino acids with aromatic or branched aliphatic side chains	Smaller peptides and amino acids
	Carboxypeptidase B		Cleaves carboxyl-terminal amino acids with basic side chains	
Peptides	Intestinal mucosal peptidases		Active transport	Amino acids
Amino acids			Activated by transport protein in microvillus membrane	

In many instances the manifestations of intestinal protein loss may be overshadowed by other aspects of the disease process. Protein maldigestion produces fewer specific clinical symptoms than either carbohydrate or fat maldigestion, and the disorder may not be appreciated; close attention to protein status is helpful. The various disorders of protein loss, digestion, and absorption and recommended dietary therapy are outlined in Table 5–11.[1, 6, 10, 25] A more detailed case example of milk-protein allergy follows.

Dietary Recommendations for Milk-Protein Allergy [26–30]

Protein intolerance causes severe vomiting, diarrhea, and weight loss in susceptible infants. Serious gastrointestinal reactions include colitis and persistent diarrhea with intestinal flat-villus lesions and documented systemic allergic manifestations. Because allergy to cow's milk protein frequently leads to small bowel damage (including atrophy of villi), mucosal permeability to other, nonallergenic proteins can result in an increased systemic uptake, an immunologic response, and

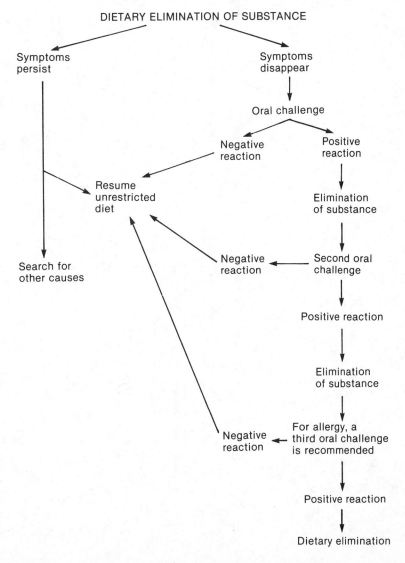

Figure 5–2. Treatment for specific defects in absorption or for dietary elimination of an allergenic substance (such as gluten, soy, or milk protein).

TABLE 5–11. Disorders of Altered Protein Digestion and Absorption that Respond to Dietary Therapy

Disorder	Mechanism	Dietary Therapy
Hepatic encephalopathy	Normal degradation by the liver is decreased	Lowered protein intake (0.5 to 1 g/kg/day)
Protein-losing enteropathies (Many disorders are associated with enteric protein loss; those listed under major headings are examples)	Disorders of intestinal lymphatics: intestinal lymphangiectasia, congestive heart failure	Replacement of long-chain fats with medium-chain triglycerides; use of amino acids or protein hydrolysate supplement, fat-soluble vitamins, and calcium
	Ulceration of a region of the mucosa of the gastrointestinal tract: regional enteritis, acute infectious enteritis	
	Demonstrable pathologic condition, but unknown mechanism: giant hypertrophy of the gastric mucosa, allergic protein-losing gastroenteropathy, eosinophilic gastroenteritis, kwashiorkor, cystic fibrosis, dermatitis herpetiformis, agammaglobulinemia	
Protein intolerance	Milk-protein allergy, soy-protein allergy, gluten-sensitive enteropathy, eosinophilic gastroenteritis	In infancy (with flat-villus lesion), Pregestimil will be required initially with advancement to a diet eliminating only the toxin or toxins. In severe protein intolerance, elemental diet may be required, with very slow introduction of nonallergenic foods

a similar allergic reaction to these proteins; thus the allergic response may be broadened. Therefore, in infants and children with clinical manifestations of allergic disease, a protein hydrolysate formula should be used. The diet should be expanded slowly to include a variety of foods and should strictly eliminate all sources of milk

TABLE 5–12. Milk Protein–Free Diet*

Foods Allowed	Foods Avoided
Milk—breast milk, formulas with elemental protein hydrolysate	All milk, milk drinks—whole, skim, low fat, dried, evaporated, and condensed milk Yogurt—any type Cream—sweet or sour Infant formulas other than those permitted Frappes, ice cream sodas
Beverages—powdered, fruit-flavored drinks; ginger ale, soda	Any made with milk—frappes, eggnog, hot chocolate
Eggs—as desired	Eggs made with milk—use specific formula; do not prepare with butter
Meats, Fish, and Poultry—any except those to be avoided	Creamed or breaded meat, fish, or poultry; prepared meats that contain dried milk solids—bologna and cold cuts, frankfurters, salami, commercially prepared fish sticks, some sausages
Cheese—none	All cheese and cheese dishes
Breads—any made without milk products	Any breads that contain milk products
Cereal—any made without milk (cooked or ready-to-eat); all macaroni, spaghetti, pasta, and rice prepared without milk	Any prepared cereal that contains dry milk solids
Vegetables and Potatoes—all cooked, canned, frozen, or fresh	Any vegetable prepared with milk, butter, milk solids, bread or bread crumbs; no cheese or cream sauces
Fruits—all	
Desserts—any made without milk or milk products—gelatin desserts, fruit crisp, snow puddings, fruit and water sherbets, pie with fruit filling, angel cake	All commercial cake and cookie mixes, ice cream, custard puddings, junket, ice milk or sherbets that contain milk; frosting made with milk or butter; dessert sauces; cheesecakes
Soup—any prepared without milk or milk products; homemade or canned (e.g., chicken rice)	All creamed soups, chowders; no cheese
Fats—milk-free margarine or "parve" margarine; oils, nuts, peanut butter	Butter, margarine, some commercial salad dressings (check labels)
Sugar and Seasonings—Sugar, honey, molasses, maple syrup, corn syrup, jelly and jam, hard candy, gum drops, marshmallow, hard peppermints, fondant; salt, pepper, spices, herbs, condiments, vinegar, catsup, relish, pickles, olives, tomato sauce, coconut, wheat germ; artificial flavoring or extracts	Any product made from milk, butter, cream—chocolate, toffee, cream mints, caramel candy, candy with cream centers
Miscellaneous	Medications that use lactose as filler or bulk agents; party dips, nonprescription vitamins; spice blends; Easter egg dyes; dietetic foods and foods advertised as "high protein" sometimes contain lactose or dry milk solids; *check all labels carefully*

Read the label carefully. Avoid any food containing milk, nonfat milk solids, skim milk, butter, cream, lactose, casein, caseinate or sodium caseinate, whey

For more detailed diets consult the following references:

Allergy Diets. Ralston Purina Company, Checkerboard Square, St. Louis, MO 63199.

Baking for People with Food Allergies. Home and Garden Bulletin No. 147, US Dept. of Agriculture, Superintendent of Documents, US Government Printing Office, Washington, DC 20402.

Meals Without Milk: Easy Appealing Recipes Using Prosobee Soy Isolate Milk. Mead Johnson, Evansville, IN 47721.

Tasty Recipes, Mull Soy Liquid in Milk Free Diets. Borden Pharmaceutical Products, 350 Madison Avenue, New York, NY 10017.

Wheat-Milk and Egg Free Recipes. Home Economics Department, The Quaker Oats Company, Merchandise Mart Plaza, Chicago, IL 60611.

Nursoy Cookery. Wyeth Laboratories, Philadelphia, PA 19101.

protein (Table 5–12). Procedures for slow introduction of nonallergenic foods appropriate for a child's age should be outlined for parents so that problem foods can be noted.

In instances of specific defects in absorption or allergy, dietary elimination of the offending agent is the treatment of choice, as shown in Figure 5–2.

NUTRITIONAL SUPPORT IN DISORDERS OF GENERALIZED MALABSORPTION AND MALDIGESTION

A variety of disorders are manifested by generalized malabsorption secondary to an insult that causes flattening of the intestinal mucosa. With flattening of the mucosa, there is quantitative and qualitative reduction in absorptive surface area, digestive enzymes, and absorptive transport mechanisms. Malabsorption of varying degrees occurs for all nutrients. Patients may present with diarrhea, weight loss, and a variety of nutrient deficiencies. In all cases, individualized dietary therapy is extremely important in order to prevent any additional disruption of intestinal function and to avoid serious nutritional consequences. In addition, prematurity, drugs, toxins, or radiation may result in generalized malabsorption. Various situations with which generalized malabsorption has been associated are shown in Table 5–13.[1, 10] Two case examples of common generalized malabsorption (prematurity and acute infectious enteritis) are outlined.

Enteral Feeding Guidelines for Premature Infants[15, 31–48]

I. Limitations of intestinal function most commonly seen in prematurity.
   A. Carbohydrate: Sucrase, maltase, and isomaltase have reached normal postnatal levels by the 28th week of gestation. Lactase begins to rise at 30 weeks and is maximal at term.
   B. Fat: Preterm infants have a decreased bile acid pool, with duodenal bile acids well below the critical micellar concentration, and decreased resorption of bile acids in the terminal ileum. The mean coefficient of fat absorption in premature infants fed human milk is significantly higher than that in

TABLE 5–13. Disorders and States that Create Generalized Malabsorption and Maldigestion

α- or β-Lipoproteinemia	Hypoparathyroidism	Primary acquired
Acrodermatitis enteropathica	Ileal atresia	hypogammaglobulinemia
Adrenal insufficiency	Immune deficiency	Pseudohypoparathyroidism
Basophilic leukemia	Inflammatory bowel disease	Radiation enteritis
Dermatitis herpetiformis	Intestinal lymphangiectasia	Reaction to bacterial toxins
Drug toxicity	Intractable diarrhea	Scleroderma
Eosinophilic gastroenteritis	Lactose deficiency	Short-bowel syndrome
Familial chloride diarrhea	(congenital)	Small bowel resection
Food allergy	Lymphoma	Small bowel ischemia (heart
Giardiasis	Malnutrition	disease, NEC, vasculitis,
Glucose–galactose	Mast cell disease	polycythemia vera)
malabsorption	Milk-protein allergy	Sucrose-isomaltase deficiency
Gluten-sensitive enteropathy	Necrotizing enterocolitis	Sucrase deficiency (congenital)
Hirschsprung's disease	(NEC)	System mastocytosis
Hormone-producing tumors	Parasitic infestation	Thyroid cancer
(Zollinger-Ellison syndrome)	Postgastrectomy syndrome	Tropical sprue
Hyperparathyroidism	Prematurity	Wolman's disease

comparable infants fed cow's milk formulas, because of the lipase present in human milk.

C. Protein: Enterokinase activity is decreased; therefore, duodenal trypsin is 1/4 to 1/10 that of children older than 1 year. Renal immaturity limits the amount of protein that should be given; however, slightly higher levels of protein in breast milk of mothers delivering preterm infants meet the increased needs for rapid growth.

II. Suggested Feeding: The infant's own mother's milk is the preferred feeding for a preterm infant. In addition to its unique composition (higher protein, sodium, and chloride content) and increased nutrient availability (breast milk lipases and increased iron and zinc absorption) breast milk has anti-infectious properties that protect the infant. Supplemental calcium, phosphorus, and vitamin E are necessary in the rapidly growing preterm infant.

If the infant's own mother's milk is unavailable, formulas made specifically for preterm infants should be used (see Tables 3–6 and 3–7). Compared with standard formulas, they contain both sucrose and lactose; they are partially composed of medium-chain triglycerides and long-chain fats with a slightly higher protein level and a whey to casein ratio similar to that of breast milk. They are calorically more dense (24 cal/oz) to meet the infant's increased requirements and contain higher levels of certain nutrients.

III. Delivery Method: Coordination of sucking, swallowing, and epiglottal reflexes of the developing infant occurs at 32 to 34 weeks. Before this time there is uncoordinated activity. In addition, stomach volume is small and the gastro-esophageal sphincter is immature in the premature infant. Initially, continuous pump-assisted intragastric or jejunal infusion is recommended, followed by advancement to small-volume bolus and then to nipple feeds.

A too-rapid increase in the rate of formula delivery appears to increase the incidence of necrotizing enterocolitis. The rate of formula delivery should be advanced slowly to full feeds over 8 or 12 days in large and small preterm infants, respectively.

IV. Feeding Guidelines for Premature Infants (Table 5–14)

TABLE 5–14. Feeding Guidelines for Premature Infants

Age	Condition	Formula	Method of Delivery
26 to 34 weeks	Without GI complications	Mother's milk Premature formula Peripheral or central alimentation to achieve 120 to 150 kcal/kg Vitamin E, other supplements, depending on feeding	Continuous infusion, advance to nasogastric or nasojejunal tube, advance to bolus nasogastric feeding, advance to bolus plus nipple, finally advance to nipple
	With renal complications	Mother's milk Dilute premature formula, SMA or PM 60/40 Peripheral or central alimentation to achieve 120 to 150 kcal/kg Vitamin E, other supplements, depending on feeding	Same as above
34 to 36 weeks	Without GI complications	Mother's milk or banked human milk Standard cow's milk formula	
Any age	Maldigestion	Pregestimil	Same as above, depending on age

TABLE 5–15. Advancement of Enteral Feedings for Infants Weighing 1.0–1.5 kg at Birth

Day	Amount (24 kcal/oz) ml/kg/3 hr	ml/kg/day	Supplemental Parenteral Alimentation
1	2	16	Yes
2	3	24	Yes
3	4	32	Yes
4	6	48	Yes
5	8	64	Yes
6	10	80	Yes
7	13	104	Yes
8	16	128	—
9	19	152	—

From Reynolds J: Nutrition of the low birth weight infant. In: Walker WA, Watkins J, eds.: Nutrition in Pediatrics: Basic Science and Clinical Application. Boston: Little, Brown, 1985.

V. Advancement of Enteral Feeds (Table 5–15)
VI. Evaluation
  A. Basic requirements
    1. Calories: 120 to 150 kcal/kg/day
    2. Fluid: 150 to 200 ml/kg/day
    3. Protein: 2 to 4 g/kg/day
  B. Growth: Low weight should be reached between 2 and 8 days of age and should be no more than 5 to 10 percent reduction in body weight.
    1. Intrauterine weight gain
      a. 28 to 32 weeks: 18 g/day
      b. 32 to 36 weeks: 38 g/day
    2. Weight gain of premature infants
      a. 1000 to 1250 g: 20 g/day
      b. 1250 to 1500 g: 25 g/day
      c. Greater than 1500 g: 30 g/day
  C. Length: As measured by described methods (see Chap. 1), length should increase on the average of 0.5 to 1 cm/week.

Suggested Protocol for Enteral Feeding in Infants Recovering from Severe Gastroenteritis[49–53]

The goal of this protocol is to maintain the structural and functional integrity of the intestine, stimulate intestinal mucosal growth, and provide adequate calories for tissue repair and growth by a feeding composition and method that reflect the alterations of intestinal function most commonly seen.
 I. Impairments in intestinal function most commonly seen following severe gastroenteritis
  A. Carbohydrate: Lactase is almost always destroyed, sucrase occasionally, and maltase very rarely.
  B. Fat: Fat malabsorption can be severe and often prolonged.
  C. Protein: Protein absorption is generally the least affected; however, the possibility of increased intestinal permeability exists.
 II. Formula composition (suggested formula: Pregestimil or Portagen)
  A. Osmolarity: < 350
  B. Protein: In the form of casein hydrolysate, to provide 8 to 14 percent of total calories (nonprotein calories should be approximately equally divided between fat and carbohydrate).

    C. Fat: Mostly medium-chain triglycerides, some long-chain fats, in order to provide essential fatty acids.

    D. Carbohydrate: Lactose-free, glucose polymers recommended to lower osmolarity.

III. Delivery Method

    A. Initially, continuous pump-assisted intragastric infusion is recommended because it maximizes utilization of limited surface area. Higher concentrations of formula are generally tolerated better when a smaller volume is continuously provided. Increase concentration of formula, then volume.

    B. Weaning from continuous infusion in some cases is a slow process. In general, keep the volume the same and slowly decrease the time over which it is given.

    C. General guidelines for weaning from continuous infusion

       1. Volume previously infused over a 3-hour period is infused over 2 hours with 1 hour off feedings. After 24 to 48 hours with good tolerance, advance to

         a. Same volume infused over 1 hour

         b. Same volume infused over 30 minutes

         c. Bolus feeds

IV. Evaluation

    A. Tolerance: Diarrhea is not necessarily an indication of intolerance. The patient's medical and clinical response in conjunction with stool output and character requires individual evaluation.

    B. Weight Gain

       1. Inefficient energy utilization and varying degrees of malabsorption increase the energy requirements of many patients.

       2. Early weight gain may be unrealistic; as long as feeds are being tolerated and advanced regularly, therapy is appropriate.

V. Common Management Problems

    A. Too rapid advancement of either formula concentration or volume, resulting in diarrhea or increased aspirates.

    B. Inappropriate or irrational formula changes, resulting in inadequate intake, diarrhea, and difficulty in evaluation of tolerance.

FEEDING GUIDELINES

For infants with gastrointestinal problems, begin with 1 to 2 days of oral rehydration solution or *bowel rest* with peripheral alimentation of a glucose-amino acid-lipid solution. Peripheral alimentation should be continued until fluid and nutrient needs are being met by the enteral formula and tolerated by the patient. Suggested formulas are presented in Table 5–16. Many times enteral feedings are stopped abruptly; therefore, it is important to continue peripheral support.

The *formula* should be lactose-free, partially composed of medium-chain oil triglyceride and a protein hydrolysate, and of low osmolarity (Pregestimil). Begin with half-strength formula, advance to full strength, then increase volume to meet requirements.

Delivery should be a continuous, intragastric infusion. Once full-strength formula is tolerated, volume should be increased slowly to meet the patient's needs.

Advancement to bolus feeds depends on the patient's clinical response to an increase in volume of continuous feeds. Many patients will tolerate a fairly rapid advance, and this holds true for changing to bolus feeds as well. For those more difficult patients, a slower progression to bolus feedings is required and at times

Text continued on page 128

TABLE 5–16. Suggested Formulas for Gastrointestinal Problems in Infancy

Gastrointestinal Problem	Suggested Formula	Rationale
Allergy		
Cow's milk protein	Protein hydrolysate	Protein sensitivity
Soy protein	(Nutramigen or Pregestimil)	
Biliary atresia	Portagen	Impaired intraluminal digestion and absorption of long-chain fats
Celiac disease	Pregestimil, soy-based formula, cow's milk formula	Flat-villus lesion causes intolerance to lactose and sucrose so that an elemental formula is required initially; advancement to a more complex formula occurs as the intestinal epithelium returns to normal
Constipation	Routine formula with increased sugar; higher fiber, solid foods	Mild laxative effect
Cystic fibrosis	Portagen	Impaired intraluminal digestion and absorption of long-chain fats and protein
	Pregestimil	Disaccharide digestion may be impaired initially
	Routine formula	With normal pancreatic function or enzyme therapy
Diarrhea		
Chronic nonspecific	Routine formula	Appropriate distribution of calories
Intractable	Pregestimil	Impaired digestion of intact protein, long-chain fats, and disaccharides
Failure to thrive	Pregestimil	Advance to a more complex formula as intestinal epithelium returns to normal
Gastroesophageal reflux	Routine formula	Smaller, thickened feedings; head up, prone position after feeding
Gastrointestinal bleeding	Protein hydrolysate	Rule out allergy, milk toxicity
Hepatitis		
Without failure	Routine formula	
With failure	Portagen (higher protein content may be a problem in some patients)	Impaired digestion and absorption of long-chain fats
Hirschsprung's disease	Routine formula	
Jaundice	Routine formula	If caused by cholestatic hepatocellular disease, fat digestion will be impaired and Portagen should be used
Lactose intolerant	Soy-based formula	Impaired digestion of lactose
Necrotizing enterocolitis	Pregestimil	Impaired digestion and absorption of protein, fat, and carbohydrate
Short-bowel syndrome		
> 100 cm remaining	Routine formula	
< 100 cm remaining	Pregestimil	Impaired end-stage digestion and absorption
Sucrose intolerance:		
Primary	Cow's milk formula	Sucrase deficiency, lactose normal
Secondary (sucrose and lactose)	Pregestimil	Advance to more complex formula as the intestinal epithelium returns to normal

Adapted from Grybowski J, Walker WA, eds.: Gastrointestinal Problems in the Infant, 2nd ed. Philadelphia: WB Saunders, 1983.

TABLE 5–17. Drug and Nutrient Interactions

Drug	Nutrient Considerations	Possible Gastrointestinal Side Effects
Alcohol	Decreased absorption of folic acid, B_{12}, and fat; increased excretion of magnesium	Gastrointestinal irritation
Analgesics		
Barbiturates	May decrease B_{12}, niacin, and folic acid absorption and increase vitamin C excretion	
Colchicine	Intestinal damage with nonspecific decrease in absorption	Constipation, or gastrointestinal irritation with diarrhea, vomiting, and nausea; GI bleeding
Morphine, narcotics	May decrease gastric and pancreatic secretions, peristalsis, and appetite; anemia may result	
Anorexics—general	Decreased nutrient intake secondary to appetite suppression	Appetite suppression, growth retardation
Antacids—general	Increased excretion of phosphate, magnesium, calcium, and fluoride by the formation of insoluble aluminum salts; high sodium content may cause fluid retention; alkalinity causes destruction of thiamine and increased absorption of iron	Constipation, diarrhea, steatorrhea
Anticholinergics—general	Possible decreased absorption of electrolytes and iron; increased absorption of monosaccharides	Nausea, vomiting, constipation, decreased taste acuity
Anticoagulants—general	Blocks the conversion of vitamin K to its active form	Nausea, vomiting, cramps, diarrhea, mouth sores, hemorrhage
Anticonvulsants	Decreased vitamin D levels; decreased absorption and competitive inhibition of folic acid and B_{12}—with megaloblastic anemia; osteomalacia or rickets caused by accelerated vitamin D and bone metabolism; vitamins K, B_6, and C, calcium, and magnesium levels decreased	Hyperplasia of gums; gastric irritation with nausea, anorexia, and vomiting
Phenytoin	Altered vitamin D metabolism with a reduction in vitamin D and calcium; decreased levels of folic acid, B_{12}, and B_6	
Primidone	Decreased levels of vitamin D and K caused by altered vitamin D metabolism	
Ritalin		Appetite suppression, depression of height and weight
Antidepressants		
Tricyclic antidepressants		Stimulation of appetite and weight gain

Table continued on following page

TABLE 5–17. Drug and Nutrient Interactions *Continued*

Drug	Nutrient Considerations	Possible Gastrointestinal Side Effects
Anti-inflammatory agents		
Aspirin	Decreased uptake of vitamin C in thrombocytes and leukocytes; decreased protein binding of folacin; loss of iron with blood loss	Gastrointestinal irritation
Corticosteroids	Increased protein catabolism, decreased glucose tolerance, increased sodium retention; decreased absorption or increased excretion of zinc, potassium, vitamin C, calcium, and iron; accelerated vitamin D metabolism; increased B_6 requirement	Increased appetite, height retardation
Antimicrobials—general	Decreased synthesis of vitamin K by gut microflora; nonabsorbed antibiotics reduce lactase levels; some are folate and B_{12} antagonists and show increased incidence of megaloblastic anemia	Diarrhea, nausea, vomiting, decreased taste acuity, lactase deficiency; damage to intestinal cell wall; steatorrhea
p-aminosalicylic acid	Inhibition of absorptive enzymes—vitamin B_{12} absorption, folic acid, iron, cholesterol	
Chloramphenicol	Altered protein and hemoglobulin synthesis; increased excretion of B_6, lowered niacin levels	
Clindamycin	Decreased potassium	
Cycloserine	Vitamin B_6 antagonist, decreased intestinal absorption of niacin, calcium, magnesium	
Gentamicin	Increased urinary excretion of potassium, magnesium	
Isoniazid	Complexation of B_6, increased excretion of B_6, lowered levels of niacin	
Neomycin	Inactivation of bile salts and decreased absorption of fat, vitamins A, D, K, B_{12}, potassium, sodium, calcium, lactose, sucrose, D-xylose, magnesium	
Penicillin	Aftertaste with food—suppression of appetite; inhibition of glutathione, increased urinary potassium excretion	
Sulfonamides	Decreased synthesis of folic acid, B vitamins and vitamin K; decreased iron absorption	
Tetracyclines	Binding to bone calcium; decreased zinc and iron	
Antineoplastics—methotrexate	Folic acid antagonists block normal metabolism, cause megaloblastic anemia in some cases; damage to intestinal wall with nonspecific decrease in absorption	Anorexia, stomatitis, nausea, vomiting, diarrhea, oral ulcerations, constipation, decreased taste acuity

Table continued on opposite page

TABLE 5–17. Drug and Nutrient Interactions *Continued*

Drug	Nutrient Considerations	Possible Gastrointestinal Side Effects
Cathartics, laxatives	Fluid and electrolyte losses may occur; lubricants decrease absorption of fat-soluble vitamins and calcium; bulk agents may bind certain trace elements	Mucosal irritation with abdominal cramps, diarrhea
Calomel	Decreased phosphorus absorption	
Mannitol	Damage to intestinal wall—absorption of glucose, water, and sodium	
Mineral oil	Interference with micelle formation and decreased vitamin A, D, E, K, carotene and calcium absorption	
Cardiac glycosides	Increased excretion of divalent cations (magnesium, calcium)	Gastric irritation, anorexia, diarrhea, constipation
Chelating agents—general	Increased excretion of heavy metals	Decreased taste acuity and aftertaste, with suppression of appetite, nausea, vomiting
Penicillamine	Chelating of metals, decreased iron, zinc, copper levels; increased renal excretion of B_6	
Diuretics—general	Increased renal excretion or retention of potassium, calcium, magnesium; decreased B_6 and thiamine, decreased carbohydrate tolerance	Gastric irritation, nausea, vomiting, abdominal pain
Furosemide	Increased renal losses of zinc	
Electrolyte repletion—potassium chloride	Decreased absorption of B_{12} secondary to decreased ileal pH	
Hypocholesterolemics—general	With increased binding of bile salts there is malabsorption of fat, fat-soluble vitamins, and calcium; B_{12}, iron, and folic acid absorption may be decreased	Decreased appetite, constipation, vomiting, abdominal pain, nausea; may decrease levels of mucosal disaccharides
Cholestyramine	Decreased absorption of potassium and fat-soluble vitamins with bile-salt depletion; binding of inorganic and hemoglobin iron *in vitro;* also decreased absorption of calcium, folate	
Clofibrate	Decreased absorption of vitamin B_{12}, D-xylose, carotene, MCT, iron, electrolytes	Decreased taste acuity; suppression of appetite
Oral Contraceptive Agents (containing estrogen)	May decrease serum B_{12}, folate (with megaloblastic anemia), riboflavin, magnesium, and zinc; decreased B_6 caused by induction of tryptophan enzyme, competition for binding sites; increased hemoglobin, hematocrit, serum vitamin A, triglycerides, iron, total iron-binding capacity, and copper; decreased absorption of vitamin C	Nausea, vomiting, cramps; mood changes may affect appetite

Table continued on following page

TABLE 5–17. Drug and Nutrient Interactions *Continued*

Drug	Nutrient Considerations	Possible Gastrointestinal Side Effects
Tranquilizers	Sodium retention may cause edema; may increase levels of serum cholesterol with chlorpromazine	Appetite increases, resulting in weight gain; dry mouth, constipation, diarrhea, decreased taste acuity

Adapted from Walker WA, Watkins J, eds.: Nutrition in Pediatrics: Basic Science and Clinical Application. Boston: Little, Brown, 1985.

going back to continuous infusion may be necessary (see Table 4–17 for a case example).

DRUG AND NUTRIENT INTERACTION[54–62]

Drug-induced nutritional deficiencies are generally slow to develop and occur most frequently in long-term drug treatment of chronic disease. General effects of drugs include.

1. Altered *food intake* secondary to a depression or increase in appetite, nausea, vomiting, or altered taste acuity (increased appetite secondary to insulin, steroids, and some antihistamines; decreased appetite secondary to amphetamines).

2. Altered *nutrient function* and metabolism caused by competition for binding sites or promotion of urinary excretion of nutrients (methotrexate blocks normal metabolism of folic acid; chelating agents bind heavy metals such as iron and zinc).

3. Increased *nutrient requirements* caused by decreased absorption of nutrients (increased intestinal motility with laxatives and cathartics, binding of bile salts with cholestyramine).

4. Decreased *nutrient synthesis* (antimicrobials decrease synthesis of vitamin K; chloramphenicol's effect on protein).

Dietary factors may also influence the absorption and metabolism of drugs. In some cases the effect on nutrient status is desirable (folic acid antagonists), and nutrient supplementation may be inappropriate. In other instances, such as protein-calorie malnutrition, sensitivity to various drugs is increased significantly.

References

1. Silverman A, Roy CC, eds.: Pediatric Clinical Gastroenterology, 3rd ed. St. Louis: CV Mosby, 1983.
2. Gray GM: Carbohydrate digestion and absorption, role of the small intestine. N Engl J Med 292:1225, 1975.
3. Gray GM: Assimilation of dietary carbohydrate. View Dig Dis 12:1, 1980.
4. Grand RJ, Watkins JB, Torti FM: Development of the human gastrointestinal tract. Gastroenterology 70:790, 1976.
5. James WP: Sugar absorption and intestinal motility in children when malnourished and after treatment. Clin Sci 39:305, 1970.
6. Freeman HJ, Kim YS, Sleisenger MH: Protein digestion and absorption in man. Normal mechanisms and protein-energy malnutrition. Am J Med 67:1030, 1979.
7. Ganong WF: Review of Medical Physiology, 9th ed. Los Altos, CA: Lange Medical, 1979.
8. Lake AM, Kleinman RE, Walker WA: Enteric alimentation in specialized gastrointestinal problems: an alternative to total parenteral nutrition. Adv Pediatr 28:319, 1981.
9. Green HL, McCabe DR, Merenstein GB: Protracted diarrhea and malnutrition in infancy: changes in intestinal morphology and disaccharidase activities during treatment with total intravenous nutrition or oral elemental diets. J Pediatr 87:695, 1975.

10. Gryboski J, Walker WA, eds.: Gastrointestinal Problems in the Infant. Philadelphia: WB Saunders, 1983.
11. Cornblath M, Schwartz R, eds.: Disorders of Carbohydrate Metabolism in Infancy, 2nd ed. Philadelphia: WB Saunders, 1966.
12. Dahlqvist A, Lindberg T, Meeuwisse G, et al.: Intestinal dipeptidases and disaccharidases in children with malabsorption. Acta Paediatr Scand 59:621, 1970.
13. Jensen RG, Clark RM, de Jong FA, et al.: The lipolytic triad: human lingual, breast milk, and pancreatic lipases: physiological implications of their characteristics in digestion of dietary fats. J Pediatr Gastroenterol Nutr 1:243, 1982.
14. Wilson FA, Dietschy JM: Differential diagnostic approach to clinical problems of malabsorption. Gastroenterology 61:911, 1971.
15. Atkinson SA, Bryan MH, Anderson GH: Human milk feeding in premature infants. J Pediatr 99:617, 1981.
16. Wood RE: Cystic fibrosis: diagnosis, treatment and prognosis. South Med J 72:189, 1979.
17. Park RW, Grand RJ: Gastrointestinal manifestations of cystic fibrosis: a review. Gastroenterology 81:1143, 1981.
18. Sproul A, Huang N: Growth patterns in children with cystic fibrosis. J Pediatr 65:664, 1964.
19. Shepherd R, Cooksley WGE, Cooke WD: Improved growth and clinical, nutritional and respiratory changes in response to nutritional therapy in cystic fibrosis. J Pediatr 97:351, 1980.
20. Kraemer R, Rudeberg A, Hadorn B, et al.: Relative underweight in cystic fibrosis and its prognostic value. Acta Paediatr Scand 67:33, 1978.
21. Chase HP, Long UA, Lavin MH: Cystic fibrosis and malnutrition. J Pediatr 95:337, 1979.
22. Roy CC, Weber AM: Nutrition of the child with cystic fibrosis. In: Walker WA, Watkins J, eds.: Pediatric Nutrition: Basic Science and Clinical Aspects. Boston: Little, Brown, 1985.
23. Hubbard VS, Mangrum PJ: Energy intake and nutrition counseling in cystic fibrosis. J Am Diet Assoc 80:127, 1982.
24. Berry HK, Kellogg FW, Hunt MM, et al.: Dietary supplement and nutrition in children with cystic fibrosis. Am J Dis Child 129:165, 1975.
25. Fisher JE, Bower RH: Nutritional support in liver disease. Surg Clin North Am 61:653, 1981.
26. American Academy of Pediatrics Committee on Nutrition: Soy protein formulas: recommendations for use in infant feeding. Pediatrics 72:359, 1983.
27. Eastham EJ, Lechauco T, Grady MI, et al.: Antigenicity of infant formulas: role of immature intestine on protein permeability. J Pediatr 93:561, 1978.
28. Iyngkaran N, Davis K, Robinson MJ, et al.: Cow's milk protein–sensitive enteropathy, an important contributing cause of secondary sugar intolerance in young infants with acute infective enteritis. Arch Dis Child 54:39, 1979.
29. Powell GK: Milk- and soy-induced enterocolitis of infancy. Clinical features and standardization of challenge. J Pediatr 93:553, 1978.
30. Udall JN, Pang K, Fritze L, et al.: Development of gastrointestinal mucosal barrier. Pediatr Res 15:241, 1981.
31. American Academy of Pediatrics Committee on Nutrition: Nutritional needs of low-birth-weight infants. Pediatrics 60:519, 1977.
32. Atkinson SA, Bryan MH, Anderson GH: Human milk: differences in nitrogen concentration in milk from mothers of term and premature infants. J Pediatr 93:67, 1978.
33. Gross SJ: Growth and biochemical response of preterm infants fed human milk or modified infant formula. N Engl J Med 308:237, 1983.
34. Bell EF, Brown EJ, Milner R, et al.: Vitamin E absorption in small premature infants. Pediatrics 63:830, 1979.
35. Caillie MV, Powell GK: Nasoduodenal versus nasogastric feeding in the very low birthweight infant. Pediatrics 56:1065, 1975.
36. Cavell F: Gastric emptying in preterm infants. Acta Paediatr Scand 68:725, 1979.
37. Canadian Pediatric Society Nutrition Committee: Feeding the low-birthweight infant. Can Med Assoc J 124:1301, 1981.
38. Gaull GE, Rassin DK, Räihä NC, et al.: Milk protein quantity and quality in low-birth-weight infants. J Pediatr 90:348, 1977.
39. Gross SJ, David RJ, Bauman L, et al.: Nutritional composition of milk produced by mothers delivering preterm. J Pediatr 96:641, 1980.
40. Lubchenco LO, Hansman C, Dressler M, et al.: Intrauterine growth as estimated from liveborn birth-weight data at 24 to 42 weeks of gestation. Pediatrics 32:793, 1963.
41. Reichman B, Chessex P, Putet G, et al.: Diet, fat accretion, and growth in premature infants. N Engl J Med 305:1495, 1981.
42. Reichman BL, Chessex P, Putet G, et al.: Partition of energy metabolism and energy cost of growth in the very low-birth-weight infant. Pediatrics 69:446, 1982.
43. Sinclair JC, Driscoll JM, Heird WC, et al.: Supportive management of the sick neonate: parenteral calories, water and electrolytes. Pediatr Clin North Am 17:863, 1970.
44. Roy RN, Pollnitz RB, Hamilton JR, et al.: Impaired assimilation of nasojejunal feeds in healthy low-birth-weight newborn infants. J Pediatr 90:431, 1977.
45. Senterre J: Net absorption of starch in low birth weight infants. Acta Paediatr Scand 69:653, 1980.
46. Stevens D, Burman D, Strelling MK, et al.: Folic acid supplementation in low birth weight infants. Pediatrics 64:333, 1979.

47. Reynolds J: Nutrition of the low birth weight infant. In: Walker WA, Watkins J, eds.: Pediatric Nutrition: Basic Science and Clinical Aspects. Boston: Little, Brown, 1984.
48. Pereira GR, Lemons JA: Controlled study of transpyloric and intermittent gavage feeding in a small preterm infant. Pediatrics 67:68, 1981.
49. MacLean WC, de Romona GL, Massa E, et al.: Nutritional management of chronic diarrhea and malnutrition: primary reliance on oral feeding. J Pediatr 97:316, 1980.
50. Parker P, Stroop IS, Greene H: A controlled comparison of continuous versus intermittent feeding in the treatment of infants with intestinal disease. J Pediatr 99:360, 1981.
51. Santosham M, Daum RS, Dillman L, et al.: Oral rehydration therapy of infantile diarrhea: a controlled study of well-nourished children hospitalized in the United States and Panama. N Engl J Med 306:1070, 1982.
52. Sherman JO, Hamly CA, Khachadurina AK: Use of an oral elemental diet in infants with severe intractable diarrhea. J Pediatr 86:518, 1975.
53. Kaschula RO, Gajjar PD, Mann M, et al.: Infantile jejunal mucosa in infection and malnutrition. Isr J Med Sci 15:356, 1979.
54. Herbert V: The vitamin craze. Arch Intern Med 140:173, 1980.
55. American Academy of Pediatrics Committee on Nutrition: Vitamin and mineral supplement needs in normal children in the United States. Pediatrics 66:1015, 1980.
56. National Research Council Food and Nutrition Board Dietary Allowances Committee, ed.: Recommended Dietary Allowances, 9th ed. Washington, DC: National Academy of Sciences, 1980.
57. American Academy of Pediatrics Committee on Nutrition: Nutritional aspects of vegetarianism, health foods, and fad diets. Pediatrics 59:460, 1977.
58. American Academy of Pediatrics Committee on Nutrition: Megavitamin therapy for childhood psychoses and learning disabilities. Pediatrics 58:910, 1976.
59. American Academy of Pediatrics Committee on Nutrition: Iron supplementation for infants. J Pediatr 58:765, 1976.
60. Grant A: Nutritional Assessment Guidelines, 2nd ed. Berkeley, CA: Cutter Laboratories, 1979.
61. American Dietetic Association: Interactions of Selected Drugs with Nutritional Status in Man, 2nd ed. Chicago: American Dietetic Association, 1978.
62. Roe DA: Drug Induced Nutritional Deficiencies. Westport, CT: Avi Publishing, 1980.

6

NUTRITIONAL SUPPORT IN PATIENTS WITH ALTERED NUTRIENT REQUIREMENTS BUT NORMAL GASTROINTESTINAL FUNCTION

A multitude of medical and surgical disorders, particularly chronic medical problems with complicated therapies, result in alteration of nutrient requirements. A comprehensive discussion of every clinical situation in which nutrition has a role is beyond the scope of this manual. Rather, five disorders are described; these represent a range of conditions to which nutritional support of sick pediatric patients may apply.

For the pediatric patient with *cancer,* nutritional support is an adjunct to primary treatment of the malignancy. The *hypermetabolic state,* which occurs following trauma, surgery, or burns, involves a complex series of metabolic changes that result in acute nutritional problems that are often overlooked. *Nonorganic failure to thrive* is included because it is one of the most common causes of growth failure in this age group. The interrelationship of disease, organ function, nutritional status, and nutritional support is demonstrated in patients with *chronic pulmonary disease.* For example, fluid restriction in the infant or child may severely limit intake, yet increased requirements exist because of increased respiratory rate. In addition, high carbohydrate loads may not be tolerated well and several dietary interventions may be necessary for adequate support of these patients. Finally, nutritional considerations for patients with *renal insufficiency* represent one of the more complicated therapies in chronic disease.

NUTRITIONAL SUPPORT IN CANCER PATIENTS

The high incidence of malnutrition in cancer patients is caused by concomitant factors. The adverse nutritional consequences of the cancer itself are well recognized, and many patients present with weight loss, fatigue, and early satiety.[1, 2] Local and systemic disease–related effects that limit nutrient intake include anorexia, metabolic changes, altered taste perception, and intestinal obstruction. In addition, the various therapies of radiation and surgery (Table 6–1)[3–7] and chemotherapy (Table 6–2),[3, 8] many times used in combination in these patients, may result in anorexia, nausea or more disturbed gastrointestinal function, decreased caloric intake, metabolic changes, and weight loss.[3]

TABLE 6–1. Effects of Radiation Therapy and Surgery on Nutrient Status

Area	Treatment	Result
Head and Upper Neck Area	Radiation therapy	Dry mouth, difficulty or pain when chewing and swallowing, burning sensation with tart, acid fluids and foods
	Surgical intervention	Difficulty in swallowing, chewing
	Radical resection	Esophagitis, fibrosis, stricture, difficulty in swallowing
Lower Neck and Midchest Area	Radiation	Difficulty or pain when swallowing, esophagitis, stricture, nausea, vomiting
	Surgery (esophageal reconstruction)	Steatorrhea, diarrhea, hypochlorhydria secondary to vagotomy, fistula, stenosis, gastric stasis
Abdominal and Pelvic Area	Radiation	Enteritis, acute and chronic, with diarrhea; malabsorption; stricture; obstruction; nausea; vomiting; constipation
	Surgery (effects are varied; may not be particular to cancer but may depend on organ removed)	Nutrient deficiencies and malabsorption depend upon degree of resection (see Chap. 5)
		Gastrectomy; dumping syndrome, malabsorption, hypoglycemia
		Intestinal resection: jejunal—decreased efficiency of absorption of many nutrients; ileal—vitamin B_{12} deficiency and bile salt losses; massive bowel resection—malabsorption and malnutrition; ileostomy and colostomy—complications of salt and water balance
		Blind-loop syndrome
		Pancreatectomy: malabsorption/maldigestion, diabetes mellitus
		Ureterosigmoidostomy; hyperchloremic acidosis, potassium depletion

Nutritional therapy alone only transiently alleviates or reverses the depleted state. However, when used in conjunction with definitive treatment for the underlying cancer, it may improve a patient's prognosis by reducing morbidity. Identification of patients at risk for nutritional complications of disease and treatment and identification of patients who would benefit from aggressive nutritional support permit optimization of cancer therapy. Nutritional assessment criteria helpful in evaluating these patients are outlined in Table 6–3. Weight loss and measurement of weight for height percentile are important prognostic factors.[9] Diet history and determination of adequacy of calorie and protein intake are helpful in predicting which patients will benefit from early nutritional intervention.[10] Aggressive nutritional support, provided before the effects of therapy decrease nutrient intake and result in malnutrition, significantly reduces the morbidity but does not change mortality in cancer patients.[11]

Guidelines for management of specific nutritional problems encountered in these patients are outlined in Table 6–4.[1, 3–8, 10] Primary nutritional support should aid the family in maintaining as normal a lifestyle as possible. For many patients, this entails receiving normal nutrition for age (see Chap. 1) and obtaining advice for coping with eating difficulties associated with illness and its therapy or with emotional responses that limit intake. For those patients unable to meet caloric requirements through a regular diet, supplementation or concentration of calories may be necessary, as detailed in Table 6–5. Those patients who are unable to meet their requirements during treatment may need enteral tube feeding (see Chap. 3) or total parenteral nutrition (see Chap. 4) to preserve nutritional status and permit optimal therapy.[11–14]

TABLE 6–2. Gastrointestinal Effects of Cancer Chemotherapeutic Agents

Drug	Stomatitis	Nausea	Vomiting	Diarrhea	Oral Ulcerations	Constipation	Gingivitis	Metallic Taste	Anorexia	Abdominal Pain
Actinomycin D	X	X	X	X	X				X	
Adriamycin	X		X						X	
Asparaginase			X						X	
BCNU		X	X						X	
Bleomycin	X	X	X						X	
Busulfan		X	X							
CDDP		X	X						X	
Cyclophosphamide		X	X						X	
Cytarabine		X	X	X	X					
Daunorubicin	X	X	X						X	
5-Fluorouracil	X	X	X	X	X				X	
Hydroxyurea	X	X	X	X		X			X	
Melphalan		X	X							
6-Mercaptopurine	X	X	X	X			X		X	
Methotrexate	X	X	X	X	X				X	
Mitomycin		X	X	X					X	
Nitrogen Mustard		X	X					X	X	
Nitrosoureas		X	X						X	
Procarbazine		X	X						X	
Vinblastine	X	X	X	X		X			X	X
Vincristine		X	X			X				X

TABLE 6—3. Guidelines for Routine Nutritional Assessment of Cancer Patients

Nutrient Intake
Intake of energy, protein, carbohydrate, fat, vitamins, minerals

Evaluation of early satiety, anorexia, fatigue, nausea,
vomiting, diarrhea, constipation

Anthropometry
Weight, weight change

Height, weight for height

Arm circumference

Triceps skinfold thickness

Laboratory Studies
Serum albumin, total protein, and transferrin

Recall skin antigen testing

NUTRITIONAL SUPPORT IN HYPERMETABOLIC STATES

Stress is defined as "the nonspecific response of the body to any demand."[15] It may be physical, as in injury, surgery, trauma, burn, or infection, or psychologic, secondary to tension or anxiety.[15] The effects of stress on nutrient status have been evaluated in surgical patients but are similar for patients in other states of stress. These effects include pre-existing nutrient depletion as a cause for postoperative malnutrition and a high correlation between percent preoperative weight loss and operative mortality rates.[16, 17] Although weight loss in convalescence has received less attention, postoperative malnutrition as a result of surgical procedures and postoperative complications are important factors in patient outcome.[18, 19] Several metabolic changes, which occur after the release of hormones in response to acute stress, influence the use of nutrients as substrates. Briefly, this complex response has three main components: (1) Catecholamine discharge inhibits insulin secretion and peripheral insulin action, and stimulates glucagon and ACTH production; (2) pituitary-adrenal and renal-adrenal stimuli increase corticosteroids, inhibit insulin activity, and increase aldosterone; and (3) posterior pituitary stimulation produces water retention and antidiuresis.[19] These responses are outlined in Figure 6–1.[19, 20] The magnitude and duration of the hypermetabolic stress, as well as the patient's previous nutritional status, influence metabolism.[15]

Wide variation exists in caloric requirements for weight gain in stressed patients (see Chap. 2). Calories should be adjusted to meet each patient's requirements for nitrogen balance once the initial corticoid phase has passed (generally 3 to 4 days after injury). Amounts of protein necessary for replenishment of visceral proteins, restitution of muscle mass, and promotion of wound healing range from 1.5 to 2 times the RDA for age.[22] Excess protein intake may not be beneficial to these patients, since it increases the renal solute load and thus the need for free water. Carbohydrate is nitrogen-sparing, but in excess in stressed patients it may increase blood sugar, interfere with fat mobilization,[23] and compound pulmonary compromise.[23] Thus, nonprotein calories should be equally divided between carbohydrate and fat. A summary of nutritional support necessary for patients with severe burns is outlined in Table 6–6.[24, 25] In addition, many patients suffer gastrointestinal complications (see Chap. 5), pulmonary compromise, and renal failure (see later); all conditions may complicate nutritional management.

TABLE 6–4. Guidelines for Specific Nutritional Problems in Cancer Patients

Problem	Cause	Recommendations
Nausea	Effects of cancer therapy (chemotherapy, radiation, surgery); possible effects of malignancy (circulating metabolites); depression, anxiety, fear, or other psychologic causes	Dietary counseling with primary concern for adequate caloric intake; encourage small, frequent meals of high caloric density, fluids throughout the day; serve bland foods at room temperature; may require parenteral support
Vomiting	Same as above	Antiemetics (phenothiazines, tetrahydrocannabinol, antihistamines); encourage bland foods; withhold solids until vomiting is well under control; may require parenteral support.
Anorexia	Same as above	Atmosphere makes a difference; avoid odors or environments that may be disagreeable; small, frequent high-calorie meals; drink high-calorie liquids with medications
Diarrhea	Radiation, chemotherapy, surgery	Small, frequent meals, decreased fiber and lactose as indicated; antispasmodics, antiemetics, anticholinergics, or antidiarrheal agents as needed; warm rather than hot foods may be better tolerated; drink liquids between, rather than with meals.
Psychologic causes of decreased food intake	Conditioned food aversions (acute malaise resulting from therapy may be psychologically associated with food eaten before therapy); intractable pain, fear, anorexia, anxiety, depression	Fast several hours before treatment; improve social context of eating; use behavior modification.
Altered taste perception	Effects of cancer therapy or possibly the effects of the malignancy; although the exact mechanism is unknown, the likelihood increases with the extent of the tumor; zinc deficiency may contribute	Most common alterations include an elevated threshold for sweet sensation and lowered threshold for bitter; seasonings should be adjusted (decrease seasonings with meats, increase with simple sugars) or alternative food selections made (turkey, chicken, eggs, and fish); acid foods may stimulate taste buds; rinse mouth before eating to clear taste
Early satiety	Surgery or tumor	Small, frequent meals of high caloric density; make sure liquids have nutritional content
Constipation	Chemotherapy	High-fiber, high-fluid intake; increase exercise; hot beverages may stimulate the bowel
Mucositis	Radiation of head and neck, chemotherapy	Attend to good dental and oral hygiene; use anesthetic mouthwashes or lozenges before meals; avoid food or drinks that cause pain (generally hot, spicy, acidic, tart, salty or caffeine-containing foods); soft, moist, bland, cool foods or food chopped in small pieces or soaked in liquids to soften are usually well tolerated; semiliquid or liquid diet
Decreased salivation	Radiation	Moist foods (stews, casseroles, addition of sauce, gravy) or pureed or blended foods; tart foods (lemon, vinegar, pickles) may stimulate saliva; serve extra liquids during and between meals; rinse mouth frequently

TABLE 6–5. Suggestions for Increasing Protein, Calorie, and Nutrient Density in Patients with Malnutrition Secondary to Chronic Illness

Milk and Milk Products

Add powdered skim milk to regular whole milk (1 qt milk with 1 c powdered milk) or use half and half, evaporated milk, or sweetened condensed milk instead of milk or water whenever possible in recipes for pudding, cocoa, milk shakes, cream soup, custard, or eggnog.

Add powdered milk to yogurt, casseroles, bread, muffins, sauces, and gravies.

Add cheese to sandwiches, meats, potatoes, salads, vegetables, rice, pasta, and cream sauces.

Offer cream cheese or cottage cheese on crackers; add these cheeses to vegetables or pasta.

Add plain or flavored yogurt to ice cream, mix with granola, use in beverages such as shakes or in whole-grain cookies.

Make instant breakfast with milk.

Yogurt may be added to fruit or desserts, and used to top cereal, pancakes, or waffles.

Protein Group

Add small pieces of cooked meat, fish, poultry, or eggs to salads, casseroles, soup, vegetables, omelets, and noodles.

Eggs may be added to French toast or pancake batter, custards, pudding, deviled sandwich spreads, cheesecake, or sponge cake.

Peanut butter can be used with all grains, spread on fruit or vegetables, blended in milk drinks, ice cream, or yogurt.

Add nuts to desserts, salads, ice cream, vegetables, or fruits.

Textured vegetable protein or legumes can be cooked and made into casseroles, soups, cheese or milk dishes.

Offer simple fried foods such as chicken or fish.

Serve meat with extra gravy or sauce when appropriate.

Fruits and Vegetables

Add mashed fruit to milk, yogurt, shakes, ice cream, or pudding.

Make gelatin desserts with juice instead of water.

Add a bit less water when reconstituting frozen juices.

Add honey or syrup to fruit in juice or vegetables.

Add dried fruits to muffins, cookies, cereal, and grains or combine with vegetables, nuts, or grains.

Serve vegetables raw with a dip or cooked creamed style.

Add small amounts of butter, sour cream, or mayonnaise to vegetables.

Grains

Make hot cereals with milk or juice instead of water.

Use high-protein noodles and grains in casseroles and soups.

Bread or flour meat before cooking.

Offer whole-grain desserts such as oatmeal, raisin-bran, or peanut-butter cookies.

Top muffins, toast, crackers, pancakes with margarine, cream cheese, syrup, jam, peanut butter, cheese, or honey.

Serve granola over ice cream, frozen yogurt, or fruit, or mix with nuts or dried fruit.

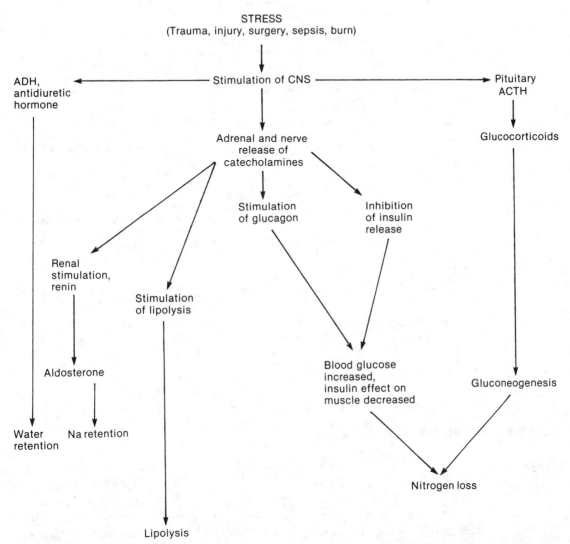

Figure 6–1. Metabolic response to stress. The hormones responsible for bringing about the metabolic response to stress are divided into 4 phases. The length of each is directly related to the severity of the stress. Phase I, the adrenergic-cortisoid phase, is shown above. The overall effects are increased metabolic rate, increased protein catabolism, and water and sodium retention. In phase II the adrenal steroid output begins to return toward normal with an associated increase in sodium excretion and decrease in potassium and nitrogen excretion. During phase III anabolic recovery begins as protein synthesis occurs and nitrogen balance becomes positive. In phase IV most of the increase in body weight is caused by fat deposition. (Adapted from Hill GL: Surgically created nutritional problems. Surg Clin North Am 61:721, 1981; Wolfe BM, Chock E: Energy sources, stores and hormonal controls. Surg Clin North Am 61:509–518, 1981, by courtesy of Marcel Dekker, Inc.)

TABLE 6–6. Nutritional Considerations in Severe Thermal Injury

	Effect of Injury	Estimation of Requirement
Calories	Increased energy requirements appear to be directly proportional to the magnitude of the burn injury (up to 60% total body surface burn)*; weight loss, delayed wound healing, and increased infections are observed if energy intake does not approximate expenditure; need for tissue repair is increased.	One recommendation for estimating caloric requirement is (25 × weight in kg) + (40 × % total body surface burn).*
Protein	Urea excretion is increased, but is sensitive to protein intake; protein synthesis and catabolism can be elevated with sufficient protein intake.	Recommendations for protein intake range from 1.5 to 2.5 g/kg.†
Carbohydrate	Glucose production is elevated; responsiveness to hypoglycemic action of insulin is depressed.	There is a limit to the amount of glucose that should be given to burn patients; nonprotein calories should be equally divided between carbohydrates and fat.
Fat	Catecholamines stimulate lipolysis; free fatty acid oxidation is increased.	The administration of intravenous fat emulsions to burn patients has not been well studied; current recommendation (as noted above) is 50% of nonprotein calories as fat.
Vitamins, Minerals, and Electrolytes	Fluid and electrolyte imbalances are common and require individualized monitoring.	Needs for vitamins and zinc are increased.

*See Curreri PW, et al.: Dietary requirements of patients with major burns. J Am Diet Assoc 65:415, 1974.

†See Molnar JA, et al.: Metabolism and nutritional therapy in thermal injury. In: Schneider HA, Anderson CE, eds.: Nutritional Support of Medical Practice, 2nd ed. Philadelphia: Lippincott, 1983.

NONORGANIC FAILURE TO THRIVE

Diagnosis

If the initial work-up for failure to thrive does not define an organic cause, the chances are only one in ten that further evaluation will determine a medical reason for growth failure. Thorough physical examination and clinical and psychosocial history are sensitive indicators of any organic component when extensive laboratory tests yield little useful information.[26] Similarly, degree of social turmoil and environmental discord are strong predictors of nonorganic failure to thrive. One set of diagnostic criteria for this condition includes:[27]

1. Weight below the third percentile and subsequent weight increase in the presence of appropriate nurturing.

2. Developmental retardation and subsequent acceleration of development after appropriate stimulation and feeding.

3. No evidence of systemic disease or abnormality to account for the initial growth failure.

4. Clinical signs of deprivation that improve in a more nurturing environment.

5. Significant environmental or psychosocial disruption.

Etiology

Although many theories exist as to the cause of this syndrome, the pathogenesis of the resultant growth failure remains obscure. The mother's character has been evaluated as a possible causal factor in this syndrome, and the following three groups have been developed by Evans.[28]

1. Mothers who have recently experienced a loss that resulted in depression and put strain on the mother-child relationship. Generally, once this mother's depression resolves, she responds well to treatment, and a favorable prognosis for growth is predicted for her infant.

2. Mothers who have depression and losses of a more chronic nature, who generally live under impoverished conditions, and who perceive their children as ill. Subsequent weight gain in these infants does not always occur.

3. Mothers who perceive their children as bad and who foster a hostile mother-child interaction. Their histories are remarkable for difficulties with interpersonal relationships and, often, neglect for their children. Foster placement for the child may be warranted, since these mothers are generally unresponsive to treatment.

There has recently been a notable evolution from the theory that places all responsibility on the mother to one that also sees the infant as an individual who may contribute to the failure-to-thrive syndrome. Feeding, a frequent, routine interaction, is an activity that must be engaged in by the infant and caretaker together. The mother may have "normal" maternal attributes with an infant who, for some reason (prematurity, small for gestational age, individual temperament), puts additional stress on the mother; this results in the mother's difficulty in forming attachment bonds and meeting the infant's needs.

Possible causes of growth retardation because of caloric and nutrient deficiency may result from (1) unavailability of food, (2) refusal by the infant to feed, (3) simple feeding difficulties, and (4) malabsorption secondary to organic cause or the infant's emotional state.

Treatment

Follow-up studies to date show that regardless of intervention strategy, children with feeding problems do not fare well in the subsequent years of childhood.[29, 30] They are at risk for having permanent stunting of growth, impaired intellectual function, and disturbances of personality development.

Because of the wide range of causal relationships, treatment and intervention must be highly individualized. Evaluation and treatment programs should be interdisciplinary in approach; the primary physician, nurse, nutritionist, and social worker should coordinate their care. Regular conferences that include other caretakers should be scheduled throughout the hospitalization and following discharge so that comprehensive treatment for the child and family can be planned. Parents must be aware of needed behavioral changes; thus, it is important to incorporate parents into the team so that they may take part in long-term management.

NUTRITIONAL SUPPORT IN PULMONARY DISEASE

Nutritional aspects of chronic respiratory illness can be divided into two major categories: (1) the effects of chronic pulmonary disease upon nutritional status,[28] and (2) the effects of nutrition on pulmonary function.[29] Pulmonary diseases that

**TABLE 6–7. Factors that Determine Energy Demands and Supply
in Pulmonary Disease**

Factors Determining Energy Demands
Work of Breathing
Minute ventilation
Compliance and resistance

Efficiency
Lung volume
Neuromuscular disease
Nutritional status
Body position

Factors Determining Energy Available
Oxygen transport
O_2 content
Blood flow

Substrate availability

Substrate stores

From Askanazi J, et al.: Nutrition and the respiratory system. Crit Care Med 10:163, 1982.

begin early in life, such as respiratory distress syndrome, bronchopulmonary dysplasia, cystic fibrosis, and asthmatic bronchitis, place a child at risk for malnutrition.[31] These patients are generally smaller than their healthy counterparts, probably because of a combination of increased metabolic needs (as respiration increases so does metabolic rate, because of the increased needs for oxygen).[32] In addition, early severe dietary restrictions or the disease process may cause decreased nutrient intake, as has been documented in cystic fibrosis.[33] Factors that may influence energy supply and demand in these patients are listed in Table 6–7. Table 6–8 outlines the diseases, their complications, and treatments that may affect nutrient needs or intake.

Malnutrition has adverse effects on various aspects of pulmonary function. Respiration is highly dependent on muscle function, and when energy utilization exceeds supply, catabolism of respiratory musculature occurs. This atrophy is enhanced in states of passive lung movement, such as in prolonged artificial ventilation.[23] Fatigue occurs more easily because vital capacity and diaphragm mass are decreased.[34] Because malnutrition reduces both respiratory muscle strength

TABLE 6–8. Nutritional Aspects of Representative Chronic Respiratory Illness

---

Asthmatic Bronchitis
Treatment may include steroid therapy, which inhibits linear growth.
Caloric intake for age is decreased secondary to anorexia and nausea.
Increased nutrient needs are caused by recurrent infections, increased work of breathing.

Bronchopulmonary Dysplasia
Cor pulmonale or cardiac failure requires fluid restriction and may decrease intake.
Bronchospasm may require steroid therapy, which inhibits linear growth.
Antibiotic therapy may damage the gastrointestinal flora.
Recurrent infections increase need for calories and protein.
Chronic hypoxemia and tachypnia occur.

Cystic Fibrosis
Malabsorption occurs secondary to pancreatic insufficiency.
Caloric intake for age is decreased secondary to anorexia, dyspnea during eating, vomiting.
Increased metabolic rate is caused by fever, infection, and increased work of breathing.
Chronic hypoxemia occurs.

Respiratory Distress Syndrome
In the premature infant, this is often seen in combination with cardiac disease (requiring fluid restriction) and gastrointestinal immaturity, which limits volume of intake and absorption.

---

and maximal voluntary ventilation, it may well impair the capacity of the respiratory muscles to handle increased ventilatory loads such as occur in thoracopulmonary disease.[35]

In addition, surfactant production decreases,[36, 37] reducing pulmonary compliance. Direct effects of semistarvation on the lung include decreased tissue elasticity and air space enlargement, which further compromise lung function.[38, 39] Low serum albumin may lead to a decrease in colloid osmotic (oncotic) pressure and pulmonary edema. Impaired cell-mediated immunity predisposes the patient to infection.[40, 41]

In summary, the effects of malnutrition on the respiratory system include respiratory muscle atrophy, decreased surfactant, decreased oncotic pressure, decreased vital capacity, inability to be weaned from the ventilator, and increased susceptibility to infection.[41]

Recently, the role of nutrition in control of ventilation has received increased attention because of the influence nutrition has been shown to have on metabolic rate—increased metabolic rate increases ventilatory drive and decreased metabolic rate decreases it. In addition, metabolic end-products of nutrient metabolism (most notably, CO_2) affect respiratory function. This is most commonly expressed as the respiratory quotient (RQ), which is the ratio of the amount of CO_2 expired to the amount of O_2 inspired.[38] When only glucose is being metabolized to meet basal requirements, the RQ equals 1.0 because the amount of CO_2 produced equals the amount of O_2 consumed. When fat is metabolized, extra O_2 is necessary for the formation of H_2O; this lowers the RQ to an average of 0.703. The average RQ for proteins is 0.82.

In starvation there is a decrease in basal metabolic rate and a resultant decrease in both O_2 consumption and CO_2 production. With glucose loading (as is often the case in total parenteral nutrition regimes) dextrose effects a shift from fat to glucose oxidation, and CO_2 production may increase to two times normal or higher.[42] Thus, excessive glucose infused in a depleted patient is converted to fat, the amount of CO_2 produced is greater than the O_2 consumed, and the RQ is increased. This is important in the patient who is being weaned from the respirator, as the excess CO_2 generated must be excreted by the lungs at an energy cost caused by an increased tidal volume and respiratory rate.[43]

For an RQ greater than 1.0, a relatively small increase in the intravenous glucose delivery rate creates a marked increase both in RQ and in CO_2 production in relation to O_2 consumption. As a result, there is a considerable increase in the volume of CO_2 that the respiratory system is required to excrete[44] and an increase in the respiratory workload.

Whether increased CO_2 production is caused by adequate calories administered primarily as glucose or by excessive calories, the end result is an increased load on the lungs, and this makes the patient with marginal pulmonary function difficult to wean.[41]

The metabolic response in differing clinical situations varies. Septic and injured patients preferentially utilize endogenous fat as an energy source, and this results in an RQ that is significantly lower.[45] Because there is a large increase in both CO_2 production and O_2 consumption, the RQ in these hypermetabolic patients is generally less than 1.0 and the ratio may not reflect these increases. In addition, although carbohydrate influences are most significant, the metabolism of both protein and fat may affect respiratory function.[35] The optimal proportions of glucose, fat, and protein needed for ventilator patients remains controversial, but the following recommendations have been suggested. Starvation, hypermetabolic states, and overfeeding may adversely affect the respiratory function of these patients. Goals should be restoration of lean body mass and, in children, promotion of growth.[34] This requires an accurate assessment of caloric requirements so that the patient can be successfully managed and weaned.

Fluid restriction and diuretics can cause large fluctuations in weight, so growth should be monitored weekly (weight, height, skinfold thickness) and intake adjusted as needed. Calories and protein should be given at requirement levels with 50 percent of nonprotein calories coming from fat and 50 percent from carbohydrate (provided that triglyceride intolerance is not present).[41]

NUTRITIONAL SUPPORT IN CHRONIC RENAL INSUFFICIENCY

The regulation of fluid and solute by the glomerulus and resorption of substances by the tubules represent the major homeostatic functions of the kidney. The effects of malnutrition on renal function are similar in both protein-energy malnutrition and anorexia nervosa, and they accompany many disease states of children in which undernutrition is a complicating factor. These changes in renal function, listed in Table 6–9, are a functional response that is reversible with improved nutritional status.[46]

In chronic renal insufficiency (CRI) many abnormalities affect the metabolism of nutrients or their metabolic products. Alterations in protein, lipid, carbohydrate, vitamin, mineral, endocrine, and acid-base status are common.[47–50] The main excretory, regulatory, and metabolic functions of the kidney and the effects of renal failure on each are listed in Table 6–9. The nutritional consequences of CRI and their interrelationships are depicted in Figure 6–2.

Growth failure occurs in an estimated 35 to 65 percent of children with CRI.[50, 51] When CRI has its onset in infancy, it appears to impair linear growth more than it does when it first occurs in older children. The multitude of dietary restrictions and the anorexia caused by illness appear to be the main causes of

TABLE 6–9. Effects of Renal Insufficiency and Protein-Calorie Malnutrition on Kidney Function

Renal Function	Protein-Calorie Malnutrition	Chronic Renal Insufficiency	Clinical Complications
Excretion			
Nitrogenous metabolites (urea, uric acid, creatinine)	↓ Glomerular filtration rate ↓ Renal plasma flow	↓ Glomerular filtration rate ↓ Renal plasma flow	Uremia
Hydrogen ions, sulphate	↓ Acid excretion	↓ Acid excretion	Acidosis
Water, sodium	↓ Sodium excretion	↓ Sodium excretion	Hypertension edema
Potassium			Hyperkalemia
Phosphate			Hyperparathyroidism
Regulation			
Water	↓ Sodium excretion	↓ Sodium excretion	Loss of homeostasis
Sodium	↓ Urine concentration	↓ Urine concentration	
Potassium, hydrogen, magnesium	↓ Acid excretion	↓ Acid excretion	
Metabolic			
Vitamin D		↓ Hydroxylation to active form	Bone loss
Erythropoietin	↓ Red cell production deficiency of specific erythropoietic factors		Anemia

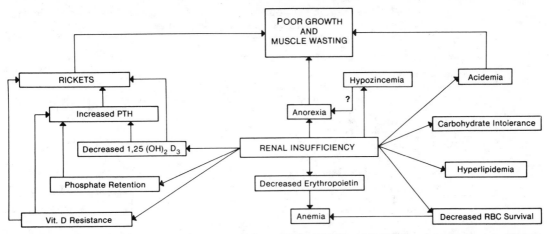

Figure 6–2. Consequences of chronic renal insufficiency. (From McVicar MI: Nutritional consequences of kidney disease. In Lifshitz F, ed.: Pediatric Nutrition. New York: Marcel Dekker, 1982. Reprinted by courtesy of Marcel Dekker, Inc.)

growth failure.[52] Studies show a significant decrease in intake of energy, protein, and vitamin D for age, and growth failure occurs when energy intake falls below 80 percent of the RDA.[52, 53] In oxygen-consumption studies corrected for weight, the values for children with CRI are similar to those of normal children, and adequate energy intake corrects growth failure in these patients; all these results indicate that these children have normal energy needs.[53, 54] However, even with careful urging, many children with CRI seem unable to attain these levels.

The objective of nutritional therapy in the patient with CRI is to minimize uremic toxicity and other metabolic disturbances and to supply adequate calories, protein, vitamins, and minerals. The clinical and metabolic complications vary greatly in CRI and are often progressive. Replacement of losses, correction of nutrient deficits, and determination of the amount of protein required to prevent net protein catabolism are highly individualized and make exact recommendations difficult.[55] There are three areas of suggestions for dietary management.

1. Calories. Energy demands must be defined and met. Generally, the RDA for age is appropriate. Decreased intake secondary to fluid and dietary restrictions, anorexia, and altered taste perception are often factors that limit nutrient intake.

2. Protein. The level of dietary protein restriction necessary to minimize metabolic complications and still maintain endogenous protein synthesis remains controversial. In infants and young children, 2 g of protein per 100 cal meets anabolic needs without increasing azotemia.[56] Supplying 1 g protein/kg of high biologic value will be adequate for most patients, although severe stress may increase requirements to 2 g/kg or more.[57] Alpha-keto acids of the essential amino acids may be substituted for whole protein.

3. Vitamins, minerals, and trace elements. Water-soluble vitamins and folate are lost in dialysate and supplementation is necessary. The severity of dietary restrictions, which limits variety and nutrient intake, will determine what supplemental nutrients are necessary in each patient.

A suggested routine for nutritional assessment of patients with CRI is listed in Table 6–10. As is the procedure with most chronic diseases in childhood, nutritional assessment should be performed at least every 6 months.

TABLE 6–10. Parameters for Routine Nutritional Assessment of Patients with Acute or Chronic Renal Failure

Nutrients
Intake of total energy, protein, carbohydrate, fat, minerals, vitamins, and water

Anthropometry
Height
Weight, percentage relative body weight, and weight change as percent of usual weight
Triceps and subscapular skinfold thickness (actual measurements and percentages of the standard values)
Percent body fat
Mid–upper arm muscle circumference (actual measurements and percentages of standard values)

Biochemical and Other Laboratory Studies
Serum total protein, albumin, and transferrin (transferrin concentrations may be estimated by [0.8 × total iron binding capacity] − 43)
Urea nitrogen appearance (UNA)
Serum sodium, potassium, chloride, and bicarbonate
Serum calcium, phosphorus, and magnesium
Creatinine and urea clearance and daily urine volume
Fasting blood glucose, serum triglycerides, cholesterol, and high-density lipoproteins
Skin tests
Lymphocyte count
Radiographic skeletal survey and photon absorption

Adapted from Kopple JD: Nutritional therapy in kidney failure. Nutr Rev 39:193, 1981.

References

1. Donaldson SS, Wesley MN, DeWys D, et al.: A study of the nutritional status of pediatric cancer patients. Am J Dis Child 135:1107, 1981.
2. Kien CL, Camitta BM: Protein-energy nutritional status of pediatric cancer patients. Am J Clin Nutr 34:2486, 1981.
3. Shils ME: How to nourish the cancer patient. Nutrition Today May/June, 1981.
4. DeWys WD: Nutritional care of the cancer patient. JAMA 244:374, 1980.
5. Donaldson SS, Jundt S, Ricour C, et al.: Radiation enteritis in children. Cancer 35:1167, 1975.
6. US Department of Health, Education and Welfare: Feeding the Sick Child. PHS Publication No. 78–795, 1977.
7. US Department of Health, Education and Welfare: Diet and Nutrition. PHS Publication No. 80–2038, 1979.
8. Visconti JA, ed.: Drug–food interaction. In: Nutrition in Disease. Columbus, Ohio: Ross Laboratories, 1977.
9. Carter P, Carr D, van Eys J, et al.: Nutritional parameters in children with cancer. J Am Diet Assoc 82:616, 1983.
10. Carter P, Carr D, van Eys J, et al.: Energy and nutrient intake of childen with cancer. J Am Diet Assoc 82:610, 1983.
11. Brennan MF: Total parenteral nutrition in the cancer patient. N Engl J Med 305:375, 1981.
12. Darbinian JA, Coulston AM: Parenteral nutrition in cancer therapy: a useful adjunct? J Am Diet Assoc 82:493, 1983.
13. Filler RM, Dietz W, Suskind RM, et al.: Parenteral feeding in the management of children with cancer. Cancer 43:2117, 1979.
14. Costa G, Donaldson SS: Current concepts in cancer: effects of cancer and cancer treatment on the nutrition of the host. N Engl J Med 300:1471, 1979.
15. Nutritional demands imposed by stress. Dairy Council Digest 51:31, 1980.
16. Kinney JM, Long CL, Gump FE, et al.: Tissue composition of weight loss in surgical patients. Ann Surg 168:459, 1968.
17. Studley HO: Percentage of weight loss: basic indicator of surgical risk in patients with chronic peptic ulcer. JAMA 106:458, 1936.
18. Rhoads JE, Alexander CE: Nutritional problems of surgical patients. Ann NY Acad Sci 63:268, 1955.
19. Hill GL: Surgically created nutritional problems. Surg Clin North Am 61:721, 1981.
20. Wolfe BM, Chock E: Energy sources, stores, and hormonal controls. Surg Clin North Am 61:509, 1981.
21. American College of Surgeons Committee on Pre- and Postoperative Care: Manual of Surgical Nutrition. Philadelphia: WB Saunders, 1975.

22. Greecher CP, Cohen IT, Ballantine TV: Nutritional care of the surgical neonate. J Am Diet Assoc 82:654, 1983.
23. Bassili HR, Deitel M: Effects of nutritional support on weaning patients off mechanical ventilators. JPEN 5:161, 1981.
24. Curreri PW, Richmond D, Marvin J, et al.: Dietary requirements of patients with major burns. J Am Diet Assoc 65:415, 1974.
25. Molnar JA, Wolfe RR, Bourbie JF: Metabolism and nutritional therapy in thermal injury. In: Schneider HA, Anderson CE, eds.: Nutritional Support of Medical Practice, 2nd ed. Philadelphia: Lippincott, 1983.
26. Holmes GL: Evaluation and prognosis in nonorganic failure to thrive. South Med J 72:693, 1979.
27. Barbero GJ, Shaheen E: Environmental failure to thrive: a clinical view. J Pediatr 71:639, 1967.
28. Evans SL, et al.: Failure to thrive: a study of 45 children and their families. Paper presented at 22nd annual meeting of the American Association of Pediatric Sources for Children, Philadelphia, PA, 1970.
29. Glaser HH, Heagarty MC, Bullard DM Jr, et al.: Physical and psychological development of children with early failure to thrive. J Pediatr 73:690, 1968.
30. Mitchell WG, Gorrell RW, Greenberg RA: Failure to thrive: a study in a primary care setting. Epidemiology and follow-up. Pediatrics 65:971, 1980.
31. Karp RJ, Bachrach SJ, Moshorvitz S: Malnutrition in chronic illness of childhood with special reference to pulmonary disease. Clin Chest Med 1:375, 1980.
32. Comroe JH: Physiology of Respiration, 2nd ed. Chicago: Year Book Medical, 1979.
33. Hubbard VS, Mangrum PH: Energy intake and nutrition counseling in children with cystic fibrosis. J Am Diet Assoc 80:127, 1982.
34. Askanazi J, Weissman C, Rosenbaum SH, et al.: Nutrition and the respiratory system. Crit Care Med 10:163, 1982.
35. Arora NS, Rochester DF: Respiratory muscle strength and maximal voluntary ventilation in undernourished patients. Am Rev Respir Dis 126:5, 1982.
36. Deitil M, Williams V, Rice T: Nutrition and the patient requiring ventilatory support. J Am Coll of Nutr 2:25, 1983.
37. Thet LA, Alvarez H: Effect of hyperventilation and starvation on rat lung mechanics and surfactant. Am Rev Respir Dis 126:286, 1982.
38. Harper HA, Rodwell VW, Mayes PA, eds.: Review of Physiological Chemistry, 17th ed. Los Altos, CA: Lange, 1979.
39. Sahebjami H, MacGee J: Effects of starvation and refeeding on lung biochemistry in rats. Am Rev Respir Dis 126:483, 1982.
40. Hunter AM, Carey MA, Larsh HW: The nutritional status of patients with chronic obstructive pulmonary disease. Am Rev Respir Dis 124:376, 1981.
41. Barrocas A, Tretola R, Alonso A: Nutrition and the critically ill pulmonary patient. Respir Care 28:50, 1983.
42. Doekel RC Jr, Zwillich CW, Scoggin CH, et al.: Clinical semi-starvation: depression of hypoxic ventilatory response. N Engl J Med 295:358, 1976.
43. Askanazi J, Nordenstrom J, Rosenbaum SH, et al.: Nutrition for the patient with respiratory failure: glucose vs. fat. Anesthesiology 54:373, 1981.
44. Wolfe RR, Allsop JR, Burke JF: Glucose metabolism in man: responses to intravenous glucose infusion. Metabolism 28:210, 1979.
45. Askanazi J, Carpentier YA, Elwyn DH, et al.: Influence of total parenteral nutrition in fuel utilization in injury and sepsis. Ann Surg 191:40, 1980.
46. Grupe W: Nutritional considerations in the prognosis and treatment of children with renal disease. In: Suskind RM, ed.: Textbook of Pediatric Nutrition. New York: Raven Press, 1981.
47. Kipple D: Nutritional therapy in kidney failure. Nutr Rev 39:193, 1981.
48. Fat-soluble vitamin nutrition in patients with chronic renal disease. Nutr Rev 39:212, 1981.
49. Decreased taste acuity in chronic renal patients. Nutr Rev 39:207, 1981.
50. McVicar MI: Nutritional consequences of kidney disease. In: Lifschitz F, ed.: Pediatric Nutrition. New York: Dekker, 1982.
51. Bergstrom WH, De Leon AS, Van Gemund JJ: Growth aberrations in renal disease. Pediatr Clin North Am 11:563, 1964.
52. Stickler GB: Growth failure in renal disease. Pediatr Clin North Am 23:885, 1976.
53. Betts PR, Magrath G: Growth pattern and dietary intake of children with chronic renal insufficiency. Br Med J 2:189, 1974.
54. Simmons JM, Wilson CJ, Potter DE, et al.: Relation of calorie deficiency to growth failure in children on hemodialysis and the growth response to calorie supplementation. N Engl J Med 285:653, 1971.
55. Hyne BE, Fowell E, Lee HA: The effect of caloric intake on nitrogen balance in chronic renal failure. Clin Sci 43:679, 1972.
56. Holliday MA: Chronic renal disease. In: Pediatric Nutrition Handbook. Evanston, IL: American Academy of Pediatrics, 1979.
57. Burton BT, Hirschman GH: Current concepts of nutritional therapy in chronic renal failure: an update. J Am Diet Assoc 82:359, 1983.

Appendix
CONVERSION TABLES *(approximate)*

Mass (Weight)

1 ounce	=	28	grams
¼ pound	=	0.11	kilograms
½ pound	=	0.23	kilograms
¾ pound	=	0.34	kilograms
1 pound	=	0.45	kilograms
1 gram	=	0.036	ounces
1 kilogram	=	2.2	pounds

To convert ounces to grams, multiply by 28; grams to ounces, divide by 28. To convert pounds to kilograms, multiply by 0.45; kilograms to pounds, multiply by 2.2.

Length

1 inch	=	2.54	centimeters
1 foot	=	30.5	centimeters
1 yard	=	0.91	meters
1 mile	=	1.61	kilometers
1 millimeter	=	0.04	inches
1 centimeter	=	0.4	inches
1 meter	=	3.3	feet
1 meter	=	1.1	yard
1 kilometer	=	0.6	miles

To convert inches to centimeters, multiply by 2.54; centimeters to inches, multiply by 0.4

Area

1 square inch	=	6.5	square centimeters
1 square foot	=	9.29	square meters
1 square yard	=	0.84	square meter
1 square centimeter	=	0.16	square inches
1 square meter	=	1.2	square yards

Liquid

1 teaspoon	=	5	milliliters
1 tablespoon	=	15	milliliters
1 ounce	=	30	milliliters
8 ounces	=	236	milliliters
32 ounces (1 quart)	=	946	milliliters
1 milliliter	=	0.03	fluid ounces
1 liter	=	1.06	quarts

To convert milliliters to ounces, divide by 30; ounces to milliliters, multiply by 30.

Temperature

Water freezes	0°C	32°F
Room temperature	22°C	72°F
Body temperature	37°C	98.6°F
Water boils	100°C	212°F

To convert Fahrenheit to Celsius (centigrade), subtract 32, multiply by 5, and divide by 9; Celsius (centigrade) to Fahrenheit, multiply by 9, divide by 5, and add 32.

Table of Equivalent Weights

Avoirdupois, lb	Metric, kg (approx.)	Avoirdupois, lb	Metric, kg (approx.)
1	0.45	51	22.95
2	0.90	52	23.40
3	1.35	53	23.85
4	1.80	54	24.30
5	2.25	55	24.75
6	2.70	56	25.20
7	3.15	57	25.65
8	3.60	58	26.10
9	4.05	59	26.55
10	4.50	60	27.00
11	4.95	61	27.45
12	5.40	62	27.90
13	5.85	63	28.35
14	6.30	64	28.80
15	6.75	65	29.25
16	7.20	66	29.70
17	7.65	67	30.15
18	8.10	68	30.60
19	8.55	69	31.05
20	9.00	70	31.50
21	9.45	71	31.95
22	9.90	72	32.40
23	10.35	73	32.85
24	10.80	74	33.30
25	11.25	75	33.75
26	11.70	76	34.20
27	12.15	77	34.65
28	12.60	78	35.10
29	13.05	79	35.55
30	13.50	80	36.00
31	13.95	81	36.45
32	14.40	82	36.90
33	14.85	83	37.35
34	15.30	84	37.80
35	15.75	85	38.25
36	16.20	86	38.70
37	16.65	87	39.15
38	17.10	88	39.60
39	17.55	89	40.05
40	18.00	90	40.50
41	18.45	91	40.95
42	18.90	92	41.40
43	19.35	93	41.85
44	19.80	94	42.30
45	20.25	95	42.75
46	20.70	96	43.20
47	21.15	97	43.65
48	21.60	98	44.10
49	22.05	99	44.55
50	22.50	100	45.00

Table of Equivalent Weights *Continued*

Avoirdupois, lb	Metric, kg (approx.)	Avoirdupois, lb	Metric, kg (approx.)
101	45.45	151	67.95
102	45.90	152	68.40
103	46.35	153	68.85
104	46.80	154	69.30
105	47.25	155	69.75
106	47.70	156	70.20
107	48.15	157	70.65
108	48.60	158	71.10
109	49.05	159	71.55
110	49.50	160	72.00
111	49.95	161	72.45
112	50.40	162	72.90
113	50.85	163	73.35
114	51.30	164	73.80
115	51.75	165	74.25
116	52.20	166	74.70
117	52.65	167	75.15
118	53.10	168	75.60
119	53.55	169	76.05
120	54.00	170	76.50
121	54.45	171	76.95
122	54.90	172	77.40
123	55.35	173	77.85
124	55.80	174	78.30
125	56.25	175	78.75
126	56.70	176	79.20
127	57.15	177	79.65
128	57.60	178	80.10
129	58.05	179	80.55
130	58.50	180	81.00
131	58.95	181	81.45
132	59.40	182	81.90
133	59.85	183	82.35
134	60.30	184	82.80
135	60.75	185	83.25
136	61.20	186	83.70
137	61.65	187	84.15
138	62.10	188	84.60
139	62.55	189	85.05
140	63.00	190	85.50
141	63.45	191	85.95
142	63.90	192	86.40
143	64.35	193	86.85
144	64.80	194	87.30
145	65.25	195	87.75
146	65.70	196	88.20
147	66.15	197	88.65
148	66.60	198	89.10
149	67.05	199	89.55
150	67.50	200	90.00

INDEX

Note: Page numbers in *italics* refer to illustrations; page numbers followed by (t) refer to tables.